SOUND THE TRUMPETS
BEAT THE DRUMS

Sound the Trumpets
Beat the Drums
Military Music through the 20th Century

**To celebrate the 25th Anniversary
of the
International Military Music Society**

by
John Ambler
Colin Dean
Brian Reynolds
Paul Taylor
Alwyn W Turner
Gordon Turner

Foreword by HRH The Duke of Edinburgh

PARAPRESS LIMITED
in association with
The International Military Music Society

Also by Gordon and Alwyn Turner: *The Trumpets Will Sound, the Story of the Royal Military School of Music, Kneller Hall*, Parapress 1996

First published in the UK by
PARAPRESS LTD
5 Bentham Hill House
Stockland Green Road
Tunbridge Wells
Kent TN3 0TJ

A catalogue record for this book is
available from the British Library.

Typeset by Vitaset, Paddock Wood, Kent
Cover design by MRM Advertising & Design

Printed in Great Britain by
Biddles Ltd, Guildford and King's Lynn

The cover painting by Charles Stadden depicts figures from the four principal reigns of the 20th century:

King Edward VII	(*1901–1910*):	State Trumpeter, Household Cavalry
King George V	(*1910–1936*):	Bugler, Royal Marines Chatham Division
King George VI	(*1936–1952*):	Drummer, 2nd Bn Grenadier Guards*
Queen Elizabeth II	(*1952– ?*):	Trumpeter, Royal Air Force

* This figure represents the late Harry Harding MBE when he took part in the King's Birthday Parade of 1939. Harry was the first Chairman of the International Committee of the International Military Music Society and the first Chairman of the United Kingdom (Founder) Branch. Sadly, Harry died shortly before the publication of this book.

CONTENTS

INTRODUCTION

See, the conquering hero comes!
Sound the trumpets, beat the drums!
Thomas Morell, libretto for Handel's oratorio, *Judas Maccabaeus*

T rumpets sounded, drums were beaten and bands played on countless occasions
throughout the 20th century, whether they were joyous or sad, or whether the
conquering hero of the day was the sovereign or the ordinary British sailor, soldier
or airman.

The great ceremonial events such as coronations, jubilees, state funerals and times
of national celebration would be unthinkable without the participation of immacu-
lately turned-out military musicians, while events such as the Royal Tournament and
the great searchlight tattoos have brought pleasure to millions and raised incalculable
sums for service charities.

In the days before the wireless and the gramophone, it was the military band
playing on the bandstand that was often the prime source of musical entertainment,
aside from the family singing around the piano. Most people could not afford to hear
orchestras playing in a concert hall but learnt to appreciate the best of the classical
repertoire from the bandstand in the local park or at the seaside.

The public profile of military bands was further enhanced during the middle part
of the century when they were heard on the wireless several times each week; this
did much to boost national morale, particularly amongst factory workers during the
war years.

Cuts in defence expenditure have taken their toll but, although bands are now
heard much less on the bandstand and the radio, their contribution to state and
national occasions remains undiminished.

Sound the Trumpets, Beat the Drums covers all these aspects, paying tribute to the
outstanding contribution that the bands made to the British way of life during the
20th century. It starts with a review of some of the major events, from the funeral of
Queen Victoria in 1901 to the 100th birthday celebrations for Queen Elizabeth, the
Queen Mother in 2000, and ends with a look at how the International Military Music
Society evolved to help support military music.

ACKNOWLEDGEMENTS

This book has been written and produced with the help of a considerable number of people and the authors would particularly like to acknowledge the contributions made by the following individuals: Margaret Ambler, James Ashton, Maurice Bradbury, George Brinckley, Ken Burns OBE, Pat Chambers, Dominic Cleydon, Major Alastair Donald RM, Major Paddy Dunn RM, Chris Eley, T John Foster, Anne Gatehouse, Harry Harding MBE, Pat Higgins, Vic Hillsdon, Matthew Little of the Royal Marines Museum, Philip Mather, Alastair Mitchell, Captain Derek Oakley MBE RM, Major Richard Powell, Alan Purdie, David Robertson, Royal Military School of Music, LV ('Curly') Shaw, Stuart Stredwick, Robert von Motz and the Band of the Welsh Guards.

Special thanks also to Linda Peabody for help with the typing.

ABOUT THE AUTHORS

John Ambler
An engineer by profession, John is the current chairman of the UK (Founder) Branch of the IMMS and has developed a considerable reputation for his expertise on the history of the Royal Marines Band Service. He wrote the narration for the much acclaimed CD 'Sound the Alert' which depicts a day in the life of a Royal Marines Bugler, and is a regular contributor to the *Blue Band Magazine*.

Colin Dean
Colin was destined to take an interest in military music and ceremonial, as his parents first met by the bandstand in Barking Park on VJ night. A Chartered Insurer, he has been a member of IMMS since its inception in 1977 and Vice Chairman of the UK (Founder) Branch since 1992. His historical articles frequently appear in *Band International* and other publications, while his photographs have graced record sleeves, tattoo programmes and magazines.

Brian Reynolds
Now retired from the insurance world, Brian devotes much of his time to researching all aspects of light music. He was the author of a regular series of composer biographies for the Vintage Light Music Society and has presented broadcasts of light music on Radio Kent for the last few years. His compositions for military band became popular and many appeared on recordings and broadcasts.

Paul Taylor
Paul is a Chartered Architect, whose career has included a long period with British Rail, where he was responsible for the design of the new Liverpool Street station in London. Since retiring Paul has been busier than ever, qualifying as a City of London Guide and undertaking a full schedule of lectures and walks on a wide range of subjects. One of his most popular lectures has been on bandstands.

Alwyn W Turner
Educated at Christ's Hospital and London University, Alwyn is a professional journalist who specialises in developing and writing games. He is also the author of *Tribute: A Salute to the British Armed Forces of World War II*, and co-author, with his father, of *The Trumpets Will Sound*, a history of Kneller Hall, and the acclaimed three-volumed *History of British Military Bands*.

Gordon Turner, MBE

Major Gordon Turner was taught at the age of ten to play the cornet in a Salvation Army Band. He joined the Corps of Royal Engineers as a junior musician at the age of sixteen and in 1958 became the youngest bandmaster in the British Army. He served as Bandmaster with 15th/19th The King's Royal Hussars and the Royal Green Jackets, and was Director of Music with the Royal Tank Regiment and the Royal Corps of Signals. He subsequently became Professor of Orchestration at Kneller Hall and has won prizes for both conducting and composition.

BUCKINGHAM PALACE.

Any national celebratory event without military music is unthinkable. Military Bands, whether on bandstands, concert halls or marching on grand ceremonial occasions, have become familiar and a much-loved element in our musical tradition.

The origin of military bands may have been in the practical need for a means of communication in camp and in action, but their development has brought them very much into the public eye. No longer restricted to marching tunes, Regimental Directors of Music and Band Masters have shown great imagination and initiative in creating a remarkable versatility in musical entertainment. Their music has come to be an essential part of all ceremony and pageantry.

I am very pleased to welcome this Jubilee Book. It marks the 25th anniversary of the International Military Music Society and I am sure that all enthusiasts will be delighted with this history of military music over the last hundred years.

Philip

CHAPTER 1

A CENTURY OF CEREMONIAL

COLIN DEAN

T he list of events in which military bands participated between 1901 and 2000 is endless and encompasses everything from the great national and state occasions to the local carnival or village fête, not forgetting great sporting events such as the Olympic and Commonwealth Games and numerous Cup Finals. This chapter looks at just a few of these great occasions with particular emphasis on bands and music. Space precludes listing the various processions in full, although sufficient detail has generally been included to give an indication of their composition and to show how the bands were positioned.

1901 – State Funeral of Queen Victoria

Queen Victoria acceded to the throne on 20th June 1837 and reigned for over 63 years until her death at Osborne House on the Isle of Wight on 22nd January 1901. Most of her citizens at that time could not remember life under a different monarch.

The Queen's death brought about the first great ceremonial event of the 20th century with a State Funeral that took four distinct parts, starting on 1st February 1901 when her coffin was borne on a gun carriage of 'Y' Battery Royal Horse Artillery from Osborne House to Trinity Pier at East Cowes. Included in the procession, according to a report in *The Globe and Laurel*, were the Bands of the Royal Marine Artillery and the Royal Marine Light Infantry, Portsmouth Division, with 40 Drummers of the RMLI, under the direction of 2nd Lieutenant George Miller, RMLI. However, an account by the then Adjutant of the RMLI Portsmouth Division refers to the RMLI Band and the Massed Drums of the RMA and RMLI.

It would appear that the Queen had left specific instructions that only Chopin's and Beethoven's funeral marches were to be played. Chopin's 'Marche Funèbre' is taken from his Piano Sonata in B♭ minor and the Beethoven march was the third movement of his Piano Sonata No 12 in A♭, not to be confused with the march attributed to Beethoven which is now played annually at the Cenotaph. *The Globe and Laurel* reported that a funeral march composed by Lieutenant Miller was also played during this procession although it would seem that this refers to the drum beatings in the intervals between marches, and as the coffin was transferred from the gun carriage to the Royal Yacht *Alberta*. This funeral march for drums had been played at the funeral of HRH Prince Henry of Battenburg in 1896 and was said to have created a most impressive sound which 'tore the heartstrings of all who heard it'.

The bands played 'The Saints of God, Their Conflict Past' as the yacht left the quay and the coffin was conveyed across the Solent, passing through lines of ships of the Royal Navy and the navies of France, Germany, Japan, Portugal and Spain. Ships' bands played Chopin's and Beethoven's funeral marches as HMY *Alberta* passed on its way to the Clarence Victualling Yard at Gosport where the coffin rested overnight.

The next morning, Saturday 2nd February 1901, a Guard of Honour from the Royal Marine Light Infantry was mounted on the jetty, supported by the Band, who played a funeral march as the coffin was placed on the train to be taken to Victoria Station in London, where it arrived at 11 am.

The second stage of the funeral was a procession through the capital from Victoria by way of The Mall, St James's Street, Piccadilly, Hyde Park and Edgware Road to Paddington Station. As is traditional for royal processions, it was formed in reverse order of seniority so that the most senior units were nearest the gun carriage:

Officer of Headquarters Staff
   Mounted Band of the Royal Horse Guards (The Blues)
   Mounted Band of the 2nd Life Guards
Yeomanry, Colonials, Militia, Honourable Artillery Company
Departmental Corps
Indian Army
Infantry of the Line, Foot Guards
Royal Engineers, Royal Garrison Artillery, Royal Field Artillery
Cavalry of the Line, Household Cavalry
Royal Marine Light Infantry, Royal Marine Artillery, Royal Navy
Military Attachés, Headquarters Staff and Field Marshals
   Band of the Royal Marine Light Infantry (Chatham Division)
   Massed Bands of the Guards (Coldstream and Scots Guards)
   Band of the Royal Engineers
   Band of the Royal Artillery
Gun Carriage drawn by eight Hanoverian creams driven by royal postillions
Royal Mourners
Sovereign's Escort

It is interesting to note that while the Royal Marines units took their precedence with the Royal Navy rather than after the Royal Berkshire Regiment, the RMLI Band was positioned according to its army precedence.*

---

* The Royal Marines took precedence with the Royal Navy when serving at sea but their precedence under the Army Act when ashore was after the Royal Berkshire Regiment (49th Foot), giving rise to their nickname, 'The Forty Ninth and a Half'. The current position is covered by Queen's Regulations 1975, Chapter 8 Para J8008 which states that 'The Royal Marines and Royal Marine Reserve should form part of the Royal Navy contingent whenever Royal Navy or Royal Naval Auxiliary Forces are on parade. When no Royal Navy or Royal Naval Auxiliary Forces are on parade, the Royal Marines and Royal Marine Reserve should parade according to their Army order of precedence.' As a result of amalgamations, their place is now shown as after The Black Watch (Royal Highland Regiment).

The two mounted bands, each 30 strong, were formed up in Piccadilly in readiness for leading the procession, which stretched right back to Victoria Station. The remaining bands were grouped together immediately ahead of the gun carriage, each of the five bands being 60 strong, with the Senior Bandmaster, (2nd Lieutenant) Cavaliere Ladislao Zavertal, Royal Artillery, having charge of the musical arrangements. The orders for the parade stated: *'The two mounted bands in front will not play; the four dismounted bands in rear will play alternately, commencing with the rear band of the group,'* adding *'Beethoven's and Chopin's funeral marches alone to be played.'*

On arrival at Paddington the coffin was placed on the royal train and taken to Windsor Central Station where it was to have been drawn on a gun carriage of 'S' Battery, Royal Horse Artillery. However, the horses had been standing still in the cold for a considerable time and, just as the procession was about to move off, one of the wheelers reared and plunged, damaging the traces to the extent that it proved necessary for the horses to be unhooked from the gun carriage. As a result the Naval Bluejackets forming the Guard of Honour took over and dragged the gun carriage to St George's Chapel in the Castle, thus giving rise to a new tradition. The procession marched by way of High Street, Sheet Street, turning left into Park Street and left again along the Long Walk to the Castle for the service in St George's Chapel and included the Bands of the Grenadier Guards and the 1st Life Guards (*dismounted*) who played alternately.

The final stage of the funeral took place at 3 pm on Monday 4th February when 'S' Battery bore the coffin from the chapel to Frogmore in a procession which again included the Band of the Grenadier Guards (and, according to some reports, the Band of the 1st Life Guards). The bands ceased playing at the gates of the Royal Mausoleum and the Queen's Pipers, Mr James Campbell and his nephew, played as the Queen's coffin was taken inside for burial alongside Prince Albert.

1902 – Coronation of King Edward VII

The Coronation of King Edward VII took place on 9th August 1902 with the procession from Buckingham Palace to Westminster Abbey led by Trumpeters of the Royal Horse Guards (The Blues) and a Squadron and Band of the 1st Life Guards, with the Sovereign's Escort found by the Royal Horse Guards. Student Bandmasters from Kneller Hall under Professor WO'Keefe acted as State Trumpeters in Westminster Abbey.[*]

A Royal Progress to celebrate the coronation left Buckingham Palace on Saturday 25th October 1902 and passed through the City of London and areas south of the river over an eight-mile route. The cavalcade was led by a military procession of:

Naval Gun Detachments
   Royal Artillery Mounted Band
'N' Battery, Royal Horse Artillery
   Band of the 2nd Life Guards

[*] From 1903 the provision of State Trumpeters became the sole prerogative of the Household Cavalry although State Trumpeters were subsequently found from the 1st King's Dragoon Guards and the 10th Royal Hussars (Prince of Wales's Own) at the Delhi Durbars in India.

Coronation Procession of King Edward VII on 9th August 1902 with the Mounted Band of the 1st Life Guards in Whitehall led, unusually, by a black drum horse. The Bandmaster, Mr Joel Englefield, can be seen on a grey horse, riding at the side of the band as was the custom at the time.

Royal Horse Guards (The Blues)
'X' Battery, Royal Horse Artillery
   Band of the 1st Royal Dragoons
1st Royal Dragoons
10th Battery, Royal Field Artillery
   Band of the 13th Hussars
13th Hussars
70th Battery, Royal Field Artillery
   Band of the 5th (Royal Irish) Lancers
5th (Royal Irish) Lancers

There followed numerous royal carriages ending with the State Coach carrying the King and Queen, with a Sovereign's Escort found by the 1st Life Guards. Despite the day being fine and warm, all troops were cloaked, which rather veiled the splendour of their uniforms and must have left them feeling quite uncomfortable. Each band played the National Anthem as it rode past Buckingham Palace from the marshalling area in Eaton Square to the start of the procession.

1910 – State Funeral of King Edward VII

After a comparatively short reign King Edward VII died on 6th May 1910. A procession conveyed his remains from Buckingham Palace by way of The Mall, Horse Guards Parade, Whitehall and Parliament Street to the Lying-in-State at Westminster Hall on 17th May:

Officer of the Headquarters Staff
Army Council, Lords of the Admiralty
1st Division of the Sovereign's Escort
Field Marshals, Admirals of the Fleet, Indian Orderly Officers, Naval and Military ADCs
2nd Division of the Sovereign's Escort
  Massed Bands of the Brigade of Guards, Drums, and Pipes of the Scots Guards
Gun Carriage drawn by the Royal Horse Artillery
His Majesty the King and his two sons, foreign sovereigns, princes of the blood
3rd Division of the Sovereign's Escort
Members of the Household
4th Division of the Sovereign's Escort

The Sovereign's Escort was dismounted, while behind came the carriages of Queen Alexandra, Queen Mary and Empress Marie escorted by a Captain's Escort (*mounted*).

The Massed Bands of the Brigade of Guards, headed by eight Drum Majors, were under the Senior Bandmaster, Lieutenant John Mackenzie Rogan, Coldstream Guards. Knowing the tremendous effect the drums can have on such an occasion, he had requested permission to use all 80 side drummers from the Brigade in addition to the 250 musicians from the four bands and the pipers of the Scots Guards.

The funeral marches were each preceded by an introductory drum roll of 48 paces, especially written by Mackenzie Rogan, which was said to have given the suggestion of the firing of musketry and the booming of artillery over the grave of a hero.

The Major General desired to know the exact time it would take for the procession to pass, so Mackenzie Rogan, always a perfectionist, personally paced out the route in slow time – it took 43 minutes. He was therefore able to ascertain the number of bars to be played, and selected the music as follows:

Buckingham Palace to Marlborough Gate
  Prelude for Drums   *Mackenzie Rogan*
  Funeral March in B♭ Minor and D♭ Minor   *attributed to Beethoven*

Marlborough Gate to Duke of York's Steps
  Flowers of the Forest (Pipes)

Duke of York's Steps to Downing Street
  Prelude for Drums   *Mackenzie Rogan*
  Marche Funèbre   *Chopin*

Downing Street to Westminster Hall
  Prelude for Drums   *Mackenzie Rogan*
  Saul   *Handel*

Left: the Massed Bands, Drums and Pipes of the Brigade of Guards, led by eight Drum Majors, approaching Westminster Hall at the head of the gun carriage bearing the remains of King Edward VII in the procession from Buckingham Palace on 17th May 1910.

Below: the Massed Bands of the Brigade of Guards conducted by Lieutenant John Mackenzie Rogan, Coldstream Guards. The bands continue to play as the gun carriage enters Old Palace Yard for the Lying-in-State of King Edward VII. In the background are Guards of Honour found by 2nd Bn Coldstream Guards and the Royal Marine Light Infantry, while behind them is the first division of the dismounted Sovereign's Escort.

The State Funeral of King Edward VII on 20th May 1910 with the procession led by the Band of the 2nd Life Guards, followed by the Band of the 1st Life Guards. The 2nd Life Guards have white sheepskin saddles and the Bandmaster, Lieutenant Charles Hall, can be seen wearing officers' uniform with a white plume and a shabraque over his saddle. This contrasts with the 1st Life Guards whose sheepskins are black and who were then led by a Warrant Officer Bandmaster, Mr George Miller, who wears a red plume (as worn by all members of the band when not in state dress up to 1951) and with no shabraque.

Following the Lying-in-State, the State Funeral took place on 20th May 1910 with the procession in London leaving Westminster Hall at 9.50 and taking two hours to reach Paddington. It took a similar form to the procession for Queen Victoria, and after the first two divisions of the Escort rode the Band of the 2nd Life Guards, immediately followed by the Band of the 1st Life Guards. The same dismounted bands were used (the Brigade of Guards bands being those of the Grenadier and Coldstream Guards) and they were again positioned together in front of the gun carriage, playing alternately.

As the procession reached Paddington it was the turn of the Royal Artillery Band to play, but orders were given by Lieutenant Mackenzie Rogan, that the Guards bands would play (out of turn) at the station and as the train moved out. This decision did not please the Royal Artillery, who felt they were entitled to this honour 'both by seniority and by turn'.

The gun carriage in London had been drawn by 'BB' Battery, Royal Horse Artillery but the Royal Navy took over for the procession through the streets of Windsor, following the tradition started at Queen Victoria's funeral. All troops were on foot, including the Sovereign's Escort found by the Royal Horse Guards (The Blues), the first two divisions being followed by:

Band of the Irish Guards
Band of the Scots Guards
Pipes of the Scots Guards
Band of the Royal Horse Guards (The Blues) (*dismounted in state dress*)

The bands played Chopin's and Beethoven's (B♭ minor) funeral marches and the pipers played 'Flowers of the Forest' during the procession and 'Land o' the Leal' as it passed through the Lower Ward of the Castle.

1911 – Unveiling of the Queen Victoria Memorial

A memorial to Queen Victoria was erected outside Buckingham Palace and unveiled on 16th May 1911 by the late Queen's grandson, King George V, accompanied by Queen Mary and the Emperor and Empress of Germany. Guards of Honour found by the Royal Navy and the King's Company, 1st Bn Grenadier Guards were formed up in the palace forecourt facing each other, supported by the Band of the Royal Marine Light Infantry (Chatham Division), 50-strong under the Bandmaster, Mr J C Hoby, and the Corps of Drums of 1st Bn Grenadier Guards.

The Massed Bands of the Brigade of Guards were positioned in The Mall facing the memorial, and detachments of Royal Navy, Royal Marines and Army with standards and colours, were positioned along The Mall.

On the arrival of the royal party, the orders stated that, 'The King will raise his baton and the General Officer Commanding will direct a "G" to be sounded on the bugle as a signal for a Royal Salute.' The National Anthem was then played by the massed bands and 'on a "G" being sounded the parade will slope swords or slope arms as the case may be.' Divine service was then taken by the Archbishop of Canterbury, including the hymn 'O God Our Help in Ages Past', after which the King unveiled the memorial. Finally the troops on parade marched past to:

Royal Navy, RMA and RMLI
    A Life on the Ocean Wave   *H Russell*

Household Cavalry and Cavalry of the Line
    Under the Double Eagle   *J F Wagner*

Foot Guards and Infantry of the Line
    The Red Feathers   *J M Rogan*

1911 – Coronation of King George V

The Coronation of King George V took place on 22nd June 1911. The first of three processions from Buckingham Palace to Westminster Abbey was led by Trumpeters, the Band and a squadron of the 1st Life Guards, followed by a Captain's Escort and carriages conveying foreign royalty. Next came a procession of members of the Royal Family, also with a Captain's Escort, and finally the King's Procession with a Sovereign's Escort. No bands other than 1st Life Guards took part in any of the processions and all Escorts were found by the Royal Horse Guards (The Blues).

The Band of the Royal Horse Guards (The Blues) returning along The Mall at the end of the Royal Progress on 23rd June 1911 to celebrate the coronation of King George V. The Bandmaster, Mr Manuel Bilton, can be seen riding a grey horse on the extreme right of the picture.

The processions on Coronation Day took the short route via The Mall and Whitehall but on the following day, 23rd June 1911, a Royal Progress was held around London, leaving Buckingham Palace and moving by way of Constitution Hill, Piccadilly, St James's Street, Pall Mall, Trafalgar Square, Strand, Fleet Street, Ludgate Hill, Cannon Street, Queen Victoria Street, King William Street, London Bridge, Borough High Street, St George's Circus, Westminster Bridge, Parliament Street and Whitehall, finally returning along The Mall to Buckingham Palace.

The Royal Progress was formed in three processions, with a band at the front and in rear of the Colonial Procession and the Indian Procession, and with a number of bands in the Royal Procession, all of which, of course, were mounted:

The Colonial Procession	**Band of the 2nd Life Guards**
	Band of the 1st Life Guards
The Indian Procession	**Band of the 2nd Dragoons (Royal Scots Greys)**
	Band of the 7th (Queen's Own) Hussars
The Royal Procession	**Royal Artillery Mounted Band**
	Band of the Royal Horse Guards (The Blues)
	Band of the 2nd Dragoon Guards (Queen's Bays)
	Band of the 4th (Queen's Own) Hussars
	Band of the 5th (Royal Irish) Lancers

1911 – Investiture of the Prince of Wales

The Investiture of the Prince of Wales, later to become King Edward VIII, took place on 13th July 1911 at Caernarvon Castle in North Wales. Massed Bands of the Royal Marine Light Infantry, Portsmouth and Chatham Divisions, 100 strong, played in Castle Square under the direction of Lt George Miller, Portsmouth Division. The programme of music was:

Ceremonial March	**Hail to the Prince**	*Miller*
Overture	**Tannhäuser**	*Wagner*
Selection	**Lohengrin**	*Wagner*
Suite	**Sigurd Jorsalfar**	*Grieg*
Marche	**Héroique**	*Saint-Saëns*
Hallelujah Chorus from	**The Messiah**	*Handel*

A Sovereign's Escort found by the 2nd Life Guards escorted the King along the two-mile processional route from Griffith's Crossing to Caernarvon Castle, and a Prince of Wales's Escort was found by the Denbighshire Yeomanry. Guards of Honour were found by 1st Bn Royal Welch Fusiliers and 1st Bn South Wales Borderers who paraded with their bands.

1919 – End of the Great War

The Triumphal March by the Household Cavalry and Foot Guards

The first of two principal celebrations in London to mark the peace of 1918 took place on the afternoon of Saturday 22nd March 1919, a time chosen to ensure that as many spectators as possible would be able to witness the occasion. The parade was described in a message from the King as a 'Triumphal March' and took place in spite of bitter winds and the imminent threat of snow. Eight thousand officers and men took part in the procession, including Captain HRH the Prince of Wales, Grenadier Guards, who was on parade as a member of the Earl of Cavan's staff.

The Major General
 Band of the 1st Life Guards
1st Life Guards
 Band of the 2nd Life Guards
2nd Life Guards
 Band of the Royal Horse Guards (The Blues)
Royal Horse Guards (The Blues)
 Band of the Grenadier Guards
1st Guards Brigade
(2nd Bn Grenadier Guards, 1st Bn Irish Guards, 2nd Bn Coldstream Guards)
 Band of the Coldstream Guards
2nd Guards Brigade
(3rd Bn Grenadier Guards, 1st Bn Scots Guards, 2nd Bn Irish Guards, 1st Bn
  Coldstream Guards)

Band of the Scots Guards
3rd Guards Brigade
(1st Bn Grenadier Guards, 1st Bn Welsh Guards, 2nd Bn Scots Guards)

Also taking part were Pipers of the Scots Guards and 2nd Bn Irish Guards. Demobilised men who had been recalled marched in plain clothes, while lorries carried those unable to march. The Bands of the Irish and Welsh Guards were positioned in the Forecourt of Buckingham Palace where King George V took the salute from a dais at 1.45 pm. The procession passed along The Mall, Marlborough Road, Pall Mall, Trafalgar Square, Strand, Fleet Street, Ludgate Hill, Cannon Street to King William Street where it halted for a short while. It then continued past Mansion House and returned along Poultry, Cheapside, Holborn, Broad Street, Shaftesbury Avenue, Piccadilly to Hyde Park Corner.

A number of bands were positioned along the route:

Mansion House:	**Canadian Composite Band**
	1st King's Dragoon Guards
South End of St James's Street:	**2nd Bn Queen's Royal Regiment (West Surrey)**
Trafalgar Square:	**2nd Bn The Buffs (East Kent Regiment)**
St Mary-le-Strand:	**2nd Bn Middlesex Regiment (Duke of Cambridge's Own)**
St Paul's Churchyard:	**3rd Bn Middlesex Regiment (Duke of Cambridge's Own)**
Holborn Circus:	**2nd Bn Border Regiment**
Junction of New Oxford Street and High Holborn:	**1st Bn Loyal North Lancashire Regiment**
Palace Theatre:	**2nd Bn Manchester Regiment**
Piccadilly Circus:	**2nd Bn Queen's Own Royal West Kent Regiment**
Hyde Park Corner:	**1st Bn Duke of Cornwall's Light Infantry**

National Peace Celebrations

The Victory March to mark the end of the Great War was held on 19th July 1919, and what was intended to be a temporary Cenotaph was designed by Sir Edwin Lutyens and constructed from wood and plaster in Whitehall to act as the focal point for the nation's homage.

Before the march an orchestra of 24 musicians and choir, under Sir Walford Davies wearing his Doctor of Music robes, came from a door of the Home Office on to the pavement opposite the Cenotaph. Their music, before the procession arrived and at intervals as it passed, included 'For All the Saints', 'Jesu, Lover of My Soul', 'Pomp and Circumstance' and Sullivan's 'Requiem'. 'Last Post' was sounded as four Guardsmen took post around the Cenotaph and rested on their arms reversed.

The parade set off from Albert Gate in Hyde Park at 10.00 am and marched via Sloane Street, Pont Street, Buckingham Palace Road, Vauxhall Station, Lambeth

The National Peace Celebrations on 19th July 1919. The Bands of the Grenadier and Coldstream Guards lead the Brigade of Guards contingents past the temporary wooden Cenotaph in Whitehall. Unusually, all four State Colours are seen on parade together – on the left in the picture is that of the Grenadier Guards (more correctly known as the King's Company Colour, the Royal Standard of the Regiment), in the centre, the two State Colours of the Coldstream Guards and on the right, the State Colour of the Scots Guards.

Road, Westminster Bridge, Whitehall past the Cenotaph, Admiralty Arch, The Mall, Constitution Hill to Hyde Park Corner. King George V took the salute at the Queen Victoria Memorial at 12.10 pm.

The Naval section which led the procession included seven bands, presumably including Bluejacket bands and the Royal Marines.

Next came the Army section, which included the following bands spread throughout the procession:

Band of 4th Bn King's Royal Rifle Corps	**Band of 2nd Bn East Surrey Regiment**
Band of the 1st Life Guards	**Band of the Royal Horse Guards (The Blues)**
Band of the Grenadier Guards Massed Pipers	**Band of the Coldstream Guards**
Band of the Honourable Artillery Company	**Band of 6th Bn City of London Regiment**

Band of the Royal Engineers
Band of 2nd Bn Royal Irish Rifles
Band of 3rd Bn Middlesex Regiment (Duke of Cambridge's Own)
Band of 2nd Bn Lancashire Fusiliers
Band of 1st Bn Royal Inniskilling Fusiliers
Band of 2nd Bn Royal Irish Fusiliers (Princess Victoria's)
Band of Royal Munster Fusiliers
Australian Band
Drums: 1st Bn Welsh Guards
Drums: 1st Bn Coldstream Guards
Drums: 1st Bn Scots Guards

Finally came the Royal Air Force, a service little over a year old which did not yet have established bands and which was therefore accompanied by the Band of 2nd Bn Royal Fusiliers (City of London Regiment).

At 7 pm that evening, a concert was given in Hyde Park by the Imperial Choir of Peace (10,000 voices) and the Massed Bands of the Brigade of Guards, all conducted by Dr Charles Harriss. Heavy rain fell and the choir wore raincoats over their white dresses but the event was a success, with the programme including:

Rejoice Today With One Accord
God Bless the Prince of Wales
March of the Men of Harlech
Soldiers' Chorus from *Faust*
Minstrel Boy
Wi' a Hundred Pipers
Hallelujah Chorus
All People That On Earth Do Dwell
Rule Britannia

1920 – Interment of the Unknown Warrior

Overwhelming public demand led to the Cenotaph being made into a permanent structure of Portland stone and this was unveiled by King George V on 11th November 1920 as the body of the Unknown Warrior passed for interment in Westminster Abbey.

The body of the Unknown Warrior was chosen to represent all those who fell during the Great War and was brought across the Channel from France in a destroyer, HMS *Verdun*, on Wednesday 10th November 1920. The *Verdun* arrived at Dover soon after 3 pm to a Field Marshal's salute of 19 guns fired from Dover Castle.

Awaiting its arrival was a Guard of Honour found by 2nd Bn Royal Irish Fusiliers with the Band under the Bandmaster, Mr L P Bradley, but the music was not a funeral march as might have been expected. Instead, the Unknown Warrior was brought home to the triumphant strains of Elgar's 'Land of Hope and Glory', although reports differ as to whether this was played as the *Verdun* drew alongside or as the bearer party approached the gangway. Bandmaster Bradley later recounted that Chopin's 'Funeral March' had originally been suggested but that he had felt something more martial was required and had therefore sought the approval of his commanding officer for Elgar's music to be played.

The coffin was taken to London by rail in a special saloon carriage which arrived at 8.32 pm at Victoria Station, where it was placed under a guard furnished by 1st Bn Grenadier Guards, the sentries resting on their arms reversed. The next morning, 11th November 1920, the coffin was placed on a gun carriage and taken in a funeral procession which moved off from Victoria in slow time at 9.40 am in the following order:

1   Firing Party – 1 Sergeant, 1 Corporal and 12 Guardsmen of 3rd Bn Coldstream Guards.

2   The Massed Bands and Drums of the Coldstream, Scots, Irish and Welsh Guards and the Pipes of the Scots Guards. A total of 4 officers and 209 other ranks including 1 Director of Music and 1 Sergeant Drummer (Drum Major) of each of the 4 regiments.

3   Gun Carriage with a team of 6 horses, together with 3 Limber Gunners on foot, furnished by 'N' Battery Royal Horse Artillery.

4   Bearers – 1 Sergeant and 8 Guardsmen of 3rd Bn Coldstream Guards.

5   Pall Bearers – 12 Distinguished Officers of the Royal Navy, Army and Royal Air Force.

6   The Mourners   Royal Navy   76 officers 150 other ranks
                    Army   174 officers 307 other ranks
                    Royal Air Force   31 officers   60 other ranks

7   Representatives of various ex-servicemen's organisations – 400 in total.

The procession marched by way of Grosvenor Gardens, Grosvenor Place, Wellington Arch, Constitution Hill, The Mall, Admiralty Arch and Charing Cross into Whitehall. As the massed bands approached the Cenotaph, which was draped with huge union flags, they passed to the east side and marched on as far as King Charles Street, counter-marched and halted facing the Cenotaph from the south. The gun carriage halted opposite the point where His Majesty King George V was standing. One Sergeant Drummer and 8 drummers of the Brigade of Guards took post on the east side of Whitehall facing the Cenotaph and two choirs were in position on either side of the entrance to the Home Office.

A short service commenced at 10.50 am with the hymn 'O God Our Help in Ages Past', after which the Archbishop of Canterbury led the Lord's Prayer. As Big Ben struck 11 the King unveiled the Cenotaph and two minutes' silence was observed, commencing with the last strike of the hour. At the end of the silence Last Post was sounded and the King and the distinguished guests placed wreaths on the Cenotaph.

The service over, the massed bands counter-marched and led the procession along Parliament Street and via the north and west sides of Parliament Square towards the North Door of Westminster Abbey. Behind the bands walked the Archbishop of Canterbury and the heads of various religious denominations, while behind the gun carriage marched the King and Royal Princes, followed by the Mourners. The gun carriage halted in Broad Sanctuary and the bearer party carried the coffin into the Abbey between the ranks of the firing party and through two lines of holders of the Victoria Cross to the point of interment.

On duty inside the Abbey were the Band and Drums of the Grenadier Guards, the band being placed immediately west of the organ loft on the south side of the nave. The Unknown Warrior was laid to rest and Reveille was sounded from the steps west of Henry VII Chapel at the conclusion of the service.

1924 – Empire Exhibition

A week of massed bands concerts began on Empire Day, 24th May 1924, at the newly built Empire Stadium at Wembley. Two concerts were presented daily with massed bands of 600 musicians, comprising the Kneller Hall Band and an average of five bandsmen from each band stationed in the UK, under the direction of Lieutenant Hector Adkins, Director of Music of the Royal Military School of Music. Sir Edward Elgar conducted the massed bands at the opening ceremony. The band was seated in a large circle with the conductor on a platform in the centre and the instruments so arranged that the full band sound could be heard in all parts of the stadium.

Amongst the music played was Bach's 'Prelude and Fugue in G Minor', 'Songs of the Gael' (Lt B Walton O'Donnell), Ethel Smyth's overture 'The Wreckers', Holst's 'Planets' Suite and the 'Suites for Military Band' by Holst and Vaughan Williams. Among the new works composed specially for the Exhibition was Vaughan Williams' 'Toccata Marziale'.

1935 – Silver Jubilee of King George V

King George V celebrated his Silver Jubilee with a Thanksgiving Service in St Paul's Cathedral on 6th May 1935. The processions from Buckingham Palace moved at what was described in the orders as a 'slow trot' and thus did not include any bands. However, a combined Household Cavalry Band led the Sovereign's Escort from Hyde Park Barracks to Buckingham Palace and, before the processions left the Palace, played along The Mall, through Trafalgar Square and into Northumberland Avenue. It then counter-marched and returned to The Mall, leaving the route at Horse Guards Approach Road and rode to Wellington Barracks via Birdcage Walk.

Guards of Honour were found at Buckingham Palace by the Royal Navy, 1st Bn Grenadier Guards and the Royal Air Force, and at St Paul's by the Honourable Artillery Company. Six State Trumpeters of The Life Guards were on the steps of the Cathedral to sound fanfares on the arrival and departure of the King and Queen, while the Kneller Hall Band under Major Hector Adkins played inside.

At 9.30 that evening there was a Tattoo on Horse Guards Parade performed by the Massed Drums of 2nd and 3rd Bns Coldstream Guards, 1st Bn Irish Guards and 1st Bn Welsh Guards, with Pipers of 1st Bn Irish Guards, in front of an estimated 40,000 spectators,

1936 – State Funeral of King George V

King George V died the year following his Silver Jubilee. The State Funeral took place on 28th January 1936 with a procession from Westminster Hall to Paddington, this time with a Royal Navy gun carriage crew in London as well as at Windsor. Following the first two divisions of the dismounted Sovereign's Escort, found by the Royal Horse Guards (The Blues), marched:

Band of the 3rd Carabiniers (Prince of Wales's Dragoon Guards)
Band of the Royal Horse Guards (The Blues) *(dismounted – in state dress)*

As on previous such occasions the remaining bands were grouped together immediately in front of the gun carriage, this time comprising:

Band of the Royal Air Force
Band of the Royal Marines (Portsmouth Division)
Massed Bands of the Brigade of Guards
Royal Engineers Band
Royal Artillery Band
Massed Pipers of:
    Royal Irish Fusiliers (Princess Victoria's)
    Queen's Own Cameron Highlanders
    The Black Watch (Royal Highland Regiment)
    Irish Guards
    Scots Guards

The Massed Bands of the Brigade of Guards in the funeral procession of King George V on 28th January 1936. The Band of the Royal Engineers can be seen at the rear, wearing a similar uniform to the Guards.

The Band of the Royal Air Force, wearing head-dress based on the early flying helmets, in the funeral procession of King George V on 28th January 1936. The Band of the Royal Marines can be seen in rear and, behind them, the Brigade of Guards.

The bands marched with a frontage of eight in what was a very long column, the Massed Bands of the Brigade of Guards (less the Coldstream Guards) alone being in 26 ranks, led by five Drum Majors. In the centre of the Guards bands were three ranks comprising the four time-beaters (bass drummers), cymbal players and side drummers from the bands as well as ten Drummers (ie from the Corps of Drums). The pipers were found from the regiments of which the late King was Colonel-in-Chief.

The bands in the procession at Windsor were positioned immediately behind the second division of the Escort:

Band of the Coldstream Guards
Band of the Life Guards (*dismounted in state dress*)
Massed Pipers of:
The Black Watch (Royal Highland Regiment)
Scots Guards

1937 – Coronation of King George VI

The Coronation of King George VI took place on 12th May 1937. Sixteen Kneller Hall Trumpeters, along with six percussionists, played in Westminster Abbey under the Director of Music, Major Hector Adkins. The trumpeters were by now using the valved fanfare trumpets, designed by Major Adkins, in the pattern that has survived to the present day. Major Adkins also composed a number of fanfares which were sounded outside the Abbey to greet the arrival of various members of the Royal Family.

The return procession from Westminster Abbey to Buckingham Palace included:

An Officer of the War Office Staff
Four Troopers, The Life Guards
Band and Bugles of 1st Bn The Rifle Brigade (Prince Consort's Own)

17

Overseas Contingents
Band of the Royal Air Force
Royal Air Force Detachment, Overseas Contingents
Band and Pipes of 1st Bn Highland Light Infantry (City of Glasgow Regiment)
Detachments from Territorial Army Units
Band and Bugles of 2nd Bn Somerset Light Infantry (Prince Albert's)
Corps of the Army, Royal Tank Corps
Band and Drums of 2nd Bn Royal Warwickshire Regiment
Detachments of Regiments of Infantry
Band, Pipes and Drums of the Scots Guards
Detachments of the Brigade of Guards, Royal Corps of Signals, Royal Engineers
Detachment of Regiments of Yeomanry and Scouts (TA), Honourable Artillery
Company
Royal Artillery Mounted Band
Detachment of Royal Artillery
Band of 16th/5th The Queen's Royal Lancers
Representative Detachments of the Cavalry of the Line
'K' Battery, Royal Horse Artillery
Detachment of the Royal Marines
Band of the Royal Marines (Chatham Division)
Detachments of the Royal Navy
Carriage Procession of Prime Ministers and Colonial Rulers
Carriage Procession of the Royal Family (Captain's Escort)
Carriage Procession of Queen Mary (Captain's Escort with Standard)
Band of the Royal Scots Greys (2nd Dragoons)
The King and Queen's Procession:
Massed Bands of the Household Cavalry
1st and 2nd Divisions of the Sovereign's Escort
State Coach with the King and Queen
3rd and 4th Divisions of the Sovereign's Escort

The Royal Artillery Mounted Band in the Coronation Procession of King George VI on 12th May 1937. The Bandmaster, obscured by a marshal, is WO1 Sam Rhodes, later to become Lieutenant Colonel and Director of Music, Scots Guards.
(Photo: Royal Marines Museum)

18

Coronation of King George VI on 12th May 1937. The Massed Bands of the Household Cavalry led by the Directors of Music, Lieutenant Samuel Smith, The Life Guards, and Lieutenant Joseph Thornburrow, Royal Horse Guards. The formation is unusual in that the drum horses each have one 'flanker' riding on the outside. Most of the band horses appear to be greys and music pouches can be seen attached to the saddles of the Life Guards musicians.
(Photo: Royal Marines Museum)

Sixteen bands were stationed along the route:

Duke of York's Steps:	**Irish Guards**
Trafalgar Square:	**Royal Engineers**
Whitehall:	**Royal Naval School of Music**
Parliament Square:	**Kneller Hall Band** (150 players including 50 trumpeters)
Embankment, junction of Horse Guards Avenue:	**2nd Bn The Black Watch (Royal Highland Regiment)**
Waterloo Place:	**Royal Artillery**
St James's Palace:	**Welsh Guards**
Piccadilly:	**2nd Bn Royal Northumberland Fusiliers**
Piccadilly Circus:	**The Queen's Bays (2nd Dragoon Guards)**
Regent Street, junction of Heddon Street:	**1st Bn Prince of Wales's Volunteers**
Oxford Circus:	**Royal Tank Corps**
Oxford Street:	**2nd Bn Middlesex Regiment (Duke of Cambridge's Own)**
Marble Arch:	**1st Bn The Green Howards (Alexandra, Princess of Wales's Own Yorkshire Regiment)**
Hyde Park, East Carriage Road:	**2nd Bn Lincolnshire Regiment**
Hyde Park Corner:	**1st Bn King's Own Royal Regiment (Lancaster) and 1st Bn Durham Light Infantry**

Bands supporting the Guards of Honour:

Buckingham Palace:	**Grenadier Guards**
Westminster Abbey:	**HM Royal Marines (Plymouth Division)**

1946 – Victory March

The principal victory celebrations after the Second World War took place on 8th June 1946 with a march through London amidst much rejoicing. The marching column left from Marble Arch at 10.35 am, moving east along Oxford Street, south down Charing Cross Road and Northumberland Avenue to the Embankment and Whitehall. The mechanised column had left Regent's Park at 9.18 and travelled as far east as Whitechapel, turning south via London Bridge to Kennington, back via Vauxhall Bridge and Millbank to Whitehall where the marching and mechanised elements merged to proceed down The Mall; here the salute was taken by the King.

The Royal Tank Regiment under Bandmaster Denis Plater in Whitehall at the Victory March on 8th June 1946. (Photo: A Pickering)

A vast number of bands took part in the procession including:

Royal Marines
Royal Artillery
Royal Engineers
Royal Corps of Signals
Brigade of Guards
Royal Army Service Corps
Royal Army Medical Corps
Central Band of the Royal Air Force
Massed Cranwell, RAF Regiment and No 1 Regional Band, RAF
Women's Auxilliary Air Force
Metropolitan Police Central Band
Band of the National Fire Service
Royal Garhwal Rifles (India)

1952 – State Funeral of King George VI

The State Funeral of King George VI took place on 15th February 1952. At the previous three sovereigns' funerals, aside from the cavalry, the bands in the procession in London had been grouped together immediately in front of the gun carriage so that only one band was playing at any one time. In 1952, however, a complete change took place and the bands were distributed throughout the procession in pairs with each band of the pair playing alternately. The Band of the Royal Marines this time took its precedence with the Royal Navy as it marched with its detachment. The bands were distributed as follows:

Officer of the War Office
    Band of the Royal Air Force
    Band of the Welsh Guards
Royal Air Force, Colonial Troops, Territorial Army, Infantry of the Line
    Band of the Irish Guards
    Band of the Coldstream Guards
Foot Guards, Corps of Royal Engineers, Royal Artillery
Royal Tank Regiment, Cavalry of the Line
    Band of the Royal Artillery
    Band of HM Royal Marines (Plymouth Group)
Royal Marines, Royal Navy
Drum Horse and State Trumpeters of the Household Cavalry
1st Division of the Escort
    Band of the Scots Guards
Massed Pipes and Drums of:
    Royal Irish Fusiliers (Princess Victoria's)
    Royal Scots Fusiliers
    Royal Scots (The Royal Regiment)
    Irish Guards
    Scots Guards

Earl Marshal
Royal Navy Gun Carriage
Mourners
2nd Division of the Escort
   Band of the Royal Engineers (Chatham)
   Band of the Metropolitan Police

The Central Band of the Royal Air Force followed by the Band of the Welsh Guards in Edgware Road at the head of the funeral procession of King George VI on 15th February 1952. (Photo: Band of the Welsh Guards)

The Band of the Scots Guards and the Massed Pipes marched immediately in front of the gun carriage playing the following:

Westminster to Horse Guards	Band:	Beethoven's Funeral March No 1
	Massed Pipes:	My Home
Horse Guards to Marlborough Gate	Band:	Chopin's Funeral March
	Massed Pipes:	Loch Rannoch
Marlborough Gate to Hyde Park Corner	Band:	Song of Death
	Massed Pipes:	Cradle Song

Hyde Park Corner to Edgware Road	Band:	Mendelssohn's Funeral March
	Massed Pipes:	Road to the Isles
Edgware Road to Sussex Gardens	Band:	Regrets
	Massed Pipes:	Mist Covered Mountains
Sussex Gardens to Paddington	Band:	Song of Death
	Massed Pipes:	Loch Duich

The gun carriage halted at platform 8 at Paddington Station and the coffin was placed on the train. The Bands of the Coldstream and Scots Guards played Chopin's Funeral March, starting one minute prior to the departure of the train to Windsor. On arrival at Windsor Station the procession took the traditional route to St George's Chapel in the Castle and included:

1st Division of the Escort
  Band of the Grenadier Guards
  Band of the Royal Horse Guards (The Blues) (*dismounted in State Dress*)
Massed Pipers of:
  Queen's Own Cameron Highlanders
  Seaforth Highlanders (Ross-shire Buffs, The Duke of Albany's)
  The Black Watch (Royal Highland Regiment)
Royal Navy Gun Carriage
Mourners
2nd Division of the Escort

The Band of the Welsh Guards followed by the Band of the Irish Guards and the Drums of 1st Bn Irish Guards and 1st Bn Welsh Guards by Admiralty Arch on the outward procession at the Coronation of Queen Elizabeth II on 2nd June 1953.
(Photo: Band of the Welsh Guards)

23

1953 – Coronation of Queen Elizabeth II

The Queen's Coronation was held on 2nd June 1953 on a particularly cold and wet day. A number of processions left Buckingham Palace and drove to Westminster Abbey by way of The Mall, Northumberland Avenue, Victoria Embankment, Bridge Street and Parliament Square. The Queen's Procession included over a thousand officers and men of the Brigade of Guards with the Bands and Drums of the Irish and Welsh Guards, The King's Troop, Royal Horse Artillery and a Sovereign's Escort of Household Cavalry with the Mounted Band of the Royal Horse Guards (The Blues).

The Kneller Hall Trumpeters were again present for the service in the Abbey, conducted by the Director of Music, Lt Col Meredith Roberts, Royal Artillery, and from their position on top of the choir screen they must have had one of the best of all views of the ceremony. A further 30 trumpeters sounded fanfares outside the Abbey.

After the service a greatly enhanced State Procession left Westminster Abbey and returned to Buckingham Palace by way of Whitehall, Trafalgar Square, Pall Mall, Piccadilly, East Carriage Drive, Oxford Street, Regent Street, Haymarket and The Mall. The Queen departed from the Abbey at 2.50 pm and arrived at Buckingham Palace at 4.30, 45 minutes after the head of the procession. The bands were mostly positioned in groups of four with each pair in the group playing alternately:

An Officer of the War Office Staff

Four Troopers, Household Cavalry

Band of 1st Bn Durham Light Infantry	**Band of 1st Bn The Gloucestershire Regiment**
Band of 1st Bn Royal Scots Fusiliers	**Band of the 4th Queen's Own Hussars**

Colonial and Commonwealth Contingents

Royal Army Medical Corps Staff Band	**Band of the 22 Regiment, Canadian Army**
No 1 Regional Band, Royal Air Force	**No 2 Regional Band, Royal Air Force**

Royal Air Force Contingent

Royal Air Force College Band	**Royal Air Force Regiment Band**
Band of the Royal Army Ordnance Corps	**Band of the Royal Army Service Corps**

Army Contingent including Corps of the Army, Territorial Army and Brigade of Gurkhas

Band of 1st Bn The Rifle Brigade	**Band of 1st Bn Duke of Cornwall's Light Infantry**

Massed Pipers of:
Irish and Scottish Regiments, the Brigade of Gurkhas and the Pakistan Army

Infantry and Royal Corps of Signals

Band of the Royal Corps of Signals	**Band of the Royal Engineers (Chatham)**
Band of the Royal Artillery (Woolwich)	

Royal Engineers, Royal Artillery, Royal Armoured Corps, Royal Horse Artillery and Household Cavalry

| **Band of the 7th Queen's Own Hussars** | **Band of the Life Guards** |
| **Band of the Royal Marines School of Music** | **Band of the Royal Marines (Plymouth Group)** |

Royal Navy and Royal Marines Contingents

First Detachment of Foot Guards

| **Band of the Welsh Guards** | **Band of the Irish Guards** |
| **Corps of Drums of 1st Bn Welsh Guards** | **Corps of Drums of 1st Bn Irish Guards** |

Second Detachment of Foot Guards

The King's Troop, Royal Horse Artillery

Carriage Procession of Colonial Rulers

Carriage Procession of Prime Ministers

Carriage Procession of Princes and Princesses of the Blood

Carriage Procession of Her Majesty Queen Elizabeth, The Queen Mother with a Captain's Escort with Standard

Her Majesty The Queen's Procession including:
Queen's Honorary Physicians, Surgeons, Dental Surgeons, Chaplains, Honorary Chaplains and Aides-de-Camp from each of the services

Band of the Grenadier Guards

Corps of Drums of 1st Bn Grenadier Guards

Air Ministry, War Office and Admiralty Staff

Air Officers Commanding-in-Chief, General Officers Commanding-in-Chief and Flag Officers Commanding-in-Chief

Marshals of the Royal Air Force, Field Marshals and Admirals of the Fleet

Air Council, Army Council and Board of Admiralty

Chiefs of Staff

The Queen's Escort of Officers from the Colonial Contingents

The Queen's Escort of Officers from the Commonwealth Contingents

The Yeomen of the Guard

The Queen's Bargemaster and Watermen

Mounted Band of the Royal Horse Guards (The Blues)

1st and 2nd Divisions of the Sovereign's Escort

State Coach with Her Majesty The Queen

Officers in Attendance

3rd and 4th Divisions of the Sovereign's Escort

The Massed Bands of the Royal Marines comprising Plymouth Group and the Royal Marines School of Music in the Coronation Procession of Queen Elizabeth II of 2nd June 1953. The Director of Music in the foreground is Major F Vivian Dunn. The bands marched immediately behind the combined bands of The Life Guards and 7th Queen's Own Hussars, and played alternately with them. (Photo: Royal Marines Museum)

Coronation Visit to Edinburgh

The Queen visited Edinburgh on 24th June 1953 and a State Procession took place from the Palace of Holyroodhouse to St Giles Cathedral by way of Abbeymount, Regent Road, Waterloo Place, Princes Street, The Mound and St Giles Street. After the service the procession returned directly to Holyrood by way of the Royal Mile and North Gate. The bands in the procession were:

Massed Pipes and Drums: **2nd Bn Scots Guards**
                            1st Bn King's Own Scottish Borderers
                            1st Bn The Cameronians (Scottish Rifles)
                            1st Bn Argyll and Sutherland Highlanders
                                (Princess Louise's)

Massed Bands: **Royal Scots Greys (2nd Dragoons)**
                            Scots Guards

Mounted Band: **Royal Horse Guards (The Blues)**

1st and 2nd Divisions of the Sovereign's Escort

Her Majesty The Queen

3rd and 4th Divisions of the Sovereign's Escort

The Pipes and Drums played alternately with the military bands; the mounted band was instructed to play at the same time as the Pipes and Drums since they were sufficiently far apart not to clash.

The request for a mounted band came from the Lord Provost, provoking an indignant letter from the Chief of Staff, HQ London District, to the War Office: '... *it is not for the Lord Provost to order a band, but if I hear from Gold Stick that a band is required I will let the War Office know.*' On 4th March 1953 a further letter was sent from HQ London District: '*As you probably know there is tremendous feeling in Edinburgh that a band should be provided and I think there will be a great deal of heart burning and trouble if they do not go.*' It was finally agreed to provide a mounted band but with the proviso that it would no longer be possible for the Household Cavalry to loan horses to the Royal Scots Greys.

1960 – State Visit of General de Gaulle

State Visits normally take place two or three times each year in London or Windsor, or more occasionally in Edinburgh. Military music naturally plays its part with bands supporting Guards of Honour for the visiting Head of State and the troops lining the route of the procession. An orchestra from the Household Division plays at the State Banquet held in the evening, at the end of which the guests are entertained by twelve pipers also normally from the Household Division, although recent cutbacks have led to other regiments sharing in this duty.

At one time the second day of a state visit included a carriage procession from Buckingham Palace to Guildhall in the City for luncheon with the Lord Mayor, something now replaced by an evening banquet with the visitor arriving by car.

A Royal Air Force band plays 'La Marseillaise' as General de Gaulle passes through Ludgate Circus in a carriage procession to Guildhall for luncheon with the Lord Mayor of London as part of his state visit in 1960.
(Photo: Royal Marines Museum)

When General de Gaulle made a State Visit in 1960 an addition to the normal programme was a Review of the Household Troops held on Horse Guards Parade on 7th April at 10 am. The parade was commanded by the Major General Commanding the Household Brigade, Major General W A G (later Sir George) Burns and was made up of The King's Troop, Royal Horse Artillery, the Household Cavalry, 3rd Bn Grenadier Guards, 1st Bn Irish Guards and 1st Bn Coldstream Guards.

Music was provided by the Mounted Band of the Royal Horse Guards (The Blues), the Bands of the Grenadier, Coldstream and Irish Guards, with the Corps of Drums and Pipes of the battalions on parade, all under the Senior Director of Music, Lieutenant-Colonel Fred Harris, Grenadier Guards.

General de Gaulle arrived at Horse Guards accompanied by HRH the Duke of Edinburgh with a Captain's Escort of Household Cavalry and was received with a Royal Salute, 'La Marseillaise'. The General then inspected the parade from a land-rover and took the salute for the march past which followed. French marches were much in evidence in the music programme:

Inspection:
La Petite Valse (Heyne), Le Père La Victoire (Ganne)

March Past of The King's Troop, Royal Horse Artillery and the Household Cavalry:
Royal Artillery Slow March, Slow Marches of the Life Guards and the Royal Horse Guards

March Past of the Brigade of Guards:
Le Rêve Passe (Helmer), British Grenadiers, St Patrick's Day, Milanollo, Marche Lorraine (Ganne)

1965 – State Funeral of Sir Winston Churchill

The State Funeral of Sir Winston Churchill took place on 30th January 1965. It had been planned over a number of years from an attic at the College of Arms in London, in what was known as 'Operation Hope Not' and was only the third occasion that a commoner had been accorded such an honour, the others being Lord Nelson and the Duke of Wellington.

The coffin was borne on a gun carriage drawn by the Royal Navy and escorted by the Royal Air Force, in a procession which left Westminster Hall at 9.45 and marched by way of Parliament Street, Whitehall, Trafalgar Square, the Strand and Fleet Street to St Paul's Cathedral. Ten bands took part and, as at the funeral of King George VI, they marched in pairs with each band of the pair playing alternately.

Central Band of the Royal Air Force
No 5 Regional Band of the Royal Air Force
Battle of Britain Aircrews
The Royal Air Force
Territorial Army
Royal Military Academy, Sandhurst
Band of the Coldstream Guards
Band of the Grenadier Guards

The State Funeral of Sir Winston Churchill on 30th January 1965 with the Bands of the Royal Marines leading detachments from the Royal Marine Reserve, Royal Marines, Royal Naval Reserve and Royal Navy along Fleet Street. The Bands are led by Drum Major Charles Bowden and Drum Major Colin Bowden.
(Photo: Royal Marines Museum)

Foot Guards
    Band of the Royal Marines School of Music
    Band of the Royal Marines (Portsmouth)
Royal Marines, Royal Navy
Drum Horse and State Trumpeters of the Household Cavalry
First Detachment of Household Cavalry
    Band of the Irish Guards
    Band of the Scots Guards
Chiefs of Staff
Orders, Decorations and Banners borne by Officers of the Queen's Royal Irish
Hussars
General Officer Commanding and Staff
The Earl Marshal, The Duke of Norfolk
Royal Navy Gun Carriage
The Family and other Principal Mourners

Second Detachment of Household Cavalry
Band of the Royal Artillery
Band of the Metropolitan Police
The Police, Fire Services, Civil Defence Corps

The music played by the bands in the procession included the 'Dead March' from *Saul* (Handel), 'Song of Death' (Oran au Aoig) by Sommer, and the Funeral Marches of Beethoven, Chopin, Mendelssohn and Panne.

Following the service in St Paul's Cathedral the procession continued along Cannon Street, Eastcheap and Great Tower Street to Tower Hill. Here the coffin was lifted from the gun carriage and carried to Tower Pier by the Bearer Party of 2nd Bn Grenadier Guards as 60 Pipers led by Pipe Major Bob Kilgour, 2nd Bn Scots Guards, played 'My Home', 'Mist Covered Mountains', 'My Lodgin's in the Cold Ground' and 'Highland Cradle Song'. The pipers were from:

2nd Bn Scots Guards
1st Bn Irish Guards
1st Bn King's Own Scottish Borderers
1st Bn The Cameronians (Scottish Rifles)
1st Bn Royal Inniskilling Fusiliers

As the coffin was taken on the launch *Havengore* the Royal Navy Guard of Honour on Tower Wharf presented arms and the Band of the Royal Marines (Plymouth) played the first section of 'Dover Castle' (Carter) as a General Salute, appropriate to the Lord Warden of the Cinque Ports. The coffin was piped aboard by the Royal Navy and as *Havengore* set off for the journey along the Thames to Festival Pier the Royal Marines Band played 'Rule Britannia' (Arne), the Massed Pipers played the lament, 'Flowers of the Forest' and a 19 Gun Salute was fired. Then came a Fly Past by Lightnings of Fighter Command and the unforgettable sight of the jibs of the cranes along Hay's Wharf being lowered as *Havengore* passed. Finally, the coffin was taken by train from Waterloo for burial at Blaydon.

1965 – Waterloo Parade

The Battle of Waterloo took place on 18th June 1815 and it was not possible to celebrate the centenary, which fell during the Great War. However, it was decided that the 150th anniversary in 1965 would be commemorated on Horse Guards Parade on Saturday 12th June, the day of the Queen's Official Birthday. The vexed question of whether to invite the losers was considered but a memo from the Foreign Office was quite clear, stating that 'An approach to the French would be fruitless since General de Gaulle certainly would not countenance French participation in a commemoration of their most resounding defeat in our hands.'

The Bands of the Royal Artillery (Woolwich), Royal Artillery Mounted Band, Royal Army Service Corps and the Royal Military School of Music, Kneller Hall, were formed in a static position in front of the Guards Memorial, while marching displays were provided by Massed Bands, Drums, Pipes and Bugles (drawn from the UK based regiments which fought at Waterloo), all under Lieutenant-Colonel Basil Brown, Director of Music, the Royal Military School of Music.

The parade started at 9 pm with the Colour Parties of all the 'Waterloo' regiments marching on from Horse Guards Arch to 'Wellington' (Zehle) played by the static bands. Displays followed by:

Drums & Fifes: San Lorenzo (Silva), Toledo (Ord Hume), Hazelmere (Birkett)
Band, Pipes & Drums of 1st Bn Royal Inniskilling Fusiliers: Killaloe, Eileen
    Allanagh, Dublin Bay
Bands & Bugles: Light Infantry (Plater), Marching thro' Georgia (arr Miller), Hark
    Forrard (Plater)
Massed Bands: Scipio (Handel), Royal Birthday (Young)
Pipes and Drums: My Home, Barren Rocks of Aden (McKellar), The Braes of Mar,
    The Kilt is My Delight, Pibroch of Donald Dhu

The displays were interspersed with fanfares sounded by Trumpeters of the Royal Artillery (Woolwich) and the Royal Military School of Music.

The Queen and members of the Royal Family had meanwhile been attending an Army Dinner in the Banqueting House on the opposite side of Whitehall, with the Orchestra of the Irish Guards in attendance. The royal party arrived at Horse Guards to watch the finale of the parade, Eckersberg's musical fantasy 'The Battle of Waterloo' performed by the massed bands with the voice of the guns of The King's Troop, Royal Horse Artillery.

Reveille signalled the dawn of the fateful day and the French army was heard approaching the battlefield. The British Army then moved into position with the Welsh regiments represented by the Band of 1st The Queen's Dragoon Guards marching on from Treasury Green, the Irish regiments (Royal Inniskilling Fusiliers) from Old Admiralty Passage, the English regiments (Drums of 2nd Bn Grenadier Guards) from the stands adjacent to Treasury Passage and the Scots regiments (Pipes and Drums of 1st Bn The Royal Scots (The Royal Regiment)) from Horse Guards Approach Road. The battle was joined amidst much gunfire and all ended with the Grand March of the Victors.

A memorial service was held on the battlefield at Hougomont Farm on 18th June 1965 and there was a massed bands display in Brussels on 19/20th June with the Kneller Hall Band and the Bands, Pipes and Drums of the Waterloo regiments stationed in BAOR, 840 all ranks, again under the direction of Lieutenant-Colonel Basil Brown. To avoid causing any possible upset, the bands were banned from playing the Waterloo music in Brussels and, indeed, it was ordered by the Ambassador that there must be no mention of Waterloo, just a band display 'pure and simple'.

1969 – Investiture of the Prince of Wales

The Investiture of Prince Charles as Prince of Wales took place on 1st July 1969 at Caernarvon Castle. A temporary railway station was erected near the premises of Ferodo Ltd and the Queen and Royal Family were received there by a Guard of

Honour found by 1st Bn Royal Welch Fusiliers, supported by the Band of 1st Bn The Royal Regiment of Wales (24th/41st Foot). The Prince of Wales travelled in a carriage procession with a Prince of Wales's Escort of Household Cavalry to the Water Gate entrance to the castle where a Guard of Honour of 1st Bn Welsh Guards with the Band of the Welsh Guards awaited. The Band had earlier played in Castle Square to entertain the spectators. The carriage procession of HM the Queen followed ten minutes later with a Sovereign's Escort.

Inside the castle, State Trumpeters of the Household Cavalry were positioned at the top of the Eagle Tower while three teams of Trumpeters from the Royal Military School of Music, Kneller Hall, occupied equally lofty perches on three other towers. The Band of the Royal Welch Fusiliers, augmented by students from Kneller Hall, under Bandmaster H C R 'Ben' Bentley was positioned in the centre of the castle. An augmented BBC Welsh Orchestra and a number of choirs performed specially composed items while the processions were taking place.

At the conclusion of the ceremony the Prince was presented at the three gates of the castle. Magnificent antiphonal fanfares, specially composed by Sir Arthur Bliss, Master of the Queen's Musick, rang out from each group of Kneller Hall Trumpeters in turn, with interludes played by the band, all under the direction of Lieutenant-Colonel 'Jiggs' Jaeger, Irish Guards.

1977 – Silver Jubilee of Queen Elizabeth II

Queen Elizabeth II celebrated her Silver Jubilee in 1977 and, as with her Grand-father in 1935, a Thanksgiving Service was held in St Paul's Cathedral on 7th June 1977. There was a mounted procession from Buckingham Palace but this did not include any bands, a fact much lamented in the press, even in those news-papers that might normally deride such things, perhaps emphasising just how much military bands are taken for granted but sorely missed when they do not appear.

However, the Kneller Hall Trumpeters played in St Paul's during the service, under Lieutenant-Colonel Trevor Sharpe, Coldstream Guards, and the Band and Drums of the Honourable Artillery Company were on duty with the Guard of Honour outside. At Buckingham Palace the Band of HM Royal Marines (Commando Forces) supported the tri-service Guard of Honour while a number of bands were positioned along the route with the streetliners.

That evening a concert was held at the Royal Albert Hall with the Bands of the Royal Artillery (Woolwich), Grenadier and Irish Guards, the Band and Trumpeters from Kneller Hall and the London Symphony Chorus, all under Lieutenant-Colonel Sharpe. The music included such fitting items as 'Cockaigne' and the 'Coronation Ode' by Sir Edward Elgar, 'Vivat Regina' by Laurie Johnson and the 'Investiture Music for the Prince of Wales' by Sir Arthur Bliss. As well as the concert items there were marching displays in the arena by the Bands of the Grenadier and Irish Guards, the Pipes and Drums of 1st Bn Scots Guards and the Band and Bugles of 3rd Bn Royal Green Jackets.

1979 – Funeral of Earl Mountbatten of Burma

Admiral of the Fleet The Earl Mountbatten of Burma was murdered on 27th August 1979 and his funeral took place in bright sunshine on 5th September. A Royal Navy Gun Carriage Crew took the coffin from the Queen's Chapel at St James's Palace, along The Mall, across Horse Guards Parade and via Whitehall to Westminster Abbey, in a procession which was formed as follows:

    Central Band of the Royal Air Force
Overseas Detachments, Women's Services,
Royal Air Force, 2nd King Edward VII's Own Gurkha Rifles
    Massed Bands of the Household Cavalry
The Life Guards, Royal Marines, Royal Navy
    Massed Bands of HM Royal Marines
Gun Carriage
Ex-Service Organisations
    Bands of the Grenadier and Coldstream Guards
The Blues and Royals

The Funeral Procession of Admiral of the Fleet The Earl Mountbatten of Burma on 5th September 1979. The Massed Bands of the Royal Marines lead the Royal Navy Gun Carriage Crew into the Mall. The drums are draped in black. (Photo: Royal Marines Museum)

The procession took over 45 minutes to march from the Queen's Chapel to the Abbey and the bands were required to play continuously, unlike at Churchill's funeral where they had been able to alternate. The Royal Marines Bands which preceded the gun carriage played two Beethoven funeral marches, the 'Dead March' in *Saul* (Handel) and finally the 'Preobrajensky March' (Donajowsky) which had been so closely associated with the Earl and his family.

As the Earl's coffin entered the Abbey, Trumpeters of the Royal Marines, positioned on the choir screen, sounded the fanfare 'Supreme Command' which had been composed in his honour some years before by Sir Vivian Dunn. Buglers of the Royal Marines sounded Last Post and Reveille during the service.

1981 – Wedding of the Prince and Princess of Wales

Prince Charles was oft quoted as saying he wanted a musical wedding, and the music for the service in St Paul's Cathedral was much enhanced by the presence of the Kneller Hall Trumpeters conducted by Lieutenant-Colonel George Evans, The Blues and Royals. The arrival of Lady Diana Spencer was greeted by Major 'Jacko' Jackson's 'Fanfare Royale' sounded by State Trumpeters of the Household Cavalry from under the portico at the west door of the cathedral, while they marked the end of the service with 'Rejoicing', specially composed by Major Tony Richards, The Life Guards, which was sounded from the Whispering Gallery.

The Band of the Welsh Guards was with the Guard of Honour formed by the Queen's Guard in the forecourt of Buckingham Palace. Outside St Paul's Cathedral was a tri-service Guard of Honour, appropriately supported by the Band of HM Royal Marines (Commando Forces) who wore the Prince of Wales's feathers as part of their cap badge. The bands with the streetliners included the 1st Bn 22nd (Cheshire) Regiment and 2nd Bn The Parachute Regiment of which the Prince is Colonel-in-Chief.

The Wedding of the Prince and Princess of Wales in July 1981. The Band and Drums of 2nd Bn The Parachute Regiment march along Farringdon Street to take up their street-lining position in Fleet Street, led by their pony mascot and the goat mascot of 1st Bn Royal Regiment of Wales (24th/41st Foot).
(Photo: Colin Dean)

A magnificent firework display took place in Hyde Park the previous evening with the Massed Bands of the Household Division under Lieutenant-Colonel Richard Ridings, Coldstream Guards, playing extracts from Handel's 'Music for the Royal Fireworks' and much other suitable music.

1982 – City of London's Salute to the Task Force

Following Argentina's invasion of the Falkland Islands on 2nd April 1982, a Task Force was quickly despatched and successfully recaptured the Islands in June. On 12th October 1982, representatives of the Task Force marched through the City of London for lunch at Guildhall with the Lord Mayor, including the following bands:

The City of London's salute to the South Atlantic Task Force on 12th October 1982.

Left: The Band of the Royal Marines, Commando Forces, with Captain John Ware, wearing Lovat uniforms with green berets.

Below: The Pipes and Drums of 2nd Bn Scots Guards.
(Photos: Colin Dean)

Band of HM Royal Marines, Flag Officer 3rd Flotilla*
Band of HM Royal Marines, Royal Marines School of Music

Band of HM Royal Marines, Flag Officer Plymouth
Band of HM Royal Marines, Commando Forces*

The Royal Artillery Band

Band of the Welsh Guards
Corps of Drums and Pipes and Drums, 2nd Bn Scots Guards*
Corps of Drums, 1st Bn Welsh Guards*

Massed Bands of the 2nd and 3rd Battalions, The Parachute Regiment
Massed Drums of the 2nd and 3rd Battalions, The Parachute Regiment*

Pipes and Drums of 1st Bn 7th Duke of Edinburgh's Own Gurkha Rifles*

Mounted Band of the Blues and Royals (Royal Horse Guards and 1st Dragoons)

Central Band of the Royal Air Force

1990 – The Queen Mother's 90th Birthday Parade

Queen Elizabeth, the Queen Mother celebrated her 90th birthday on 4th August 1990 but the principal celebration took place on Horse Guards Parade on 27th June. Music naturally took a central part with a large orchestra and choir positioned on a huge stage in front of the Guards Memorial. In front were the Massed Bands of the Royal Marines, Guards Division and Royal Air Force, flanked by the Mounted Bands of the Household Cavalry, all under Wing Commander Barrie Hingley, Principal Director of Music RAF.

Queen Elizabeth arrived in an open carriage escorted by a Captain's Escort with Standard of the Household Cavalry, and inspected the parade as the massed bands, orchestra and choir combined for Parry's great anthem, 'I Was Glad'. The march past was led by representatives from units of the armed forces of Britain and the Commonwealth with which Her Majesty is connected, with the music rapidly changing from one regimental march to the next. Next came representatives of countless civilian organisations, including a host of celebrities, and even racehorses.

It is a considerable tribute to the talent of Wing Commander Hingley, and probably a unique honour for a Director of Music, that he should compose the words and music for a special birthday song to be performed on this prestigious occasion. 'The Sound of the Pipes' was a great success and brought together the massed bands, pipes and choirs.

*units which took part in the conflict

O, the sound of the pipes as they play for our lady
Recall youthful years in the land of her birth
O, the sound of the pipes as they play for our lady
Bring smiles and salutations on this joyful happy day!

The Captain's Escort marched past and made a hasty exit along The Mall before the guns of The King's Troop were fired to the accompaniment of a peal of church bells. Her Majesty finally departed as the pipes played 'Will Ye No Come Back Again?'

1991 – Welcome Home Parade for the Gulf Forces

A considerable number of bands from all three services took part in the Gulf War of 1991 to secure the liberation of Kuwait. The Gulf Forces were honoured by the City of London on 21st June 1991 with lunch at Guildhall after marching from Armoury House via Mansion House where the Queen took the salute. The Band of the Scots Guards played outside Mansion House with Trumpeters from the Royal Air Force College, and the Orchestra of the Life Guards played inside Guildhall.

The parade was led by Brigadier Patrick Cordingley, a commentator at many of the Wembley Pageants, and the following bands were included in the procession, all of whom took part in the conflict:

Band of HM Royal Marines, Commander-in-Chief, Fleet
Bands of the 5th Royal Inniskilling Dragoon Guards and the
Queen's Royal Irish Hussars
Pipes and Drums of the Queen's Royal Irish Hussars and the
1st Bn Queen's Own Highlanders (Seaforth and Camerons)
Central Band of the Royal Air Force

1990–95 – Fifty Years On

Anniversaries of the major events of the Second World War are commemorated at frequent intervals, but the 50th anniversaries were to become a particular time for national celebrations and remembrance.

Battle of Britain

The first of these major events was held on 15th September 1990 to mark the 50th anniversary of the Battle of Britain. The Royal Air Force mustered on Horse Guards Parade and marched down The Mall, led by the massed bands. The massive parade formed in Queen's Gardens outside Buckingham Palace included 4 Queen's Colours and 17 Squadron Standards representing all Battle of Britain Squadrons still in existence, while the Queen's Guard, found by the Queen's Colour Squadron, Royal Air Force and augmented to a full Guard of Honour, was in position in the forecourt. As well as the RAF bands, the Royal Artillery Band also took part, representing the Gunner anti-aircraft units who also made a significant contribution to the battle.

Following a spectacular fly past the Queen inspected the parade from a land-rover as the massed bands, under Wing Commander Barrie Hingley, played specially commissioned music by Ron Goodwin simply called 'September 15th 1940'. Then came the moving climax of the day as veterans of the Battle of Britain, known to us all simply as 'The Few', appeared from Constitution Hill to march past their Sovereign to the stirring sounds of the March from Sir William Walton's 'Battle of Britain Suite'. Finally the parade marched past to the 'Royal Air Force March Past' and returned along The Mall with the massed bands, while after a final Royal Salute, the Royal Artillery Band led the Queen's Guard, Guard of Honour back to St James's Palace.

D-Day

The next major commemoration was of D-Day (6th June 1944), when Whale Island, Portsmouth, was the setting for Beating Retreat on the evening of Saturday 4th June 1994. This was held in pouring rain in the presence of the Queen Mother with bands from Canada, France and the USA as well as the Royal Marines School of Music and Royal Corps of Signals. The bands gave individual displays and joined together, appropriately playing Sousa's 'Hands Across the Sea', for the finale under Lt Col John Ware, OBE, Principal Director of Music, Royal Marines.

The Band of 2nd Bn Princess of Wales's Royal Regiment (Queen's and Royal Hampshires) with the bandmaster, WO1 Jerry Young, leading veterans to the D-Day commemoration service on Southsea Common on 5th June 1994. (Photo: John Ambler)

The sun came out the next day for a drumhead service which was held on a very wet and muddy Southsea Common with the Band of HM Royal Marines positioned on a large stage in the centre of the Common. We are all accustomed to the immaculate precision of the Royal Marines Corps of Drums but this ceremony gave them the opportunity to enhance their standing further by the impeccable manner in which they piled drums on which the flags of fourteen allied nations were laid.

The celebrations then moved across the Channel to Pegasus Bridge, the site of the first glider-borne allied landings on D-Day, where the newly formed Band of the Army Air Corps led veterans of this action across the bridge playing 'Colonel Bogey' (Alford).

The climax of the D-Day celebrations was held on the rather wet beach at Arromanches in Normandy, as veterans paraded with the bands of HM Royal Marines (Commando Training Centre), Royal Artillery, 1st Bn Princess of Wales's Royal Regiment (Queen's and Royal Hampshires) and the Army Air Corps, all under Major Terry Davis, Royal Artillery. The National Standards of the Royal British Legion and the Normandy Veterans Association were marched on to the beach from one of the landing craft which formed a back-drop to the parade as the bands played Kelly's appropriately titled march 'Arromanches'. The Queen and the Duke of Edinburgh inspected the parade and then took the salute as thousands of veterans marched past, the music rather curiously starting with a German march, 'Alte Kameraden' (Old Comrades) by Carl Teike.

VE Day

The 50th anniversary celebrations of VE Day (Victory in Europe) started in Hyde Park on Saturday 6th May 1995 with an opening ceremony held in glorious sunshine, with the Mounted Bands of the Household Cavalry, the Bands of the Grenadier and Welsh Guards, the Royal Marines School of Music and the Central Band of the Royal Air Force, with the Pipes and Drums of 1st Bn Scots Guards, 1st Royal Tank Regiment and 2nd Bn Royal Canadian Regiment, all under Lieutenant-Colonel Richard Waterer, Royal Marines. Buglers of the Royal Marines sounded Last Post and, after two minutes' silence, Reveille was sounded, unusually, by mounted State Trumpeters of the Household Cavalry.* That evening tri-service bands joined with the Central Band of the Royal British Legion for a concert of celebration on the massive stage built in Hyde Park.

The Queen attended a service at St Paul's Cathedral on Sunday 7th May and was received with a tri-service Guard of Honour supported by the Band of the Royal Air Force Regiment, while the Band of the Scots Guards played inside the cathedral. A ceremony for heads of state took place in Hyde Park in the afternoon, beginning with trumpeters from the three services playing Aaron Copeland's 'Fanfare for the Common Man', conducted by Lt Col Cliff Ross, Welsh Guards, Principal Director of Music (Army).

The 50th anniversary itself was on 8th May 1995 with the Massed Bands of the Household Cavalry, dismounted in state dress, forming part of tri-service massed bands in the forecourt of Buckingham Palace, conducted by Major Bob Garrity, The Blues and Royals. The bands accompanied Dame Vera Lynn, Sir Harry Secombe, Cliff Richard and a daylight fireworks display, all in the presence of HM The Queen, HM Queen Elizabeth, The Queen Mother, and HRH The Princess Margaret. The closing ceremony of the celebrations took place in Hyde Park that evening with

*As far as is known this was the first time that Reveille was sounded by mounted trumpeters at such an occasion. Mounted State Trumpeters sounded Last Post and Reveille outside St Paul's Cathedral during the Lord Mayor's Show on 11th November 1995, Armistice Day.

Major Stuart Watts, Welsh Guards, directing the massed bands to end three days of very long and tiring work for the bands, with rehearsals for each of the events as well as the performances themselves taking place in considerable heat.

VJ Day

Victory in Europe did not end the war and so the final commemorations were reserved for VJ Day (Victory in Japan). A Service of Remembrance and Commitment to mark the 50th Anniversary of the end of the Second World War took place outside Buckingham Palace on 19th August 1995 with the Massed Bands of the Household Cavalry, dismounted in state dress, under the baton of Major Bob Garrity, The Blues and Royals, positioned on the Queen Victoria Memorial.

Cavalry Last Post was sounded by four State Trumpeters and during the silence which followed came the unforgettable sight of a Lancaster bomber flying low above The Mall dropping thousands of poppies as it passed. Pipers of 3rd Bn Royal Gurkha Rifles then played 'Heroes of Kohima' as a lament, before Reveille rang out from the State Trumpeters.

After the Service Her Majesty and the Royal Family moved to a saluting dais in The Mall to take the salute as the veterans marched past, led by holders of the Victoria Cross and the George Cross. The procession was led by the Band of the Royal Marines School of Music and the Central Band of the Royal Air Force, playing 'The Standard of St George' and 'Burma Campaigners'. The Band of the Brigade of Gurkhas led the Indian Army Association, marching past to 'Colonel Bogey'.

The Band of the Brigade of Gurkhas leading the Indian Army Association into The Mall during the VJ Day commemorations on 19th August 1995. (Photo: John Ambler)

The Bands of the Coldstream and Scots Guards played next to the saluting base as the remainder of the column passed, including the Duke of Edinburgh who marched with the Burma Star Association. The bands then stepped off to lead the first section of the Regular and Reserve Forces past the saluting base to 'The Army the Navy and the Air Force' (Darewski) and 'Commonwealth on the March' (Jaeger). The second detachment followed, led by the Band of the Grenadier Guards with the Pipes and Drums of 3rd Bn Royal Gurkha Rifles.

The following evening a parade was held on Horse Guards Parade with the tri-service massed bands under Lieutenant-Colonel David Price, Scots Guards, and an orchestra and choir under Sir David Willcocks. As the Queen arrived the bands were playing Parry's great coronation anthem 'I Was Glad', and there followed selections of verse and music including 'Pomp and Circumstance No 4', 'River Kwai March', 'Road to Mandalay', 'Jerusalem' and 'Pie Jesu'. To Roger Quilter's 'Non Nobis Domine' the Queen and Prince Philip were led by the two Queen's Gurkha Orderlies through a cross formed by school children to the dais in front of the orchestra. Drummers of 1st Bn Grenadier Guards sounded Last Post and, after the silence, Buglers of the Royal Marines replied with Reveille.

At the end of the parade all the participants marched down The Mall to Bucking-ham Palace, the mounted bands, massed bands, a car with Her Majesty and Prince Philip followed by the choirs and children, with music including Kenneth Alford marches honouring each of the three services, 'HM Jollies', 'Eagle Squadron' and 'The Great Little Army'.

Back at Buckingham Palace the Queen and the Duke of Edinburgh stood on a dais in the centre gateway with the massed bands facing them, the mounted bands behind them and the choirs on the Queen Victoria Memorial, for a Sunset ceremony. 'O Valiant Hearts', 'Abide with Me', 'The Day Thou Gavest' were sung, and following the playing of 'Sunset', Pipers of the Royal Gurkha Rifles played 'Heroes of Kohima' from the roof of the Palace. After a short while the Queen appeared on the balcony and the mood changed as the massed bands and choirs struck up 'Rule Britannia', 'Land of Hope and Glory' and 'Auld Lang Syne'.

Simultaneous celebrations were held at Edinburgh Castle, Cardiff Castle and Carrickfergus Castle, each featuring massed bands from the three services and attended by members of the Royal Family.

Army Benevolent Fund

Mention should also be made of another important 50th anniversary, that of the foundation of the Army Benevolent Fund. This took the form of a Drumhead Service of Thanksgiving in Figure Court at the Royal Hospital, Chelsea, on 30th June 1994. Music was provided by the Bands of the Coldstream and Scots Guards, the Pipes and Drums of 1st Bn Royal Scots (The Royal Regiment), Kneller Hall Trumpeters and the Choir of the Royal Regiment of Wales (24th/41st Foot), all under Major David Marshall, Coldstream Guards.

The In-Pensioners marched on to 'Boys of the Old Brigade' after which came the unique spectacle of the Standard, Guidon, Colour and Truncheon parties of all regiments of the British Army marching onto parade. Two guns of The King's Troop represented the Royal Regiment of Artillery, four buglers represented the Royal

Green Jackets and there were representatives of all the Corps of the Army, some with piled drums.

Her Majesty Queen Elizabeth, The Queen Mother entered to 'Pomp and Circumstance No 4' in a Royal Procession which included eight Field Marshals, including the Duke of Kent, for a service which culminated with the sounding of Last Post and Reveille by buglers high on the roof of the Hospital.

1995 – The City of London Privileged Regiments

The 'Freedom' has been granted to many regiments, corps and even a band by towns and cities throughout the country while, conversely, there has been talk of what have been termed the more loony councils banning the presence of the military. Whilst the granting of the Freedom is a cherished honour, the Queen's troops can, of course, proceed along her highway as they wish – except in the City of London. This unique situation dates back to a charter granted by King Edward III to the Mayor and Commonalty of London in 1327 which provided that no citizen should be compelled to go to war out of the City. This was confirmed by Cromwell's Commonwealth Parliament in 1647 although there were a number of subsequent challenges including one in 1842 when it was upheld that the Lord Mayor and Citizens had the right established by treaties to close the City's gates against the Sovereign's troops.

This remains the case to this day and troops can only enter the City of London with the agreement of the Lord Mayor or when invited to do so on occasions such as the Lord Mayor's Show. No regiments have the *freedom* to march though the City but there are a small number of Privileged Regiments who are able to march with

The Minden Band of the Queen's Division in King Street on 20th October 1995 when the City privileged regiments marched to Guildhall. (Photo: Colin Dean)

'Drums Beating, Colours Flying and Bayonets Fixed', subject to prior notice having been given to the Lord Mayor.

This privilege is exercised from time to time, normally when one of the regiments is celebrating a particular anniversary, the most recent such occasion being on 21st June 2000 when the Coldstream Guards marked the 350th anniversary of the founding of the regiment. The regiment is met at the City boundary by the City Marshal on horseback who will challenge them with 'Who Goes There?'. The Commanding Officer replies, after which the City Marshal will state that he has the authority of the Lord Mayor to escort them through the City.

A rare, if not unique, spectacle took place on 20th October 1995* when all City of London Privileged Regiments marched through the City from Armoury House to Guildhall, past Mansion House where the Salute was taken by the Lord Mayor of London accompanied by the Duke of Edinburgh.** All troops marched with Drums Beating, Colours or Guidon Flying and Bayonets Fixed.

Band of HM Royal Marines, Royal Marines School of Music, Royal Naval Reserve, Royal Marines

Mounted & Armoured Detachments of The Blues and Royals (Royal Horse Guards & 1st Dragoons)***

Band of the Grenadier Guards, 1st Bn Grenadier Guards, Number 7 Company Coldstream Guards***

Minden Band of The Queen's Division, The Princess of Wales's Royal Regiment (Queen's and Royal Hampshires), Royal Regiment of Fusiliers

Band of the Honourable Artillery Company, Honourable Artillery Company

Drums and Pipes of the London Regiment, The London Regiment

2000 – The Queen Mother's 100th Birthday

The 20th Century opened with a very sad and solemn occasion but its last great event was one of much joy and celebration to mark a milestone unique in the history of the Royal Family, the 100th birthday of Her Majesty Queen Elizabeth, the Queen Mother. The celebrations started with a Service of Thanksgiving in St Paul's Cathedral on Tuesday 19th July 2000. Military participation outside was limited to a step-lining party but the Band of the Coldstream Guards played inside the cathedral before and after the service. Twelve State Trumpeters sounded a fanfare from the Whispering Gallery as the Queen entered the cathedral and trumpeters of the Coldstream Guards joined with the National Anthem at the conclusion.

Her Majesty had departed from Horse Guards Parade after her 90th Birthday Parade with the pipes playing 'Will Ye No Come Back Again?', and she did just that on 19th July 2000 for a parade which took a similar format although turned about so

---

*There was no particular significance in the date for the parade although the author of this chapter tried hard to convince people that it had been specially arranged to mark his 40th birthday!

**The Lord Mayor takes precedence over everyone other then the Sovereign whilst in the City of London.

***The Band of The Blues and Royals was touring North America and the Band of the Coldstream Guards was touring Japan.

that the dais was positioned by the Guards Memorial. Tri-service massed bands were once again on parade, this time under Lieutenant-Colonel Richard Waterer, OBE, Royal Marines, along with the Royal Philharmonic Orchestra and a host of choirs. The Standard, Guidon and Colour Parties, and representative detachments from units associated with the Queen Mother marched past, followed by The King's Troop, Royal Horse Artillery and the Captain's Escort with Standard of Household Cavalry, the latter followed by the two mounted bands.

A Pageant of 100 Years followed, with representations of the past ten decades passing by, accompanied by popular tunes of those days. Next came representatives of the many civilian organisations with which Her Majesty is associated in what was described as a 'March, Skip and Dance Past', again to the sound of suitable well known melodies.

The pageant on Horse Guards Parade on 19th July 2000 to mark the 100th Birthday of H.M. Queen Elizabeth, the Queen Mother. (Photo: Margaret Ambler)

The Battle of Britain Memorial Flight, a Bristol Blenheim and the Red Arrows paid tribute in their own inimitable manner and the crowd rose as one to salute holders of the Victoria Cross and George Cross who passed by in vintage motors, and, of course, for the Chelsea Pensioners. Wing Commander Hingley was invited to compose a special birthday song, 'A Hundred Years', which combined the massed bands, pipes and drums, orchestra and choirs, and he arranged much of the music for the pageant along with WO2 Mick Dowrick, Royal Marines. Her Majesty again departed to 'Will Ye No Come Back Again?' – who knows?

In Edinburgh, the occasion was celebrated with a Royal Tribute on the Castle Esplanade on 27th July with Massed Pipes and Drums from the Scottish Regiments, along with eight regiments from the Commonwealth. Their programme included 'Scotland's Salute to The Queen Mother', specially composed by the Director of Army Bagpipe Music, Major Gavin Stoddart, MBE, BEM, Royal Highland Fusiliers. The Massed Military Bands followed and combined with the pipes for the finale with 'The Sound of the Pipes' and 'Land of Light', conducted by Major Bob Owen, Scots Guards.

On the day itself, 4th August 2000, The King's Troop ranked past Her Majesty at Clarence House, followed by the St James's Palace Detachment of the Old Guard with the Band of the Irish Guards playing 'Happy Birthday'. Following the delivery of the traditional telegram, opened courtesy of the Equerry's sword, the Queen Mother drove by carriage to Buckingham Palace, passing between the Old and New Guards. After the guard changing, the Band of the Coldstream Guards remained in the forecourt to play suitable music, saluting the newly honoured Garrison Sergeant Major 'Perry' Mason, MVO, MBE with 'Perry's Pride'* and, of course, playing 'Happy Birthday' as Her Majesty appeared on the balcony with her family.

Appendix

There are frequent references in this chapter to various Escorts furnished by the Household Cavalry which are normally formed as follows, although they may vary depending on the availability of horses:

Sovereign's Escort
7 officers and 109 other ranks, commanded by a field officer. Formed in 4 divisions, each of 1 officer and 24 men, with a standard party, a farrier rank and an advance and rear guard.

Captain's Escort With Standard
3 officers and 58 other ranks commanded by a Captain or above. Formed in 2 divisions each of 1 officer and 24 men, with a standard party, a single farrier and an advance and rear guard.

Captain's Escort Without Standard
2 officers and 32 other ranks commanded by a Captain or above. Formed in 2 divisions, each of 12 men, with a warrant officer and farrier in rear, and an advance and rear guard.

Prince of Wales's Escort
1 officer, 1 warrant officer and 30 other ranks. Formed in 2 divisions of 12 men with an advance and rear guard.

Travelling Escort
2 officers and 14 other ranks, although since 1985 a Standard party has been added for certain occasions.

*An arrangement of 'Blaydon Races' by Captain (now Major) Ian McElligott, Coldstream Guards.

CHAPTER 2

THE GREAT ANNUAL OCCASIONS

COLIN DEAN

Sovereign's Birthday Parade

The origins of the Sovereign's Birthday Parade, or Trooping the Colour, really stem from the basic practicalities of soldiers mustering on a suitable open ground and being allocated their duties for the day. In London this took place daily on Horse Guards Parade until the spring of 1817, between April and September from 1817 to 1856 and then from 1st May to the day of the Queen's Birthday Parade. Until fairly recently, Guard Mounting from Horse Guards would normally be held on five days during May with each of the Foot Guards battalions in London District taking its turn to provide the Escort and with a different band each time playing its own programme of music.

One of the particularly interesting aspects of this parade until 1989 was the part played by the Corps of Drums in the forming-up procedure on Horse Guards Parade. After the Guards had formed into line, the warrant officer of each Guard recovered arms and advanced across the parade with the drums playing 'Dashing White Sergeant'. The drums then beat the Assembly (three strokes on the side drums followed by three beats from the bass drummer, each beat followed by a pause note on the flutes and a crescendo roll from the side drummers) as the officers fell in and drew swords. The officers and warrant officers then slow marched across the parade ground with swords and rifles at the recover, to join their Guards. Sadly, this parade has now lost much of its individuality and has become little more than a rehearsal for the Birthday Parade.

It is generally thought that it was in about 1805 when it became the custom to mark the Sovereign's birthday by including flank companies from each of the Foot Guards regiments at the Guard Mounting, and it is from this custom that today's Birthday Parade has evolved. Although Queen Victoria did not officially attend the parade in London, it has since been the custom for succeeding Sovereigns to take the salute whenever possible.

Music forms an integral part of the parade and is provided by the Mounted Bands of the Household Cavalry, the Massed Bands of the Guards Division, and the Corps of Drums and Pipes and Drums of the battalions on parade. It has often been asked why the Foot Guards bands form up in their particular order and why some directors of music appear to be marching with the *wrong* band. It is usual in the army for regiments to form up in order of seniority from the right of the line, but the Guards Division form up in what is termed 'Brigade Order'. The senior regiment on parade will form up on the right flank, the next senior on the left flank, the next, second from the right and so on. Thus at the Queen's Birthday Parade, when all five bands are normally on parade, their order will be:

left				right
Coldstream Guards	Irish Guards	Welsh Guards	Scots Guards	Grenadier Guards

The Senior Director of Music now always marches with the Band of the Welsh Guards so as to be in a central position. The Director of Music, Welsh Guards (if he is not the senior) will therefore march with the Senior Director of Music's band in order to balance the number of musicians. The second senior Director of Music marches with the Coldstream or Irish Guards so that he is in the correct position to signal the left half of the massed bands to turn about during the three spin-wheels. If he is not from the Coldstream or Irish Guards, this will result in a further change.

There is, of course, a further complication in that the Corps of Drums will not necessarily be in the same order as the bands, as not all regiments will be represented. The senior side drummer of the battalion finding the Escort will always march on the left flank, so as to detach himself during the Quick Troop to beat Drummers Call.

Since 1971 both Household Cavalry bands have taken part, normally led by the Director of Music of the regiment whose Sovereign's Standard is on parade. Prior to 1971 the bands usually took turns to appear, although massed mounted bands were on the parade in 1938 (led by both Directors of Music) and on the 1919 and 1920 parades which were held in Hyde Park because wartime huts had been built on Horse Guards Parade. All three Household Cavalry bands were on the 1919 parade (1st Life Guards, 2nd Life Guards and Royal Horse Guards (The Blues)).

The Royal Procession rides from Buckingham Palace along The Mall and arrives at Horse Guards Parade at 11 o'clock. The order is given, 'Royal Salute, Present Arms' and the bands play the National Anthem, after which the Queen inspects the front rank of the Guards while a slow march is played softly by the massed bands so as not to unsettle the horses as the procession passes in front. The music is often in 3/4 time and in recent years has normally been based on national airs appropriate to the regiment whose Colour is to be trooped, often specially arranged by the respective Director of Music, with titles such as:

		Arranger:
Grenadier Guards	**Summer Air**	Lt Col Stuart Watts
	British Folk Song Medley	Lt Col Philip Hills
Coldstream Guards	**Patriotic Airs**	Major David Marshall
Scots Guards	**Melodies of Scotland**	Major Jimmy Howe
	Auld Scotch Songs, Songs of Scotia	Lt Col Duncan Beat

Irish Guards	**Songs of the Emerald Isle,**	
	Paddy's Songs	Lt Col Mick Lane
	Paddy Reilly	Major Mick Henderson
Welsh Guards	**Sounds Welsh**	Lt Col Peter Hannam
	Welsh Airs and Graces	Major Terry Davis

The last medley was arranged for the 1998 parade by Major Terry Davis, Welsh Guards, who sadly died a few weeks before the parade, aged just 47. 'La Plume Rouge' (The Red Plume), written by Lt Col Richard Ridings, Coldstream Guards, was played at this point on four occasions between 1976 and 2000.

As the Queen passes the left flank of the Guards the music cuts out and changes to a quick march while she inspects the rear rank and the mounted troops. Again, this march will often reflect appropriate connections and, amongst recent innovations, the drums and flutes of the Corps of Drums joined with the bands in 1990 for 'Sospan Fach Patrol', arranged by Lt Col Peter Hannam, Welsh Guards. In 1995 the pipes combined with the bands for the first time at this point in 'Brentwood Bay' (arr. Lt Col David Price) and 'The Crags of Tumbledown Mountain'. The latter march has particular significance for 2nd Bn Scots Guards, as it was composed by Pipe Major James Riddell on the slopes of the mountain just a few days after the battle in 1982. The original score, written on the side of a ration pack, can now be seen in the Guards Museum at Wellington Barracks.

King George V returns to the saluting base after the inspection of the line. This photograph illustrates how the two troops of Household Cavalry formed up until 1936; the Mounted Band of the Life Guards can be seen on the extreme right

When the Royal Procession has returned to the saluting base, the Field Officer-in-Brigade-Waiting gives the command 'Troop' which signals three beats from the senior time-beater, followed by a pause note. The massed bands then slow-march across Horse Guards Parade to the wonderfully stirring sounds of 'Les Huguenots', arranged by Lieutenant Dan Godfrey, Bandmaster of the Grenadier Guards from

1856 to 1896 and based on themes from Meyerbeer's opera of that name. It is believed that 'Les Huguenots' was first played on the Birthday Parade in 1869 and it has since been frequently used as the slow troop. The last parade on which it was *not* played was the one and only parade for King Edward VIII in 1936, when the 'Grand March from Aida' was used.

It has often been asked why 'Les Huguenots' is now played on the parade each year and there appears to be no reason other than common usage, as it is such splendid music that perfectly suits the dignity of the occasion. The Huguenots were French Protestants, many of whom fled to England to escape persecution and settled in the area where Wellington Barracks now stands, giving the name to the road alongside, Petty France.

The Quick Troop by the Massed Bands. Prior to the last war musicians wore tunics embellished with gold lace, similar to those still worn by Drum Majors. Most of the musicians in this photograph are from the Grenadier Guards who also wore distinctive patterned cuffs at that time.

The bands then step off to a quick march which has often included the flutes of the Corps of Drums joining in the trio in such marches as 'Children of the Regiment' (Fucik), 'St Patrick's March' (Bidgood), 'Pentland Hills' (Howe) and 'Coronation Bells' (Partridge). In 1996 the pipes joined with the bands in playing 'Killaloe'.

During the quick troop a side drummer marches to the right of the line and, as soon as the massed bands cease playing, beats Drummers Call. The Escort for the Colour then marches forward, executes a left form and halts opposite the Colour. The bands play 'The British Grenadiers' at this point irrespective of which regiment has found the Escort, because the right flank company of all Guards battalions was once a Grenadier Company.

For the same reason, the 'Grenadiers March' is played as the Queen's Colour is trooped along the ranks, although until 1920 a second march was played at this point, normally 'Coburg'. In order to avoid the considerable repetition of the

The King's Birthday Parade 1925. The first spin wheel by the Massed Bands, Drums and Pipes as the Escort for the Colour, found by 1st Bn Irish Guards, march forward. Note there are six Drum Majors on parade and the percussion rank is at the rear of the bands, immediately in front of the Corps of Drums.

(Photo: Royal Military School of Music)

'Grenadiers March', the Senior Director of Music, Major Richard Ridings, Coldstream Guards, made a new arrangement for the 1978 parade to be played as the Escort to the Colour steps off to the point when the music cuts out for the remaining Guards to present arms. The march is appropriately called 'Escort to the Colour' and is based on Waldteufel's waltz, 'The Grenadiers', thus maintaining the Grenadier association with this part of the ceremony.

The massed bands meanwhile carry out a spin-wheel, which results in them changing direction by 90 degrees while occupying the same area of ground. When the wheel is complete, the left half of the band is facing to the rear until a Director of Music gives a signal for that half to turn about. The bands halt and the music cuts out for the Field Officer to order the remaining Guards to present arms. This is a particularly difficult moment, as the Senior Director of Music must carefully watch the feet of the Escort in order to signal the timebeater to pick up their step and for the bands to step off playing the 'Grenadiers March'.

Next comes the march past, and it is appropriate at this point to reflect on the role of the Household Cavalry on the parade. Until 1936 they were represented by a

Above: Part of the Massed Bands of the Guards Division, including two ladies, on Horse Guards Parade in 1998. (Photo: Colin Dean)

Below: The march past in 1932 led by the Mounted Band of the Royal Horse Guards (The Blues). The Director of Music, Lieutenant W J 'Paddy' Dunn, MC, can be seen on the extreme right of the picture.

mounted band and two troops who took up position before the Royal Procession arrived, in the south east corner of the parade to the right of the massed bands. In the early part of the century the first troop would ride under the arch at the end of the parade to take over the duties as the King's Life Guard. The Household Cavalry led the march past, headed by the mounted band playing the Regimental Walk March, which was sometimes preceded by the trumpet call 'Flourish'. They wheeled to the left after passing the saluting base, to take up position to the left of the massed bands.

It will be a surprise to many that the regimental marches were the only music played for the march past until as recently as 1958, when the first 'neutral' slow and quick marches were added to lessen the repetition. 'Golden Spurs', composed by the Senior Director of Music, Lt Col Sam Rhodes, Scots Guards, and the quick marches 'Old Comrades' (Teike) and 'Sons of the Brave' (Bidgood) were used that year, a second neutral slow march not being added until 1964.

The regimental marches are as follows:

	Regimental Slow March:	Regimental Quick March:
Grenadier Guards	Scipio (Handel)*	The British Grenadiers
Coldstream Guards	Figaro (Mozart)	Milanollo (Hamm)
Scots Guards	Garb of Old Gaul (Reid)	Hielan' Laddie
Irish Guards	Let Erin Remember**	St Patrick's Day
Welsh Guards	Men of Harlech	Rising of the Lark

When the Escort to the Colour is found by the Scots or Irish Guards, the pipers move to the front of the massed bands to play them past with the appropriate regimental march. There was an innovation in 2000 in that Numbers 5 and 6 Guards, found by the Scots Guards, were played past with the pipers playing although they remained at the rear of the bands. The march past over, the massed bands and drums turn to their right and move away from the saluting base to the music of the pipes or, in their absence, the Corps of Drums.

The role of the Household Cavalry on the parade was changed in 1937 and they now provide a Sovereign's Escort to accompany the Royal Procession to Horse Guards Parade, although the walk-past has only taken place in its current form since 1950, the trot past being added the following year. In recent years the march past has normally, but not exclusively, started to the music of the 'Preobrajensky March' (Donajowsky) when the Sovereign's Standard of The Life Guards is on parade. Also known as the 'March of the Russian Imperial Guard', this was once the march of the bodyguard of Peter the Great and was played a number of times by the massed bands on the Birthday Parade in the 19th century. It came to be associated with Earl Mountbatten of Burma through family connections and was frequently played in his honour after the Earl was appointed Colonel of The Life Guards in 1965. Similarly, when the Sovereign's Standard of The Blues and Royals is on the parade, the Grand March from Verdi's opera *Aida* is usually played, as this forms part of the regimental quick march.

*The Grenadier Guards marched past in slow time to 'The Duke of York' (Eley) from 1886 until about 1927 and again from around 1936 until the mid 1950s.
**The first two Birthday Parades in which the Irish Guards took part were in 1901 and 1902 when they marched past in slow time to 'Come Back to Erin'.

The regimental slow marches of The Life Guards and Royal Horse Guards (The Blues) are often attributed to HRH The Duchess of Kent, the mother of Queen Victoria. Although no evidence of this has been found it is interesting to note that a Court Circular in 1851 records that the Band of the 1st Life Guards played at a royal dinner party in Buckingham Palace and commenced its programme with the 'Grand March of the 1st Life Guards' with the composer shown as 'Her Royal Highness The Duchess of Kent'. While this is not conclusive proof, the Court Circular is issued by the Royal Household and the Duchess was present at the dinner, so it seems highly unlikely that the march would have been credited to her erroneously. It is, of course, possible that this may have been a different march.

The tunes regularly played for the trot-past include 'Moneymusk', composed by Daniel Dow who was a music teacher who died at Edinburgh in 1783, a tune simply called 'Anonymous' of which nothing is known, and the Tyneside air, 'The Keel Row', which is the regimental trot. In 1975 eight State Trumpeters formed the front row of the massed mounted bands and the trot tune 'Guildhall' was specially composed for them by Major Tony Richards, The Life Guards, who also rearranged the Regimental Slow Marches and 'The Keel Row' to include trumpet parts.

Perhaps the greatest change in the history of the parade came in 1998 when The King's Troop, Royal Horse Artillery took part on Horse Guards Parade. This was the first time that troops from outside the Household Division had been involved,

The Massed Mounted Bands of the Household Cavalry, led by Major Tony Richards, The Life Guards, at the Queen's Birthday Parade 1975, the one and only such occasion that State Trumpeters formed the front rank of the bands. (Photo: T John Foster)

The Massed Drums playing 'Prussian Glory' (Piefke) as the Guards form close column at the 1983 Birthday Parade. (Photo: Colin Dean)

although the Troop had ranked past at Buckingham Palace after the parade since 1973. They march past to the 'Royal Artillery Slow March' which is also believed to have been composed by the Duchess of Kent, and share 'The Keel Row' as the regimental trot.

Since 1972 the Corps of Drums has been used to assist the forming-up for the march off, when the Guards form into close column. 'Prussian Glory' (Piefke) has generally been played at this point although Hazelmere (Birkett) has been used on two occasions and 'Dashing White Sergeant' was played in 1999. Further use of the drums came from 1990 since when they have played as the Guards form back in preparation for the march past, it is said, at the suggestion of the Duke of Edinburgh. This was extended the following year to the form-back prior to the march off. 'Hazelmere' and 'The Adjutant' have frequently been used at this point, both of which were composed by Tom Birkett who was Drum Major of 3rd Bn Coldstream

The King's Birthday Parade 1925. The Guards march off parade led by King George V accompanied by Marshal Foch. Part of the Massed Drums can be seen, along with the Pipes and Drums from the Scots and Irish Guards. (Photo: Royal Military School of Music)

Guards after the last war, subsequently transferring to the Royal Air Force as Drum Major and later becoming Bandmaster.

The final stage is the march back down The Mall with the massed bands alternating with the drums and/or the pipes. Up until just after the Second World War the massed bands would form up one behind the other, each eight abreast, with all the timebeaters (percussion) in the centre, the drums and pipes in rear and the Directors of Music marching outside the ranks on the left flank. Today, the massed bands march with a frontage of 20 in a sight and sound spectacular which for many spectators is the highlight of the day.

The Massed Bands, Drums and Pipes of the Brigade of Guards lead the Guards into The Mall after a King's Birthday Parade between the wars. At that time the bands marched one behind the other, with a frontage of eight, all the time-beaters (percussion) in the centre, the Drums and Pipes in rear and with the Directors of Music marching outside the ranks on the left flank

At the far end of The Mall the massed bands wheel to the right of the Victoria Memorial towards Canada Gate, counter-march and play as the Guards march past. The mounted bands, positioned opposite the Palace, take over as The King's Troop and the Sovereign's Escort rank past. The bands then march independently into the Palace forecourt, in recent years to the music of the Corps of Drums or the Pipes, to play a programme of music while the normal Guard Changing ceremony takes place. Until quite recently the bands stood in concert formation, playing from music stands in the north side of the forecourt. Today, with no spare musicians to put out the stands and distribute music, the bands remain in marching formation on the south side of the forecourt, playing from music cards.

The Massed Bands of the Guards Division playing their programme of music in the Forecourt of Buckingham Palace after the 2000 Queen's Birthday Parade. The bands are conducted by the Senior Director of Music, Lt Col Philip Hills, Grenadier Guards. (Photo: Colin Dean)

Garter Ceremony

One of the most colourful of all occasions is the Ceremony of the Order of the Garter which takes place in Windsor Castle. The Order was founded in 1348 by King Edward III and festivals were held at St George's-tide in April with varying degrees of regularity, perhaps the most notable in recent times being on 23rd April 1948 to celebrate the six hundredth anniversary of the Order.

The ceremony is now held on the Monday of Ascot week and any new knights are invested in the State Apartments during the morning. Music for the luncheon that follows is normally provided by the orchestras of The Life Guards and The Blues and Royals in alternate years.

At 2.40 pm a procession is formed of the Constable and Governor of Windsor Castle, the Military Knights of Windsor, the Officers of Arms (i.e. Heralds and Pursuivants), the Knights of the Garter, the Officers of the Order and the Sovereign, with a detachment of the Yeoman of the Guard in rear. The procession walks slowly through the castle by way of the Quadrangle and Norman Arch, through the Middle and Lower Wards to the gateway to the Horseshoe Cloisters and the west door of St George's Chapel, where a Service of Thanksgiving takes place. State Trumpeters are positioned inside the west door to sound fanfares as the Queen enters and leaves the chapel.

The Band of The Blues and Royals (Royal Horse Guards and 1st Dragoons) marching from Windsor Castle after the Garter Ceremony 1980. The band is led by Corporal Major Tony Whennell.
(Photo: Colin Dean)

The first part of the processional route is lined by the Foot Guards with a band positioned in front of Henry III Tower, close to the Round Tower. The Household Cavalry line the rest of the route and march through the castle to their position led by a band (i.e. the band not providing the orchestra), which takes up a static position in front of the guardroom. This is the only annual occasion when a Household Cavalry band appears on foot wearing state dress, and the stately pace necessitated by their jack-boots greatly enhances the spectacle. Both bands play incidental music prior to the procession and sometimes as the procession passes.

Lord Mayor's Show

Lord Mayor's Day in the City of London was traditionally celebrated on 9th November, but the show has been held on the second Saturday in November from 1960 in order to reduce the disruption to traffic and to enable more spectators to witness the event.

The new Lord Mayor rides in procession from Guildhall to Mansion House, where he takes the salute as the procession passes. He then joins the end of the procession and continues by way of Poultry, Cheapside, New Change, St Paul's Churchyard and Fleet Street to the Royal Courts of Justice in the Strand where he takes an oath of allegiance before the judges, a requirement dating back to 1215. The procession returns to Mansion House in the afternoon along Victoria Embankment and Queen Victoria Street.

It is thought that minstrels would have accompanied the Lord Mayor and his entourage in this procession from the earliest days and that this gradually expanded over the centuries into the pageant we see today. Military bands have long played their part, for example those in the procession on 9th November 1923 were:

Royal Artillery Mounted Band
Band of the 1st Cadet Division Royal Fusiliers (City of London Regiment)
Band of Training Ship *Warspite*
Band of the 7th Bn (City of London) Regiment (Post Office Rifles)
Band of the 1st London Divisional Royal Engineers
Band of the Corps of Commissionaires
Band of the Scots Guards
Band of the Grenadier Guards
Band of the Royal Hospital School, Greenwich
Band of the Duke of York's School
Band of the Royal Air Force
Band of the Royal Air Force School
Band of the Coldstream Guards
Band of the Honourable Artillery Company
Mounted Band of the Royal Horse Guards (The Blues)

The Band of the Corps of Royal Engineers marching along Queen Victoria Street in the return procession of the Lord Mayor's Show 1999, led by Drum Major Gary Ormston and Captain Ed Keeley, the latter on one of his first appearances with the band.
(Photo: Colin Dean)

There is more emphasis today on youth bands, but leading military bands from all three services still take part, those in the 2000 procession being, in order of march:

Central Band of the Royal Air Force
Corps of Drums and Pipes and Drums of the London Regiment
Band of the Royal Yeomanry (Inns of Court and City Yeomanry)
Band of H.M. Royal Marines, Britannia Royal Naval College
Band of the Coldstream Guards
Band and Drums of the Honourable Artillery Company
Mounted Band and State Trumpeters of The Blues and Royals (Royal Horse
    Guards and 1st Dragoons)

The Lord Mayor's coach is preceded by a mounted band and state trumpeters from the Household Cavalry who wear state dress, as they are in attendance on the Lord Mayor, the only commoner to be accorded this privilege. Mention should also be made of the impressive sight and sound of the massed corps of drums, which have been provided for several years now by our sister organisation, the Corps of Drums Society.

Above: Lord Mayor's Show 1996. State Trumpeters and Mounted Band of The Blues and Royals (Royal Horse Guards and 1st Dragoons) wearing state dress, as they are in attendance on the Lord Mayor of London.

Below: The Massed Drums representing the Corps of Drums Society at the start of the Lord Mayor's Show 2000. (Photos: Colin Dean)

The Royal British Legion Festival of Remembrance

The armistice that ended the Great War took effect from the 11th hour of the 11th day of the 11th month of 1918, a time that has since become synonymous with the Nation's remembrance for those who lost their lives.

The Festival of Remembrance began on Friday 11th November 1927 when the *Daily Express*, in conjunction with the British Legion, promoted an ex-servicemen's reunion at the Royal Albert Hall in London, with 10,000 men gathered to sing songs from the war years. Amongst them was the Prince of Wales (later King Edward VIII) and at the end of the evening he led the entire audience on a march from the Royal Albert Hall to the Cenotaph.

The Festival was repeated the following year, the tenth anniversary of the armistice, in the presence of the King and Queen and other members of the Royal Family, and, as this was a Sunday, a service of remembrance was included. Excerpts from the address by the President of the British Legion, Admiral of the Fleet Earl Jellicoe, and Chopin's Funeral March played by the massed bands, were recorded and issued on a 78 rpm record.

Since 1929 the Festival has been solely organised by what is now the Royal British Legion, and the programme for 'A Festival of Empire and Remembrance' held on 11th November 1933 shows that the basic pattern had already emerged. The scene was set by the Massed Bands of the Coldstream, Irish and Welsh Guards playing the following selections:

March Memories	**The Passing of the Regiments**	*arr. Winter*
	Conductor: Captain Andrew Harris,	
	Welsh Guards (Senior Director of Music,	
	Brigade of Guards)	
Selection	**Sullivan Operas**	*arr. Dan Godfrey*
	Conductor: Lt J L T Hurd, Irish Guards	
Potpourri	**Other Days**	*arr. Gordon-Mackenzie*
	Conductor: Lt J C Windram,	
	Coldstream Guards	

The Festival commenced at 7 pm with a fanfare sounded by Trumpeters of the Royal Horse Guards (The Blues) followed by the National Anthem and continued with:

Entry of the Legion Standards: Pack up your Troubles (Powell)
Regimental Marches: British Grenadiers, Dumbarton's Drums, The Coldstream March, Men of Harlech, Highland Laddie, Wait for the Wagon

March of the Chelsea Pensioners: The Boys of the Old Brigade (Myddleton)

March of the Women's War Services and the Nursing Services: The Great Little Army (Alford)

Entry of the Union Jack with the Banners of St George, St Andrew and St Patrick: Drums and Fifes of 3rd Bn Coldstream Guards, 1st Bn Irish Guards, 1st Bn Welsh Guards.

Entry of the Divisional Signs: Tipperary (Douglas)

March of the Services:

Royal Air Force	RAF March Past (Davies/Dyson)
The Overseas Forces	
The British Army	Soldiers of the King (Stuart)
The Merchant Navy and Fishing Fleets	A Life on the Ocean Wave (Russell)
The Royal Naval Volunteer Reserve	
The Royal Naval Reserve	
The Royal Marines	
The Royal Navy	Heart of Oak (Boyce)

March of Boy Scouts and Girl Guides: Boys – Be Prepared

Massed Bands, Organ and Audience: Rule Britannia (Arne) and Jerusalem (Parry)

March of Service and Empire Flags: Old Comrades (Teike)

Next came some wartime choruses sung by the audience accompanied by the massed bands: 'The Long, Long Trail', 'Ship Ahoy', 'Who's Your Lady Friend', 'John Brown's Body', 'Keep the Home Fires Burning', 'Good-Bye-Ee', 'If You Were the Only Girl in the World', 'Take Me Back to Dear Old Blighty', 'Are We Downhearted?', 'Here's a Health unto His Majesty'.

Pipers of 1st Bn Irish Guards then marched on, after which the bands played some songs of the British Isles and the first part of the Festival came to an end with 'Some Ribbons of the Great War' comprising 'Conquering Hero' (Handel), a display by the Drums and Fifes and finally 'Land of Hope and Glory' (Elgar).

The second part commenced with the bands and organ playing a Lament from The Keltic Suite (Foulds) and a Recessional with words by Rudyard Kipling. An Act of Remembrance then took place commencing with a roll of drums and Last Post sounded by Drummers of 3rd Bn Coldstream Guards. 'To the Fallen' was spoken by HRH The Prince of Wales, Patron of the British Legion, and Choristers of St Michael's Church, Chester Square sang 'The Supreme Sacrifice' as 1,104,890 poppy petals fell in memory of the Empire's dead. A second roll of drums preceded Reveille sounded by Trumpeters of the Royal Horse Guards (The Blues) and finally the massed bands, organ and audience combined in 'Abide with Me' (Monk) and 'God Save the King'.

The Festival was not held from 1939–42 but resumed in 1943 with columns of Home Guard in tin hats forming an aisle up to the stage for the service of remembrance. The Festival is now held on the eve of Remembrance Sunday with an afternoon and evening performance and, while the detail changes from year to year (and there were considerable changes in 1999), the basic format remains the same. It is, perhaps, the muster that is most readily identifiable with the Festival, no more so than with the entry of the 132 representative Standard Bearers of the Royal British Legion who, since around 1966, have marched to Thomas Bidgood's fine march, 'British Legion'. 'Fame and Glory' (Matt) was used prior to this while 'Trafalgar' (Zehle) and 'The Standard of St George' (Alford) were played in addition to 'British Legion' in 1986 and 1999 respectively.

Next come representatives of the Royal Navy, Army and Royal Air Force with their reserve forces, along with a number of voluntary organisations including the Red Cross, St John's Ambulance and even, in comparatively recent times, the Home

The Band of the Royal Marines (Commander-in-Chief, Fleet) at the Royal British Legion Festival of Remembrance at the Royal Albert Hall in 1986. (Photo: Royal Marines Museum)

Guard. The war widows are now represented and cross the arena to the trio from Elgar's 'Pomp and Circumstance March No 4'.

No muster would be complete without the In-Pensioners of the Royal Hospital, Chelsea – the Chelsea Pensioners. The lights are dimmed, the cadets salute, the audience rise to their feet and the massed bands play Myddleton's 'Boys of the Old Brigade' as these fine gentlemen in their scarlet coats and tricorn hats march slowly and proudly across the arena to take their places on the platform.

After the muster come the service displays, which have included a Royal Marines Band for as long as most can remember. In 1953 the Band of HM Royal Marines (Plymouth Group) under Captain R H Stoner included a March Fantasia – 'August Bank Holiday 1914' by Kenneth Alford, the pen name of the band's previous Director of Music, Major F J Ricketts. The fantasia depicted a scene at Victoria Station in the early stages of the 1914–18 war when troops of numerous regiments were entraining for France.

The Portsmouth and Plymouth Bands both appeared regularly, but from the early 1970s up to 1987 the honour generally went to the Band of the Commander-in-Chief Fleet, a major staff band which was stationed at Chatham and later Northolt, thus conveniently placed for engagements in London. Since 1988 the Principal Director of Music has taken charge with the Band of the Royal Marines School of Music until its disbandment, and from 1996 with the Portsmouth Band, now known as the Royal Band.

The army generally provides a musical contribution to the arena displays, often featuring pipes and drums from one of the Scottish regiments. The Pipes and Drums of the Ulster Defence Regiment appeared in 1982, the Band, Bugles, Pipes and Drums of 2nd Bn Royal Irish Rangers in 1984 and the Royal Irish Regiment in 1999. The Bands and Bugles of the Light Division are always a particular favourite. They march at 140 paces to the minute, as do another special favourite, the Band or Pipes and Drums from the Brigade of Gurkhas, or both combined as in 1994.

The Central Band of the Women's Royal Air Force was often to be seen, its farewell appearance at the 1972 Festival being just two days before its disbandment. The Western Band of the RAF took part in 1984 to accompany a drill display by the Queen's Colour Squadron and an RAF Band has appeared regularly since 1987. The Band of the RAF College appeared in 1988 and the RAF Regiment in 1995 but otherwise this honour has gone to the Central Band. Their displays have varied considerably in format, from a complex marching display to a static presentation of music such as 'Speedbird Salutes the Few' (Hope) in 1990, 'Fighter Command' (Alwyn) in 1991 and a version of Bach's 'Toccata in D Minor' in 1996.

The Central Band of the Royal British Legion appeared in 1996 under Captain Ted Whealing, MVO, with a highly amusing rendition of 'Helter Skelter' on the xylophones and 'Post Horn Galop' played on everything from a rifle to a watering can!

One popular item in 1997 brought together the Massed Bands of the Guards Division on the platform with the Band of HM Royal Marines (Portsmouth) and the Central Band of the Royal Air Force in the arena, in an arrangement by Warrant Officer 'Mac' McDermott, Royal Marines, on the theme of 'Anything You Can Do I Can Do Better'. This was conducted by the Senior Director of Music, Guards Division, the Director of Music, Coldstream Guards and the Principal Directors of Music of the Royal Marines and RAF – all at the same time!

The Festival's origins go back to ex-servicemen singing songs from the war years and this has remained a feature ever since with community singing, which in recent years has often included a service choir. The Choir of the 1st Bn Welsh Guards took part in 1988 and 1991, while that of 1st Bn Royal Regiment of Wales (24th/41st Foot) appeared in 1996, resplendent in green blazers with dragons embellishing their bow ties, conducted by none other than the commanding officer himself, a former Oxford choral scholar.

The Junior Choir of the Royal Marines School of Music appeared in 1989 with a medley of war songs including 'Kiss Me Goodnight Sergeant Major', during which one member of the choir took the part of a 'drunk' serenading Garrison Sergeant Major 'Perry' Mason, Coldstream Guards, who stood at the top of the steps appearing to be distinctly unamused!

Finally, the mood changes and the Royal Albert Hall takes on a cathedral-like aspect for the Service of Remembrance. A hymn is sung as the choir and clergy walk in procession through the arena to take their position on the platform. At the climax of the service four State Trumpeters sound Cavalry Last Post and silence is observed as poppy petals fall from the roof – one petal for each life lost – to cover the heads and shoulders of the servicemen and the floor of the Royal Albert Hall. The State Trumpeters sound Reveille and a final hymn is sung as the clergy depart, the Festival ending with three cheers for Her Majesty.

Armistice Day and Remembrance Sunday

The Cenotaph in Whitehall forms the focal point of the Nation's remembrance for those who gave their lives in both world wars and in the later conflicts. On parade on 11th November 1921, a year after its unveiling, were 100 men of the Royal Navy, 100 from the Royal Marines, 500 from the Brigade of Guards, 100 from the Territorial Army and 200 from the Royal Air Force, along with 200 ex-servicemen. Wreaths were laid on behalf of the Royal Family, two minutes' silence was observed from the last stroke of 11 o'clock and the hymn 'O God Our Help in Ages Past' was sung to the accompaniment of the Massed Bands of the Brigade of Guards. Buglers of the Royal Marines, positioned to the south and facing the Cenotaph, then sounded Reveille.

Armistice Day at the Cenotaph between the wars with the Massed Bands of the Brigade of Guards in the foreground. Buglers of the Royal Marines and Trumpeters of the RAF are positioned immediately in front of the bands.

The Central Band of the Royal Air Force marching to the Cenotaph in 1986 led by Drum Major Terry McCarthy and Squadron Leader (later Wing Commander) Barrie Hingley. (Photo: Colin Dean)

The 11th November continued to be kept as Armistice Day but, following the Second World War, the ceremony at the Cenotaph was moved to Remembrance Sunday, which is now designated as the second Sunday in November. The parade today commences with contingents marching to the Cenotaph from Wellington Barracks as follows:

Band of the Royal Marines; Royal Navy; Royal Marines; Queen Alexandra's Royal Naval Nursing Service; Royal Fleet Auxiliary; Merchant Navy; Fishing Fleets; HM Coastguard.

2 Bands of the Foot Guards; Household Cavalry; The King's Troop, Royal Horse Artillery; Foot Guards.

2 Bands of the Foot Guards; Pipes and Drums,* Royal Logistic Corps; Adjutant General's Corps; Territorial Army.

Central Band of the Royal Air Force;** Queen's Colour Squadron, Royal Air Force; Women's Royal Air Force; Princess Mary's Royal Air Force Nursing Service; Royal Auxiliary Air Force; Merchant Air Service.

---

*The Pipes and Drums are normally found by a Foot Guards Battalion although one year during the 1960s this duty fell to the London Scottish. The Pipes and Drums of the 1st Bn Royal Gurkha Rifles took part in 1998, 1st Bn The Black Watch (Royal Highland Regiment) in 1999 and 1st Bn The Royal Scots (The Royal Regiment) joined with 1st Bn Scots Guards in 2000.

**The Band of the Royal Air Force Regiment in 1995.

A contingent from the Civilian Services joins the parade from King Charles Street, and the ex-servicemen's contingents, organised by the Royal British Legion, march from Horse Guards Parade. A contingent from London Transport marches from 55 Broadway to join the parade, in accordance with instructions given by King George V to recognise the contribution made by LT bus drivers in France during the Great War. A more recent addition has been the Bevin Boys, wearing their distinctive white miner's helmets.

The Massed Bands of the Brigade of Guards, now the Guards Division, commence their programme of music at 10.36 and precise timing is required by the Senior Director of Music to ensure that the bands finish at exactly two minutes before 11 o'clock.

It would appear that in the early days the music played before the service was changed from year to year and comprised a selection of anthems and hymns such as the anthem 'I Will Rise and Go to My Father' which was played just before the service in 1929. The music was standardised in 1930 to include traditional national airs. It is said that the son of the Home Secretary, Mr Clynes, suggested that 'When I am Laid in Earth' and 'Solemn Melody' be played and it seems likely that the Senior Director of Music, Captain Andrew Harris, Welsh Guards, may have helped make the selection, which now consists of:

Massed Bands:	**Rule Britannia** – composed in 1740 by Thomas Arne as part of the music for his masque *Alfred*. This was first included at the Cenotaph in 1946.
	Heart of Oak - the March Past of the Royal Navy, this was composed in 1759 by William Boyce for a pantomime, *Harlequin's Invasion*.
	The Minstrel Boy – an ancient Irish air also known as 'The Moreen' with words written by Thomas Moore (1779–1852).
	Men of Harlech – this first appeared in print in 1794 when it was included in *Musical and Poetical Relics of the Welsh Bards* edited by the harpist Edward Jones. It is believed to commemorate the heroic defence of Harlech Castle by the Earl of Pembroke during the Wars of the Roses.
Pipes:	**Skye Boat Song** – commemorates the departure of Bonnie Prince Charlie to the Isle of Skye after the Battle of Culloden in 1746.
Massed Bands:	**Isle of Beauty** - a wistful air of unknown origin.
	David of the White Rock – an ancient Welsh air which is said to have been composed by a bard called David on his deathbed for playing at his funeral. It was first published in *Relics of the Welsh Bards* in 1794.
	Oft in the Stilly Night – the *Lights Out* call best known to Irish infantry regiments
Pipes:	**Flowers of the Forest** – there are a number of versions of this lament which is believed to have been composed in memory of the Scots killed at Flodden Field in 1513.
Massed Bands:	**Nimrod** – surely amongst the most haunting and beautiful of all music, this has been played at the Cenotaph since 1945, and perfectly captures the dignity of the occasion. Nimrod is the ninth of the Enigma Variations composed by Sir Edward Elgar in 1899 and portrays the composer's friend A J Jaeger. Nimrod was the mighty hunter and Jaeger is German for hunter.

When I am Laid in Earth – Dido's Lament, taken from the end of Act 3 of the opera *Dido and Aeneas*, composed by Henry Purcell in around 1689.

The Supreme Sacrifice – The hymn 'O Valiant Hearts' is the most recent addition to the Cenotaph music, having been introduced in 1990. Composed by the Reverend C Harris.

Solemn Melody – composed by Sir Walford Davies, the first Organising Director of Music of the Royal Air Force. Solemn Melody was originally composed in 1908 for organ and strings.

The introduction of the SA80 rifle in 1988 led to interruptions in the music programme after 'Rule Britannia' and again after 'Flowers of the Forest', to enable the order to be given for the parade to change arms to relieve the considerable weight of a heavy rifle which cannot be rested on the ground. This problem was resolved in 1999 with the introduction of a new stand easy position in which the rifle is held with both hands.

Her Majesty The Queen and other members of the Royal Family take their position just before the two minutes' silence which begins at 11 o'clock and is signalled by the firing of a gun on Horse Guards Parade by The King's Troop, Royal Horse Artillery. Immediately following the silence, Last Post is sounded by Buglers of the Royal Marines.

Up until the mid 1960s, 12 Apprentices from No 1 School of Technical Training, Royal Air Force Halton, sounded Infantry Last Post on E♭ cavalry trumpets and Buglers of the Royal Marines sounded the Naval Reveille, known as the 'Charlie' reveille due to the unofficial words of 'Charlie Charlie, Get out of Bed'. This was never a particularly satisfactory arrangement since the Infantry Last Post was written for the B♭ bugle and the correct notes could not be played on the cavalry trumpet. The Senior Director of Music, Lieutenant-Colonel 'Jiggs' Jaeger, Irish Guards, with the blessing of his opposite numbers in the Royal Marines and RAF, put forward recommendations to alleviate the problem by reversing the roles so that the Royal Marines in future sound Last Post while the RAF sound the call Rouse.

Buglers of the Royal Marines and Trumpeters of the Royal Air Force at the Cenotaph on Remembrance Sunday in 1982.

(Photo: Royal Marines Museum)

An addition to the music programme was made in 1999 when a short extract from Handel's *Berenice* was played prior to the first wreath being laid by the Prince of Wales, to enable BBC television to insert footage showing the Queen laying her wreath in South Africa. After the Royal wreaths have been laid, the parade is stood at ease as the politicians, high commissioners and service chiefs lay their wreaths while the massed bands play:

Massed Bands: **Funeral March No 1** – this march has been played at this point since the Second World War and is attributed to Beethoven, although it has been suggested that the real composer may have been a military bandmaster named Johann Heinrich Walch. The original music used at this point was Schubert's 'Ave Maria', while 'Chanson Triste' (Tchaikowsky) was used in 1929 and Chopin's Funeral March from 1930.

The Bishop of London then conducts a short service which includes the hymn sung every year since the Cenotaph was unveiled in 1920:

Massed Bands: **O God Our Help in Ages Past** – composed in the early 18th century by William Croft to words by Isaac Watts

Trumpeters of the Royal Air Force then sound Rouse. The Halton Apprentices ceased to perform this duty in the late 1970s and the trumpeters are now drawn from the Central Band of the Royal Air Force.

After the National Anthem, members of the Royal Family and those who have laid wreaths leave Whitehall, and further wreaths are laid by the President of the Royal British Legion and ex-service representatives to the music of:

Massed Bands: **Trumpet Voluntary** – composed by Jeremiah Clarke, born in London in 1670.
                       Fame and Glory – composed by Albert Matt (1864–1941), a former professor of trombone at Kneller Hall and member of Queen Victoria's Private Band.

It was often necessary to repeat 'Fame and Glory' several times until the signal was received that the Royal Family had departed and the march past could begin, but from 1986 a selection has been played by the Pipes and Drums at this point to give the bands a short rest The two Guards bands on the outer flanks take post to the north of the Cenotaph, ready to lead the 8,000 ex-servicemen in the march back to Horse Guards Parade while the remaining bands play for the very long march past which in 2000 took over 35 minutes to pass the Cenotaph.

The traditional music for the march past comprises 'Tipperary', 'Pack up your Troubles' and 'There'll Always Be An England', the latter having been added after the last war. The rest of the music has varied over the years and at one time largely included songs from the war years such as 'Keep the Home Fires Burning', 'Mademoiselle from Armentières', 'Take Me Back to Dear Old Blighty', 'Run Rabbit Run', 'Kiss Me Goodnight Sergeant Major', 'Hang out the Washing', 'Wish Me Luck', 'Lili Marlene' and many more.

The Senior Director of Music, Lieutenant-Colonel 'Mick' Lane, Irish Guards, revised the selection in the late 1980s and the Bands of the Royal Marines and the Royal Air Force were brought in to give the Guards a break from what is certainly a very long blow. In 2000 the music for the march past was:

Guards Division:	**It's a Long Way to Tipperary**	*Douglas*
	Pack Up Your Troubles	*Powell*
RM and RAF:	**There'll Always Be An England**	*Parker and Charles*
	The Army, the Navy and the Air Force	*Darewski*
	Ship Ahoy	*arr. Mackenzie*
Guards Division:	**Soldiers**	*arr. Lane*
	Colonel Bogey	*Alford*
	Sons of the Brave	*Bidgood*
	The Contemptibles	*Stanley*
	The Liberators	*Ancliffe*
	Bond of Friendship	*Mackenzie Rogan*

Meanwhile the outer flank bands will have reached Horse Guards Parade, where they take post on either side of the Guards Memorial as the ex-servicemen march past

Royal Navy Bands were on the parade before the last war, and up to the 1960s the Metropolitan Police Band also took part. In 1974 the Senior Director of Music was Major Jimmy Howe MBE, Scots Guards, on his last day of service, since he retired the following day, 11th November 1974, which was his 57th Birthday. Major Howe's successor, Captain Duncan Beat, was on parade with the Band of the Scots Guards.

One final thought: it is almost impossible fully to appreciate the scale of the loss of life which Remembrance Sunday honours, but perhaps a television commentary once came close. It reflected that if all the British and Commonwealth troops who gave their lives in the two world wars could come back and march past their memorial in Whitehall in column of fours, as the head of the column approached the Cenotaph, the rear of the column would be in Edinburgh. *Lest we forget*.

CHAPTER 3

ALL AT SEA!

Fleet Reviews and the involvement of Royal Marine Bands

JOHN AMBLER

R oyal Marine Bands, as suppliers of music to the Royal Navy since 1903, are required to perform ceremonies such as Trooping the Colour and Beating Retreat, as are Army bands. However there is a type of ceremony, perhaps better described as a collection of ceremonies, that is peculiar to the Royal Navy and thus to the Royal Marine Bands – the Fleet Review. The reigning monarch, or a senior member of the royal family, very often carries out the Review and the event usually takes place either out of sight of the general public or, at the very best, at a distance that probably prevents the band or bands being heard or the detail being seen.

Fleet Reviews have provided the opportunity for the might of the Royal Navy, or one or more of its fleets, to be seen at its most potent, whilst also presenting the opportunity for the Senior Service to pay tribute to the Sovereign who is also the Lord High Admiral. Traditionally, major reviews have taken place in the waters off Portsmouth known as Spithead. Bands have played an important part in this ceremony, especially during the first half of the 20th century when a great many ships had their own bands. The bands not only play an important part in the traditions but also have a significant input to the panoply of such an occasion.

Probably the most magnificent of these naval spectacles occurred in 1897 on the occasion of Queen Victoria's Diamond Jubilee Review at Spithead. This was claimed to be the largest assembly of warships ever gathered at an anchorage. Fifty battle-ships were amongst the one hundred and sixty-four British ships arrayed in lines seven miles long. This gave a total of more than thirty miles of ships to be reviewed, the combined crews numbering 35,000 officers and men. The Prince of Wales, later to become Edward VII, inspected the Fleet on his mother's behalf and was surprised to see the experimental *Turbinia* weaving in and out of the rows of ships as if to show that further British Naval developments were at hand.

At this time all ships' bands comprised Royal Navy musicians. Very often the bandmasters were foreign and many of them adopted attitudes that alienated the Royal Navy officers, who were partly responsible for the financial upkeep of such bands. In 1874 the connection of Navy bands with the Royal Marines had begun, albeit somewhat tenuously, when the bandmasters of the Royal Marines divisions commenced inspecting the Training Ship Bands.

Descriptions of a few of the more significant 20th Century Royal Reviews, particularly those held at Spithead, are given here, together with random notes about the bands, military music and other matters of interest. The 1935 and 1977 Silver Jubilee Royal Reviews are described in great detail to give an indication of the planning and the co-ordination that is required for a traditional ceremony that covers several square miles of sea. These two dates have been chosen since they also illustrate the differences resulting from the reductions in the numbers of Royal Marine ships' bands.

16th August 1902 – Coronation Fleet Review – King Edward VII

Whilst the three Royal Marine Light Infantry and the Royal Marine Artillery Divisional Bands plus the Depot Band Royal Marines were part of the Coronation ceremony in London (being located at strategic points along the route), ships' bands were plentiful and much in use during the Fleet Review. However, at that time some ships' bands were of dubious quality. This was the eve of the formation of the Royal Naval School of Music at Eastney, an organisation that would transform the music, and musicians, of the Royal Navy.

24th June 1911 – Coronation Review – King George V

Petty Officers and men of the foreign fleets were guests at dinner at the Royal Naval Barracks, Portsmouth where they were entertained by the Combined Bands of HMS *Excellent* (Whale Island) and HMS *Victory* (now HMS *Nelson*) on the evening of 22nd June. The bands under Warrant Officer W C Windram (Bandmaster, HMS *Excellent*) played: Coronation March 'Le Prophète' (Meyerbeer); waltz from 'The Merry Widow' (Lehar); selection from 'The Dollar Princess' (Fall); intermezzo 'Flirtation' (Steck); two-step 'The Teddy-Bears' Picnic' (Whitney); three dances from *Henry VIII* (German); Egyptian Serenade 'Amina' (Lincke); 'Two Norwegian Dances' (Grieg); selection from 'The Girl on the Train' (Fall) and the waltz from 'The Quaker Girl' (Monckton).

18th July 1914 – Grand Mobilisation of the Home Fleets — King George V

This was a test mobilisation of the Royal Fleet Reserve. Twenty men of the Royal Marine Artillery Band including Lieutenant B S 'Ben' Green MVO, the officially appointed Royal Yacht Band, were on board the *Victoria and Albert*. (Prince Louis of Battenberg, First Sea Lord, countermanded the order for the dispersal of the Fleets after this Royal Review and this decision enabled the Reserve to be well prepared for mobilisation in time for the 1914–18 War.)

16th July 1935 – Silver Jubilee Review – King George V

At 7.45 on the morning of Tuesday, 16th July 1935, bugles sounded and bosuns piped 'Guard and Band'. Depending upon the precise routine of each type of ship, Royal

Marines guards fell-in at the for'ard end of the quarterdeck, whilst the Royal Marine Band formed up nearby. The guards and bands were inspected, bayonets fixed and the guards stood at ease. The bands trooped in slow and quick time, playing martial music, up and down the deck for five minutes before halting alongside the guards. All awaited the signal to move into position for 'Colours'. At 7.55 the Preparative pennant was hoisted in the flagship. Immediately every ship followed suit and the duty yeomen, standing by their ensign staffs, reported 'Five minutes to Colours, Sir'. This was the signal for the guard commanders to bring their guards and bands to attention, the guards sloped arms, and the bands were brought to the 'ready'. On the orders of the guard commanders and with bands playing they marched aft and, by a series of wheels, the guards halted opposite their ship's ensign staff; and the bands countermarched to halt in their rear. Having taken their dressing, guards and bands were stood at ease until the duty yeoman reported 'One minute to Colours, Sir' at which time the Guard Commander brought the parade to attention, the guard sloped arms and the band were brought to the 'ready' again.

At 8 am, on the Preparative pennant of the flagship being hauled down, all ships followed suit and duty yeomen reported 'Eight o'clock, Sir'. This was the signal for buglers to sound the 'Alert', quartermasters to pipe and order over the tannoy 'Attention on the upper-deck, face aft and salute'; bosuns' mates to strike eight bells and finally guard commanders to order 'Guard, general salute, present arms!' Whilst the bands played the first verse of the National Anthem ensigns were slowly hoisted in time with the music and, with everyone remaining at the salute, the National Anthems of all foreign warships present followed. When the final anthem ended, buglers sounded and quartermasters piped the 'Carry-on', guard commanders ordered slope arms and Royal Marine guards and bands marched off saluting their Captains, if present, as they left the quarterdeck to the Regimental March, 'A Life on the Ocean Wave'.

Ships' bands on board aircraft carriers have a slightly different routine. Whilst the guard falls-in on the flight deck, the band falls-in on a lowered aircraft lift and rises, playing, to flight deck level. When the guard is composed of Royal Navy ratings, rather than a Royal Marine detachment, the guard is marched off to 'Heart of Oak' and then 'A Life on the Ocean Wave' following the command 'Guard, by the left and Band, by the centre, quick march'.

At 1 pm gunfire sounded across the Solent. It was the signal for the review area to be cleared in anticipation of the arrival of the Sovereign. An hour later the Royal Yacht, *Victoria and Albert,* commanded by Rear-Admiral D B N North, slipped from South Railway Jetty in Portsmouth Dockyard and followed the Trinity House Vessel *Patricia* out through the harbour entrance. During this period ships' Royal Marine detachments including bands would be paraded, facing the side that the Royal Yacht would pass, ready for the Review. Buglers, apart from one with the band, would be in groups near the direction of approach of the Royal Yacht. The Fleets rode at anchor in seven long lines of ships (lines A–G) that stretched from a point opposite Southsea Castle, past Gosport, and almost to Lee-on-Solent and, as the Royal Yacht approached, HMS *Queen Elizabeth,* flying the Flag of the Commander-in-Chief Mediterranean Fleet, Admiral Sir William Fisher GCB CVO, fired a 21-gun Royal Salute. Ten minutes before the Royal Salute, ships' buglers would have sounded the call 'Guard and Band' and then, one minute before firing began, the bugler on board

HMS *Queen Elizabeth* sounded the 'Alert'. Following the twenty-first gun he sounded 'Cease Fire', the guard presented arms and the band played the National Anthem after which the 'Carry On' was sounded.

On board the Royal Yacht was the Royal Yacht Band, part of the Portsmouth Division Royal Marines Band, under Lieutenant F V Dunn. The band played on the after-deck as she made her way to a point at the end of the lines of ships where she secured to moorings to allow the King to receive the Board of Admiralty and the Flag Officers who would be flying their flags at Spithead. *Victoria and Albert's* Royal Marines Guard and Band paraded and the Band played musical salutes as the visitors came aboard. ('Rule Britannia' would have been played for Lords Commissioners of the Admiralty, Admirals and Commanders-in-Chief, 'Iolanthe' for Flag Officers and, if required, 'Garb of Old Gaul' for other entitled officers). The Band would also have provided background music until, at 4 pm, when moorings were slipped, the *Patricia* led the *Victoria and Albert* towards the review lines, making to pass between Lines D and E. The Fleet would be dressed overall at this point with crews manning ship, officers on parade and guard and band (when carried) also on parade. The tradition of manning ship is now only used on occasions of major ceremonial apart from entering and leaving harbour. The tradition is based upon the simple theory that if all of the crew are lining the side of the ship at close intervals then they cannot be manning the guns – which is similar to the tradition of the hand salute.

The first ship that the Royal Yacht passed was on her port side. This was the Fleet Flagship HMS *Queen Elizabeth*. As the Royal Yacht came towards her, the Royal Yacht Band ceased playing. Major E E Johnson, Officer Commanding Royal Marines (OCRM) of HMS *Queen Elizabeth* ordered the Royal Salute and the Royal Marines Band under Commissioned Bandmaster A C 'Jimmy' Green played the National Anthem. Timing had to be exact since, following the National Anthem, three cheers had to be given whilst the Royal Yacht was still passing abreast. This was to be repeated by every ship with a guard and band. The Royal Yacht then passed between the battleship HMS *Royal Sovereign* (Captain H A Bass OCRM) to port and the cruiser HMS *London* to starboard. Both ships, like the *Queen Elizabeth*, had bands of fifteen, that of HMS *London* being under Bandmaster II A O White. The next ships were the cruiser HMAS *Australia* to starboard, which had neither RM detachment nor band, and the battleship HMS *Ramillies* to port whose OCRM was Captain H A Tracey and bandmaster was Bandmaster II A Howden. Next were the cruiser HMS *Devonshire* to starboard (Captain C E C Ransome OCRM) and the battleship HMS *Revenge,* (Major J E Leech-Porter OCRM) to port, both with bands playing, as were those in the cruiser HMS *Shropshire* and battleship HMS *Resolution* (OCRM Captain Picton-Phillipps). These were the last capital ships of the Mediterranean Fleet, and next to salute the King (after the Training Ship HMS *Iron Duke*) were the first elements of the Home Fleet. First, on the port side, the battle cruisers HMS *Hood* and HMS *Renown* and the aircraft carrier HMS *Courageous* whose guard and band were on the flight deck under the command of Major R S Burgess (OCRM) and the baton of Bandmaster I, V H Alley. Then came, also on the port side, another aircraft carrier HMS *Furious* (Captain G R Hawkins OCRM and Bandmaster II D F Joyce), then the cruisers HMS *Orion*, HMS *Neptune*, HMS *Achilles* and HMS *Leander* all with bands playing, the latter under Bandmaster II R A Joslin.

Taken from the aircraft carrier HMS Courageous *during the 1935 Fleet Review. On the flight-deck can be seen the ship's crew manning ship, which is dressed overall, with Petty Officers drawn up and senior officers in full ceremonial uniform. The Royal Marines Band under Bandmaster I V H Alley is behind the Royal Marines guard commanded by Major R S Burgess (OCRM). The band is about to come to the 'ready' for the Royal Salute as the Royal Yacht* Victoria and Albert *(in background) comes abeam. In the line of capital ships on the right of the picture are HMS* Renown, *HMS* Hood, *HMS* Iron Duke, *and, furthest away, HMS* Resolution. Southsea can be seen on the left horizon. (Photo supplied by Colin Bowden)

The Royal Yacht then passed between smaller ships without bands. This would probably have required Lieutenant Dunn and the Royal Yacht Band to play as the ship made her way past a further eleven pairs of warships before making a 180° turn to port to return between lines F and G. For a while she again passed between ships without bands until she reached major ships of the Home Fleet. On the starboard side were cruisers, whilst to port were the battleships. First was HMS *Cardiff* (Bandmaster II E H Weller) to starboard and HMS *Valiant*, Captain S C Wooley OCRM, to port. Next to starboard was HMS *Frobisher* (Bandmaster II B A Steven) and to port, HMS *Barham* (Major L Mercer OCRM and Bandmaster II F C Roe). After these came HMS *Vindictive* and HMS *Rodney* (Captain B W Leicester OCRM and Bandmaster II G J Styles) positioned to starboard and port respectively. Then, to starboard, came HMS *Hawkins* before the final pair of major Home Fleet ships HMS *Effingham* (Bandmaster I J W H Heathcote) and HMS *Nelson* (Captain J L R Pym OCRM and Bandmaster II R Moncur) the flagship of the Commander-in-Chief, Home Fleet, Admiral the Earl of Cork and Orrery KCB.

With the time now at 5.30 pm the Royal Yacht returned to her mooring at the head of the assembled Fleets in time for the Fly Past by Fleet Air Arm aircraft. Following this, at 6 pm, a signal gun was fired to indicate that the Review area was re-opened and crews, including guards and bands, could be stood down.

A dinner party was held on board the Royal Yacht at which the Royal Yacht Band played as an Orchestra until just before the King and his guests went on deck to witness the illumination of the Fleet, which lasted from 10 pm until midnight. During this dinner party, guards and bands would have paraded to salute the ensigns as they were lowered during the daily ceremony of 'Sunset'.

Next morning, some time after morning colours, the *Victoria and Albert* led the combined Fleets to sea for exercises. She then made her way back to her berth at South Railway Jetty in Portsmouth Dockyard at 2.40 pm.

So, at the 1935 Fleet Review there were twenty-five ships with Royal Marines Bands on board in addition to Lieutenant F V Dunn and the Royal Yacht Band.

The Royal Yacht Band, part of the Band of the Royal Marines Portsmouth Division, on board the Royal Yacht Victoria and Albert. *The ship is manned and the ship's officers are awaiting the arrival of the guests. The Director of Music, Lt F V Dunn is prepared to bring the band to the 'ready' to play the appropriate salutes when the guests arrive.* (Photo supplied by Major Paddy Dunn)

20th May 1937 – Coronation Review – King George VI

As well as detachments, bands and buglers, the Royal Marines were also responsible for providing the pilot who led the Fleet Air Arm Fly-Past during this Review. He was Lieutenant B W de Courcy-Ireland of 810 Squadron, Naval Air Service.

15th June 1953 – Coronation Review – Queen Elizabeth II

HMS *Surprise* (frigate) acted as Royal Yacht and had a detachment of Royal Marines from 45 Commando embarked as well as Major F V Dunn and the Royal Yacht Band. The Commander-in-Chief's orchestra under the Fleet Bandmaster, Senior Commissioned Bandmaster A O 'Alf' White, provided music for the dinner for HM the Queen on board HMS *Vanguard*. HMS *Eagle* (aircraft carrier) and HMS *Swiftsure* had bands whilst the aircraft carrier *HMS Illustrious* had a Sea Cadet Band.

28th June 1977 – Silver Jubilee Review – Queen Elizabeth II

The aircraft carrier HMS *Ark Royal* was the flagship and this meant that the ship's Royal Marines Band under WOII (Bandmaster) J Whelton played the major role in the ceremonial. The ship herself was responsible for the returning of salutes from foreign warships joining the review and for the co-ordinating and firing of Royal Salutes, all of which required the Royal Navy Guard, under the command of a petty officer and a lieutenant, and the Royal Marines Band to be paraded on the flight deck. Guard and band were paraded for morning colours on the 24th – 29th June inclusive. Rehearsal of the Royal Salute and the Review rehearsal on the afternoon of the 27th also required them to be paraded. When guests arrived by sea the guard and band paraded on the quarterdeck. (On an aircraft carrier the quarterdeck is located at the stern of the ship two decks below the flight deck.) They were paraded on the flight deck itself when guests were flown in. During this arrival period a second Royal Marines Band was on board but this band was later transferred to undertake Review duties elsewhere.

During the Review itself HMS *Ark Royal's* guard and band were paraded for the firing of the 21-gun Royal Salute. As the sound of gunfire died away the Royal Yacht approached the Fleet. *Ark Royal's* crew were manning ship and the ship herself was dressed overall. Guard and band were drawn up on the flight deck at the stern. As the Royal Yacht came abeam, prior to making a turn to starboard to cross the bows of *Ark Royal* and enter the Review Lanes, the 'Alert' was sounded and the guard and band stepped off and marched to the bow of the ship where they arrived with customary precision. They ceased playing after the National Anthem, in time for the ship's company to respond to the orders 'Off caps' and 'Three cheers for HM the Queen' as the Royal Yacht crossed *Ark Royal's* bows.

The Royal Marines Band and Royal Navy guard of HMS Ark Royal *march from the stern of the flight deck to take position at the bow in time for the Royal Salute as the Royal Yacht* Britannia *passes. The yacht can be seen making her approach in the background.*
(Photo: Blue Band Magazine)

Guard and Band were also paraded for the firing of the Royal Salute as the Royal Yacht *Britannia* weighed anchor in the Fleet lines and returned to Portsmouth Harbour. The Queen's Colour of the Fleet with a Royal Guard of Honour was paraded during the rehearsal and the Review. As the Royal Yacht passed through the lines of ships a lone Scottish piper could be seen on a submarine's casing whilst a whole row of them were on the bridge of a destroyer. Gurkhas were on board the ship of the same name whilst another ship carried a Hussar!

On the evening of the 28th the Queen dined on board HMS *Ark Royal* and the Royal Marines ship's band performed as a small orchestra. (This included using an upright piano that had to be wheeled in and continuously tuned to compensate for the varying atmospheric conditions in the giant hanger!) A short distance away, on Southsea Common, displays by the Royal Navy and the Royal Marines were a prelude to the Fleet being 'lit up'.

On the occasions that the Royal Yacht left and re-entered Portsmouth Harbour, Royal Salutes were provided by a guard and band on each side of the harbour. The Royal Marines C-in-C Fleet Band under Captain C Taylor, with the Queen's Colour of Naval Home Command, was at HMS *Vernon*, the Torpedo School, whilst another band, (probably Royal Marines School of Music), with the Queen's Colour of Submarine Command, was at HMS *Dolphin*.

5th June 1994 – D-Day Review – Queen Elizabeth II

HMY *Britannia's* band embarked in the Royal Yacht on Saturday 4th June. The following day the Royal Yacht sailed from Portsmouth with the Band playing on the after-deck. The military band was part of the D-Day Review in the waters of the Solent. During the Royal luncheon the Royal Marines provided a Dixie band.

These glimpses of Fleet Reviews provide an indication of the traditions and the customs that, linked together, form complex, difficult and unique pieces of pageantry.

CHAPTER 4

MUSIC IN THE PARKS

How do you make a bandstand? – *Take their chairs away.*

PAUL TAYLOR

Origins

S amuel Pepys, the well-known seventeenth century diarist, had a great love of music and attended a variety of performances in the open air. He writes in his diary on 28th May 1667 how *'presently comes Creed and he and I by water to Foxhall and there walked to Spring Gardens … to hear fiddles and there a harp.'* Spring Gardens, opened in 1660, was laid out with tree-lined gravel paths and brightly lit. Music was provided by popular composers and performers, with free admission. By 1731 a circular two-storey building had been erected with the orchestra positioned in the upper storey. In 1749 Handel rehearsed his 'Water Music' here with an orchestra of 100 and an audience of 12,000. The Gardens, later to be known as Vauxhall Gardens, closed in 1859.

Cremore Pleasure Gardens, Fulham opened in 1843 in competition with Vauxhall. In 1847 a band house (one of the original descriptions of a bandstand) was erected. It was in the form of a *'monster pagoda'* with slender columns of cast iron, and seated up to 50 players. Around it was a circular platform, which could accommodate 4,000 dancers. Cremore Gardens closed in 1877.

One of the very first public parks in Britain, as distinct from the private gardens like Vauxhall and Cremore, opened in Birkenhead in 1847. Laid out by Sir Joseph Paxton of Crystal Palace fame, one of the major features of this large park was an ornamental lake together with a boathouse, above which was a band house. Originally it had a steeply pitched roof and was an important feature in the design and layout of the park. It is the earliest known bandstand still in existence in Great Britain, although no longer in use.

One of the most important developments in the history of bandstands as we know them today, was the erection in 1862 of two band pavilions (yet another early name) at the Royal Horticultural Society Gardens and Great International Exhibition, Kensington, the site of which is now the Victoria and Albert Museum. These were the largest and indeed the grandest formal gardens ever laid out in

Birkenhead Park, Birkenhead. (Photo: Paul Taylor)

Clapham Common, London. (Photo: Paul Taylor)

Britain. Their design was by the well known landscape architect W A Nesfield. After the exhibition the band pavilions were moved to Peckham Rye and Southwark Park in London but later demolished. Constructed in octagonal form of cast iron on a circular base they became the forerunners of the most common type of bandstand that is found throughout Britain and indeed all over the world. They were designed by Captain Francis Fowkes of the Royal Engineers who also designed the Royal Albert Hall. It is likely that he had been inspired by a pavilion he had seen at the Industrial Exhibition in Paris in 1855. Indian and Turkish architectural styles were popular in the mid-nineteenth century and could explain the unusual design of roof. They clearly were well liked, because in 1890 on Clapham Common the London County Council had a replica erected at a cost of £600 which still exists.

Music was played in parks before band pavilions were introduced, but their erection gave a focus to this activity as well as providing cover for the musicians. By the end of the century bandstands were very popular and indeed *'no park large or small is considered complete without one'*. They were such a feature in parks that they had *'acquired the quality of almost sacred precedent'* and symbolised many happy hours of entertainment. Visitors either sat down to listen to a concert or else strolled around. Music was seen as an important moral influence. The bandstand was now rarely a focus for dancing as it had been in the pleasure gardens such as Vauxhall and Cremore. In 1861 more than 50,000 people gathered in Corporation Park, Blackburn for a concert to celebrate the end of the Crimean War. Some 149 musicians, from 11 local works bands, played a wide range of classical music including a rousing finale. Music in parks was seen by the Victorians as an aspect of the reforming potential of open public spaces. These were regarded by the Victorians as places where *'the workers could feast for free on clean air and natural beauty before returning to the City's satanic mills. If they happened to mingle with the educated middle classes and hear the music so much the better.'*

Bandstands were erected throughout Britain but do not appear to predominate in any one area or another. They were remarkably well spread throughout cities and towns and even villages. At Nairn in the north of Scotland, a bandstand was built in 1884 on The Links, which still exists in fine condition. Later in the sub-tropical Morrab Gardens of Penzance at the opposite end of Britain, a bandstand was built in 1905. In 1893 the London County Council formed its own band and by 1906 the Council records list thirty parks with permanent bandstands. A clear indication of the popularity and support of band concerts can be gained from Glasgow Corporation archives, which indicate in their detailed records that in 1894 there were 245 performances during the 'summer season' in their parks attended by 770,380 people. By 1908 their records show that about one third of band engagements were played by military bands. In 1913 just before the outbreak of World War One, the number of performances had risen to 392 attended by 1,896,970 members of the public.

Locations

Bandstands usually had a dual purpose; the main function was to provide a raised platform and cover for the musicians, but they also give a point of interest and accent whether it is in a park, on the sea front or in a town centre. Their shape, height and form were used by nineteenth century landscape gardeners to create a focus at the

Morrab Gardens, Penzance. (Photo: Paul Taylor)

junction of avenues or paths in their layouts. This can be seen for instance at Battersea Park, London where the bandstand was the termination of specially designed vistas. The Park was laid out in 1858 and although the original bandstand has gone, it was replaced in 1987. At Chapelfield Gardens, Norwich the timber bandstand with its unusual octagonal roof turret, erected in 1890 along with a large Chinese-style pagoda (since demolished), were both major features in the original design of this fine park. In Victoria Gardens at Neath, South Wales the bandstand is the central feature of an elaborate system of flowerbeds together with park seats, laid out in 1890.

Bandstands could also be centred on terraces as a major feature where gardens were laid out on sloping sites. This arrangement is to be seen at Hanley Park, Stoke on Trent, where Thomas Mawson, a leading figure in park design in his day, laid it out in 1891. Another example of this type of planning is Upper Castle Park, Colchester, opened in 1892. However not all parks were formally laid out with avenues and terraces and in these instances bandstands were incorporated in the layout quite informally as at Carmarthen Park, South Wales in 1900 and Royal Victoria Park, Bath in 1903. In the 1920s some municipal authorities provided catering and other facilities around the bandstand. Eaton Park, Norwich built in 1928, is a very good example of this type of arrangement and one of the most elaborate in Britain.

Chapelfield Gardens, Norwich. (Photo: Paul Taylor)

Eaton Park, Norwich. (Photo: Paul Taylor)

At The Groves, Chester a bandstand was built in 1882 alongside the River Dee with terraced seating on either side, and the sound of the music reflected off the surface of the water. It has remained in use ever since. One of the most remarkable bandstands to use water as a reflector is at Scarborough in Peasholm Park. Originally designed in 1912 by the borough engineer Harry W Smith, the park was laid out in Japanese style as a large garden complete with pagoda and other buildings with far-eastern features. In 1929 a floating bandstand along with more Japanese style features was added to the park. The musicians are rowed out to the bandstand in a boat and Lieutenant-Colonel Rodney Bashford has remarked, *'That Lake must hold many a music stand, music folio and all manner of lesser musicalia dropped overboard by bandsmen.'* The music reflects over the water to the spectators seated on the terraces around the lake. On a very much smaller scale, Gheluvelt Park, Worcester has a bandstand dating from 1923 which sits on a small island in an ornamental lake accessed by a low wooden bridge. By contrast in the 1890s a fine octagonal cast iron bandstand was built on a large island in Sefton Park, Liverpool and the public can only gain access by a narrow lockable entrance.

Arboretums became popular in the early twentieth century, and some incorporated bandstands as part of their layout. Examples can be seen in Derby, Nottingham and Walsall. The bandstand at Walsall was rebuilt in 1924 and is not dissimilar to Royal Victoria Park, Bath in design but built in cast iron and glass and not stone. It backs onto a lake and faces a terrace incorporating raised benches. It was restored in 1999.

Stepped terraces in the form of an arena with a stage-type bandstand were also

Peasholm Park, Scarborough. (Photo: Paul Taylor)

developed in the 1920s. A good example at Clitheroe in the Castle grounds, was originally built in 1923 and restored in 1987. In Glasgow in the mid-1920s the Corporation demolished at least three of their fine cast iron octagonal bandstands and replaced them with large stage-type bandstands complete with extensive arena-style terraced seating. This clearly gave much improved cover and facilities for the musicians and at the same time projected the sound towards the audience.

The concept of a bandstand as a prominent feature is to be seen realised in many town centres. An excellent example exists at The Carfax, Horsham built in 1892. Town Square, Johnstone near Glasgow, 1892 and Lord Street, Southport, 1984 (replacing a much earlier model), are other examples. Since the Second World War, bandstands have been erected in town centres such as Barking, Bracknell, Caerphilly, Corby, Cwmbran, Falkirk, St Albans and Sheffield.

The Carfax, Horsham. (Photo: Paul Taylor)

The advantages of the seaside as a place for pleasurable activities featured greatly in Victorian times and it is no surprise to find bandstands prominently located on the piers or promenades of seaside towns. In the early 1870s Eastbourne Council used the end of the pier for their first bandstand. It was then moved in the later 1870s to the middle of the pier and removed altogether after the Second World War. In 1882 the Council erected a bandstand known as the Birdcage on the Grand Parade. Access for the players was by a steep metal staircase from the beach. This bandstand was removed in 1933 and replaced by the present one in 1935. In 1894 a similar Birdcage-type bandstand was erected on the Royal Parade and this was subsequently moved to the Redoubt in 1922. Brighton also used its piers for bandstands and followed these in 1894 with a very ornate example on the Royal Parade, near the West Pier. At Clevedon, a bandstand was erected in 1887 as a prominent feature high above the sea front. In Scarborough on the South Bay in 1858, Sir Joseph Paxton built the Spa together with a separate circular bandstand. A major fire in 1876 destroyed Paxton's Hall but the bandstand remained until it was rebuilt in its present oval form in 1913 by the architect Sir Edwin Cooper. There were many bandstands erected in seaside towns throughout Britain in the nineteenth and twentieth centuries and recently there has been a revival of bandstand building and examples can be seen at Blackpool, Saltburn, Southsea and Tenby.

Bandstands are not only to be found in parks and gardens but also in unusual locations such as the two at Ascot racecourse, one at Alton Towers and one sandwiched between a bowling green and a swimming pool at Hathersage in Derbyshire that was moved there from Loxley Park, Sheffield in 1936. A bandstand from Saltwell Park, Gateshead has been re-erected at the Beamish Museum near Durham and similarly one from Longfield Park, Manchester has been moved to the National Tramway Museum, Crich near Derby.

Types and Construction

One of the most interesting aspects of bandstand design is the extraordinary range of shapes, sizes and materials used in their construction. This applies not only in Britain but wherever they are found throughout the world. Indeed there are few types of buildings which span so many countries and exhibit such a variety of architectural styles. Some of the most extravagant types are to be seen in Europe, especially in France, but other remarkable specimens can be seen in Australia, Bermuda, India, South Africa and the USA.

Royal Victoria Park, Bath. (Photo: Paul Taylor)

Undoubtedly the octagonal shape that Fowler used in 1862 at the Kensington Exhibition had a profound influence on the subsequent British designs, and wherever the bandstands were exported, which included most parts of the British Empire. However as music in parks became more and more popular, bandstands changed from being open on all sides to the much more practical stage type which gave better shelter to the musicians and at the same time helped project the sound towards the audience. One of the earliest examples of this more functional design; while still retaining the attractions of the ornamental cast iron, was the Royal Victoria Park bandstand in Bath built in 1903. It has a shell shaped canopy, which reflects the sound towards the audience seated on the grass. A version of this theme in Tunstall Park, Stoke on Trent, also built in 1903, has a raised rectangular brick and timber structure and tiled pitched roof. This was followed, as has been noted already, in a number of parks in Glasgow using a stage-type bandstand similar to Tunstall but with terraced seating like a Roman open-air theatre. An interesting partially pre-fabricated timber system evolved in Lancashire and Yorkshire, which produced a curved rear wall to the stage, which was an even better reflector of the sound. Examples in parks exist at Rochdale 1913, Todmorden 1914, Clitheroe 1923 and Accrington 1929. The more severe weather in these northerly towns clearly led to the development of the stage-type bandstand. Possibly the ultimate stage-type design is on the seafront at Eastbourne. Here the need to protect the musicians and the audience from inclement weather, and the sea itself, produced a design complete with movable side screens. It was designed by Major Leslie Roseveare, the borough engineer of Eastbourne and built by G Percy Trentham. It provides cover for 1,000 people, and a further 2,000 can be seated in the open.

Grand Parade, Eastbourne. (Photo: Paul Taylor)

Although the octagon has proved to be the most popular shape for bandstands over the last 150 years, some have six or twelve sides. At Jubilee Park, Middleton near Manchester, there is even a seven-sided bandstand built in 1890. One of the most memorable of the twelve-sided bandstands is at Deal, erected in 1993; it has the names of the eleven Royal Marines who were killed by a terrorist bomb inscribed on the sides of the base, and the steps up to the bandstand are on the twelfth side.

Examples of other shapes are: square – Alexandra Park, Hastings in timber 1902 and Waterloo Park, Norwich in concrete 1933; oval – The Spa, Scarborough in stone and glass 1913; circular – Clifton Park, Rotherham 1928, Stanley Park, Blackpool 1929 and Jubilee Park, Woodhall Spa 1935, all with concrete columns and domed roofs; rectangular – the Park, Gloucester 1934 in brick. Some of these bandstands are of the open freestanding type and others are based on the stage principle.

Methods of construction and the remarkable range of building materials all contribute to variety in the design and appearance of bandstands. The most popular method of construction was from a kit of parts made of cast iron, selected from a manufacturer's catalogue, erected on a base which acted as the foundation to the cast iron frame. Aluminium, brick, concrete, steel, stone and timber were all used in the construction of bandstands, irrespective of their shape. Roofs were another opportunity to vary the design, and materials such as copper, felt, slates, thatch, tiles and zinc were used to add variety to the overall concept.

Manufacturers

Walter Macfarlane & Co of Saracen Foundry, Glasgow was the firm whose name is linked to bandstands all over the world. In the nineteenth century this firm was one of the major cast iron manufacturers of every conceivable kind of ironwork, from shop fronts to rainwater gutters. Established in 1850, they were taken over by Allied Ironfounders in 1965 who subsequently went into liquidation in the 1980s. Macfarlane's catalogues and price lists were widely available and were sent all over the British Empire. The first edition was published in 1858 and drawings of bandstands, together with prices, began to appear in 1882. In their eleventh edition, photographs of completed bandstands were also included.

One of the earliest Macfarlane bandstands to be built is in Priory Park, Great Malvern. It was their model No 279, erected in 1876, still in use and in good condition. This particular model was produced until at least 1907. In the Municipal Park at Warrenpoint, Northern Ireland there exists a bandstand dating from 1907, complete with all external decorative features including the town's crest, all in excellent condition. Macfarlane's most popular model was No 249, and in 1911 the 20-feet diameter model complete with roof but no ceiling, sold as a kit of parts, was £173.7.0d. A 25-feet diameter model cost £191.2.0d. To these figures had to be added the cost of building the base of the bandstand together with erection costs and ceiling. About 25 examples of No 249 still exist in Britain and in 1999 a replica was erected in Dane John Park, Canterbury to replace the one that had been demolished after World War II. In all, nearly 50 Macfarlane bandstands still exist out of a total of about 450 bandstands of all different types to be found in Britain in 2001. Morrab Gardens, Penzance and The Carfax, Horsham are both good examples of model No 249.

The Industrial Revolution resulted in many foundries springing up in the Glasgow area, and George Smith's Sun foundry was one of the earliest. The bandstand in the Arboretum, Lincoln was built by this firm in 1872 and the Clapham Common replica erected in 1890.

Another major manufacturer was the Lion Foundry Co Ltd of Kirkintilloch near Glasgow. This firm was established in 1880 by Robert Hudson, who had previously worked for Macfarlane's. About 15 of their cast iron bandstands still exist, all built in the early 1900s. They were also well known manufacturers of telephone kiosks. The firm finally closed in 1984.

McDowall, Steven & Co were the manufacturers of the bandstand in The Quarry. Shrewsbury. It was erected in 1879 at a total cost of £233.5.2d, as gift from the Shropshire Horticultural Society and they funded the enlargement of the bandstand by adding an outer circle of columns and a widened roof in 1887. An identical model can also be seen in West Park, Wolverhampton.

Hill & Smith Ltd of Brierley Hill erected the bandstand at Bedwellty Park, Tredegar and one of their earliest bandstands exists in Abington Park, Northampton, erected in 1897. Their work is to be found mainly in the Midlands and Wales.

With the resurgence of interest in Britain's industrial heritage, and monies from the Heritage Lottery Fund being granted for the restoration of public parks, a number of firms are now both manufacturing new bandstands and restoring old ones. Dorothea Ltd of Buxton, Ollerton Engineering Services Ltd of Preston and Heritage Engineering of Glasgow have all been involved in such projects. Grange Gardens, Cardiff is a replica of the original bandstand built in the early 1900s in the Gardens by the Lion Foundry.

Grange Gardens, Cardiff. (Photo: Paul Taylor)

Military Connections

The pioneers for the provision of outdoor music were the spa towns. In Bath as early as 1651 *'a Band of Musick consisting of viols and oboes performed in the Orange Grove'* and by the 1830s, for subscribers, the attraction of the Pump Room was *'the high enjoyment it affords from the recently introduced first-rate military band which performs daily during the season, from two till four o'clock, the choicest productions of Rossini, Auber, Strauss and other composers.'*

In 1814, the Royal Pump Room, Leamington Spa, designed and built by C S Smith of Warwick at a cost of £30,000, was officially opened. The Pump Room gardens were originally laid out and enclosed for the exclusive use of patrons *'to afford them pleasant promenades.'* A bandstand was erected and military bands played in the evening during in the summer *'for the gratification of the subscribers.'* In 1875 the Pump Room gardens became public. This bandstand was subsequently demolished as it was too small and a new bandstand, which still exists, was opened in May 1909, an event the *Leamington Spa Courier* describes as *'out of the ordinary course with the spic and span new bandstand prettily decorated with geraniums and palms and other foliage plants.'* The newspaper went on to say of the opening concert given by the band of the Queen's Own Yorkshire Dragoons that *'no combination of musicians could have given greater pleasure, nor could a programme of a more varied and acceptable character have been submitted.'*

In general British bandstands have tended to be smaller, both in height and diameter, than French or other continental ones. This could have been the result of the War Office Regulation of 1821, which limited military bands, with the exception of the Royal Artillery, to ten players only. Even when later in the century the average size increased to 20 players, the typical British bandstand was often of a modest size but adequate for most of the town and works bands. Even the Royal Artillery when it did give a concert on the bandstand in the Lincoln Arboretum in 1888 used only 28 players.

As has already been noted, pleasure gardens such as Vauxhall suffered competition from newer developments. In 1836 the Royal Surrey Gardens opened at Walworth and *'the splendid band of the Coldstream Guards occupied for the first time a new orchestra* [bandstand] *built for the occasion.'* In 1856 the Archbishop of Canterbury wrote to Palmerston, the Prime Minister, warning him of the danger of allowing bands to play in parks on Sundays in Kensington Gardens. Palmerston agreed to the ban, but as a result of public protest the Keeper of the Privy Purse observed that too much fuss was being made: *'The practice only began a year ago and as far as the gardens are concerned, very few working men ever availed themselves of the opportunity offered them. Military music is a new want which has hardly been known to the working classes.'* Regimental bands had been giving regular concerts in Kensington Gardens and drew very large audiences on Sundays. The *Illustrated London News* reported in 1855 that *'the band played between 4pm and 6pm and 72–73,000 people were counted through the various gates.'* Even larger crowds were reported from Regent's Park, where in the final concert of the 1856 season nearly 200,000 entered the park. In 1869 the Band of the Life Guards played in Hyde Park on a specially built raised platform and stood to play their music. It was in this same year that a bandstand was built in Kensington Gardens, which was subsequently moved in 1886 to its present site in Hyde Park.

One of the earliest recorded continuous links between military bands and

The Quarry, Shrewsbury during the Shrewsbury Flower Show. The Band of the Coldstream Guards conducted by Lt John Mackenzie Rogan, c. 1905

bandstands in Britain was in 1879, when the Grenadier Guards and the Shropshire Militia performed at the newly opened bandstand in The Quarry, Shrewsbury for the Shrewsbury Flower Show. In 1882 three bands, Royal Horse Guards, Grenadier Guards and the 3 KSLI, appeared at the bandstand, a custom which in the main has continued to this day but with different bands.

Eastbourne also has a long tradition of military bands playing on bandstands. Records indicate that the Band of the Royal Horse Artillery played informally at the Royal Parade bandstand from 1894. Very large concerts were held regularly in Devonshire Park from 1894 when the municipal orchestra played as a 'military band'. In 1906 the Coldstream Guards, the 2nd Sussex RGA Volunteers and the pipers of the Scots Guards are recorded as playing at the Royal Parade bandstand. The town guide of 1908 states that this bandstand was occupied constantly during the summer and autumn months by military and other bands. The opening of a new bandstand was often the opportunity to engage a military band to perform at the first concert. In 1900 the Band of the Prince of Wales [*sic*] Own Norfolk Regiment played at the official opening of the Wellington Pier Gardens, Great Yarmouth. The *Yarmouth Mercury* describes it as '*a fine bandstand … which gives ample accommodation for thirty men and a total seating under cover for about 700 persons.*' In 1902 the Ripon Spa Gardens bandstand was opened by the Mayor with the Ripon Detachment of the 1st Battalion The West Yorkshire Regiment giving the opening concert. The recently restored bandstand in Victoria Gardens, Chatham was originally opened in 1903 with a concert by the 4th Battalion The Rifle Brigade with the opening march 'Whistling Rufus' conducted by J F Brady. In 1923 the Band President of the 1st (Depot) Battalion, Tank Corps wrote to the Borough of Swanage stating '*The Commanding*

Officer (Lt Col T C Mudie DSO) has consented to allow the Band to play at the opening of your new Bandstand. The fee for the Band will be £15.15.0d, plus £174.2.0d travelling expenses.' The opening of a new bandstand was also the opportunity for a band to process through the streets of the town prior to the opening concert. This took place in Leek in 1924 where the Band of the 2nd Battalion The North Staffordshire Regiment (The Prince of Wales's) carried out these duties. In the same year the Royal Marines gave the first concert at the Can Bank bandstand in Mansfield, which according to the local newspaper was *'A bandstand of pleasing design and in the selection of which the advice of Lt Col J Mackenzie Rogan has been sought.'* The opening ceremony of the bandstand in Vale Park, New Brighton, August 1926 was attended by an audience of over three thousand and was followed with a concert by a Royal Air Force Band. The bandstand, which is still in use, has an unusual feature in that the names of six famous musical composers are inscribed in high relief around the frieze.

A remarkable connection between a bandstand and a military band is to be seen at Bedwellty Park, Tredegar. This celebrates the gift of the bandstand, which is not unusual, but for the band and the conductor to be commemorated is extremely rare if not unique.

Bedwelty Park, Tredegar. (Photo: Paul Taylor)

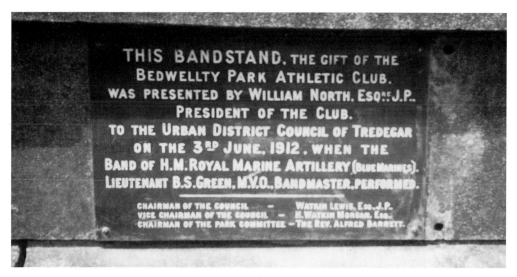

The plaque on the bandstand in Bedwelty Park, Tredegar. (Photo: Paul Taylor)

Sources:
Wroth W *Cremore and the later London Pleasure Gardens,* 1907
Jekyll G *Public Parks and Gardens,* 1918
Bradbury, Maurice *Pavilions for Music Bandstands,* 2001
Searle, M *Spas and Watering Places*
Leamington Spa Courier, May 1909
Yarmouth Mercury, 1900
The Mansfield and North Notts Advertiser, August 1895
Archives of the Museum and Art Centre for the Isle of Purbeck

CHAPTER 5

THE CONCERT PLATFORM

Military band concerts have taken place everywhere from local park bandstands to the best concert halls in the land, with a repertoire that covers virtually all kinds of music. To illustrate the concert aspects, this chapter takes a look at concert series given by bands from each of the three services.

Concerts at Kneller Hall
by Alwyn W Turner & Gordon Turner

Exactly when the Kneller Hall Summer Promenade Concerts first started is not known but they were certainly being held in the 1880s. In the early days the daily routine was broken up by a twice-weekly afternoon performance in the grounds, when the public were invited to come to listen to the students' band play. As the experience and reputation of the School grew, however, this became a more formal affair. During the summer, public concerts were given on an island in the middle of the lake, with visitors paying a penny for a programme and a chair, which they could place where they wished. This was the origin of the successful summer concert series that has become so much a part of Kneller Hall life.

The earliest programme recorded as being played in the 20th century is for 18th July 1900 and consisted of the following items:

March	Surinam	E A Barratt
	conducted by the composer, Std E A Barratt	
Overture	Leonore No 3	Beethoven
	conducted by Std A Parkes	
Solo for Flutes and French Horns	Das Waldvöglein	Doppler
	conducted by Std J Dought	
Selection	Aida	Verdi
	conducted by Std W Taylor	
Symphony	The Ocean	Rubinstein
	conducted by Std J Amers	
Morceau	Simple Aveu	Thome
	conducted by Std C W Ancliffe	
Valse	Stephanois	W S Hawkins
	conducted by Std J Slattery	

Whilst it is unlikely that the items were played in the order given, it does give some idea as to the type of music being performed.

1907 was an important year for the School, being the 50th anniversary of its foundation, and a Jubilee concert attended by over 8000 people was given on the evening of 25th September. Students conducted all items on the programme:

Fest March	Tannhäuser	Wagner
	conducted by Std J Goodered	
Overture	William Tell	Rossini
	conducted by Std C Hindmarsh	
Suite	Scènes Alsaciennes	Massenet
	conducted by Std G O Walker	
Idyll	The Forge in the Forest	Michaelis
	conducted by Std F J Ricketts	
Cornet Solo	Mia	Hartmann
	conducted by Std E Adams	
American Sketch	Down South	Myddleton
	conducted by Std A E Noble	
Two short pieces:		
a) Idyll	Bells on the Water	Watson
b) Song	The Rosary	Nevin
	conducted by Std A L Wallace	
Selection	The Merry Widow	Lehar
	conducted by Std H B Lovell	
Whistling Valse	Wiener Mädchen	Ziehrer
	conducted by Std H Stockey	
Grand Fantasia	The Battle of Waterloo	Eckersberg
	conducted by Std H Dudley	
	God Save The King	
	The Last Post	

The *Richmond and Twickenham Times*, reporting on the concert, was particularly impressed by the finale:

> 'The Battle of Waterloo' was an almost desperately realistic affair. With the free use of bombs and rifles, star shells and coloured fire, and the marching of detachments of the band, from various parts of the park to the central bandstand, the whole business was most exciting. The noise and glare of it woke up the country for a long way round.

With the outbreak of war in 1914 many of the student bandmasters, and pupils who were of age, were sent back to their regiments to bolster the numbers of fighting soldiers. The Kneller Hall concerts, however, continued, the only change being that in addition to 'God Save The King' being played at the end of each performance the national airs of our allies were included. Amongst those were Belgium, France, Italy, Japan, Russia, Servia, America, Portugal and Roumania.

It was the normal practice for a student to announce an item and then make his way to the rostrum to conduct, thus involving seven or eight students per concert. During the 1922 season, however, the new director of music Lieutenant Hector Adkins decided to change conductors for each movement in a suite, with the result that in some concerts there could be a dozen or more students ascending the rostrum for three or four minutes. The students were not happy about the state of affairs and with such war veterans as Stds George Wooley MM, Fred Allsebrook MM and Ron Botting MM DCM in the student body there were complaints that they were being treated as children.

One of 'Adko's' aims was to build a new repertoire for military band, and this is evident from a concert given on 3rd October 1923, with the following programme:

1	Overture	Othello	H A Keyser
		conductor – Student L Pay LRAM ARCM	
2	Russian Dance	Gopak	J Verney
		conductor – Student W Fitz-Earle	
3	Suite	Three Roundels:	Herbert Bedford
		a) The King of Spades	
		b) The Queen of Hearts	
		c) The Knave of Diamonds	
		conductor – Student R Marshall	
4		Toccata and Fugue in C Major	Bach
		arranged by Student D Plater LRAM ARCM	
		conducted by the arranger	
5	Suite	The Planets	Holst
		a) Mars	
		b) Mercury	
		c) Jupiter	
		arranged by Students L Pay LRAM ARCM and	
		G Smith	
		conducted by the Director of Music	
6		Variations on Two Short Themes	J Verney
		conductor – Student B Grumbley	
7		Folk Song Suite:	Vaughan Williams
		a) Seventeen Come Sunday	
		b) Sea Songs	
		c) My Bonnie Boy	
		d) Folk Songs From Somerset	
		conductor – Student S W Webber ARCM	
8	Prelude	Beatrice	Percy Harrison
		conductor – Student W C Windram	

Items 1, 2 and 8 had all been sent in response to a request for original compositions, but the real coup was to secure Dr Vaughan Williams' first piece for

Lieutenant Hector Adkins conducting at a rehearsal for a summer concert 1924. (Photo: RMSM)

military band. Curiously the printed version of the 'Folk Song Suite' does not include the second movement, 'Sea Songs', though it does exist as a separate march. When interviewed just before his 97th birthday, Stanley Webber, who conducted the suite at the 1923 concert, remembered Sea Songs being a part of the suite for several years.

This attempt to take military bands towards more serious concert material was possible to some extent only because Mr Adkins was himself a talented and educated musician, and he was greatly encouraged in these pursuits by the then Commandant, Colonel J C Somerville, who was evidently a keen amateur appreciator of music.

It was not until 1937 that the fanfare trumpeters began to appear regularly in the concerts and at first it was more to boost the 'Adkins' image than anything else. The Grand Concerts (held on the last Wednesday of every month) now commenced with two or three fanfares, specially composed to be used by the Kneller Hall Trumpeters outside Westminster Abbey on Coronation Day 1937.

With the outbreak of war, the School was moved to Churchill House, Aldershot and the concerts ceased. By the end of 1946 the School was once more back home in Whitton and on 7th May 1947 the concerts recommenced. The first item to be played publicly was a march 'Canada Overseas' conducted by the composer, Std BM Jerry Gayfer.

Wednesday, 5th July 1950 was a red-letter day as the new school march, a combination of 'Blow Away the Morning Dew' and 'Near London Town', received its first public performance. Until then 'Rule Britannia' had been used to end concerts and as the school march-past.

Percy Grainger conducting the Kneller Hall Band in one of his compositions during the School's Centenary year, 1957. (Photo: RMSM)

1957 was the centenary of the School's foundation, and a week of concerts in June saw the major bands of all three services playing at Kneller Hall in acknowledgement of the beneficial effect that the School had had on military music generally in Britain. The week started with a performance on the afternoon of Saturday 8th June by the massed military bands of the Royal Artillery, the Royal Engineers and the Royal Signals, followed in the evening by an orchestral concert by the same three bands, one of the very few occasions on which the three senior corps in the British Army have come together for such a performance. The programme consisted of the overture 'Carneval' (Dvořák), ballet suite 'Pineapple Poll' (Sullivan-Mackerras), 'Night on the Bare Mountain' (Moussorgsky), 1st movement 'Piano Concerto in A minor' (Grieg), 'The Emperor Waltz' (Strauss), ballet music 'Sylvia' (Delibes) and a symphonic suite 'The Western Desert' composed by an ex-bandmaster, Leo Paul Bradley. Later in the week there were concerts by the massed bands of the Royal Marines School of Music and the Royal Air Force, by the massed bands of the Household Brigade and by the massed bands of the Aldershot District. The series of performances culminated on 16th June with an open-air Service of Thanksgiving.

The mood and style of the concerts has varied according to the preference of the current directors of music, with some aiming at being 'audience friendly' whilst others appear to be striving to 'educate' the audience. On one concert the trombone section was featured playing '76 Trombones' whilst marching round the bandstand. Although the soloists were two paces behind each other it did prove necessary for them to run once they had disappeared from view in order to catch up with the tail end. By the time they reached the final note there were visible signs of lack of breath.

Due to the various cutbacks in bands, and in particular those brought about with 'Options for Change' there are now insufficient musicians studying at Kneller Hall to stage the concerts. The concert season has gradually dwindled from almost two dozen performances in the 1950s to six in 2000. Each concert now also features two or three visiting bands to boost the Kneller Hall musicians.

Mountbatten Festival of Music
by John Ambler

The Bands of the Royal Marines are as well known for their concert performances as they are for their immaculate marching displays. Both are epitomised by white helmets, straight lines, Fanfare Team and the Corps of Drums. The annual high point of the concert year occurs when the Massed Bands of the Royal Marines appear at the Royal Albert Hall. This first occurred in 1973, when a single concert was played for the benefit of the Royal Academy of Music. Landmarks in the development of these concerts are as follows:

1973 First concert for the Royal Academy of Music.
1974 Concert for the benefit of the Royal Marines Museum.
1975 Beneficiaries became Malcolm Sargent Cancer Fund for Children, and Service Charities.
1976 A theme used for the first time: 200th Anniversary of American Declaration of Independence.
1977 Silver Jubilee of Queen Elizabeth II celebrated.
1978 The Queen and the Captain General attended. 75th Anniversary of Royal Marines Band Service celebrated.
1979 Marine Band of the Royal Netherlands Navy took part. First LP recording through an arrangement with the Royal Marines Association.
1980 Tribute to recently murdered Life Colonel Commandant, Admiral of the Fleet, Earl Mountbatten of Burma. Sir Vivian Dunn was a guest conductor. Concerts now held on two nights and would be known as 'The Mountbatten Concerts' after this year.
1983 Commando Forces Band, recently returned from the fighting to reclaim the Falklands, took part. Concerts renamed 'The Mountbatten Festival of Music'.
1984 All previous attendance records broken. Tribute to Sir Vivian Dunn played, as was, for the first time, the Royal Marines Band Service Memorial Fanfare 'To Comrades Sleeping'.

1985   Warrant Officer Bandmaster conducting opening fanfare in tunic and peaked cap, a Deal tradition, changed when WOI (Bandmaster) Peter Rutterford took the podium in mess kit. A vocalist from the Band Service was featured.

1986   The Pipes and Drums of the 1st Battalion, The Argyll and Sutherland High-landers took part.

1987   The massed bands sang 'The Battle Hymn of the Republic' and the Corps of Drums gave their first ceremonial display in these concerts.

1988   Concert extended to three nights and all seats were sold. BBC Radio broad-cast the concert. It was recorded as usual and also video-recorded.

1989   Marine Band of the Royal Netherlands Navy took part for the second time.

1990   Included a tribute to the RMSM musicians murdered at Deal.

1992   Concert shared with 'The President's Own' US Marine Corps Band – a coup!

1995   Tribute to the veterans of Second World War in line with National commemorations.

1996   Lieutenant-Colonel Richard Waterer acknowledged that the concerts were 'The largest musical military festival' in the world. Totally produced and directed by the Royal Marines Band Service including lighting and sound.

1997   25th consecutive year at the Royal Albert Hall, Band Colour Sergeant Jon Yates being only man to have appeared in them all – many as featured soloist.

1998   First appearance of a Royal Marines Band Service piper.

2000   Stage extended to give a larger area for displays and to allow dancers to become a part of the show.

The Bands

The Band of the Royal Marines School of Music provided a continuous thread of appearances throughout the period 1973 until 1996, supported in the main by the other Staff Bands of Commander-in-Chief Naval Home Command and Commander-in-Chief Fleet. Following the demise of the Staff Band of the Royal Marines School of Music in 1996, the Royal Marines Bands from Portsmouth, Plymouth and Scotland plus either the Band from Commando Training Centre or from Britannia Royal Naval College have performed at these concerts. Junior Musicians took part in the first concert as well as those in 1981, 1982 and 1985, and on six occasions since 1988 they have taken part as a choir. The Massed Corps of Drums and the Fanfare Team have featured on a regular basis, whilst the orchestra and the Big Band have also contributed.

The Music

These concerts present a microcosm of the development of the music of the Royal Marines Band Service during this period of just over a quarter of a century. Guest vocalists such as Owen Brannigan, John Lawrenson and Beverley Humphreys, as well as guest instrumentalists and the bands mentioned earlier made occasional special appearances. These, and themes such as the 200th Anniversary of the American Declaration of Independence (1976), the Queen's Silver Jubilee (1977) and the end of Second World War (1995) automatically provided variety to the type of music played and the style and shape of the concerts.

Mountbatten Festival of Music 1987 The Massed Bands of the Royal Marines conducted by Captain Peter Heming. (Photo: Royal Marines Museum)

Three major developments took place during the years 1973–2000. The first was the introduction in 1987 of a Ceremonial Display by the Massed Corps of Drums who, until then, had rarely had an opportunity to demonstrate their individuality in these circumstances. This was established as a regular feature that became more and more complex, and eventually included the re-introduction of a Bugler playing bass drum and the innovation of a Bugler playing percussion kit. Stick drill also became more and more complex probably reaching a high point in 1996 with 'Riverdance' although subsequent displays have been equally effective and have introduced new movements and tempos. The second development has been the increase in the music composed or arranged by members of the Royal Marines Band Service. During the 1970s about a quarter of the music played was from this source whilst during the 1980s it increased to almost a half and during the 1990s it almost averaged 60% with a peak, if the items conducted by the American guest conductor are excluded, in 1996 of 75%. Whilst marches, overtures and traditional finales are retained, the composing and arranging talents of such as Captain David Cole, Lieutenant Ray Woodfield and WO Michael McDermott have enabled modern film and show themes, big band music, and suites such as 'Festival of the Sea' to be included. The most recent innovation was the inclusion of dancers and singers in 2000 to produce an all-round entertainment.

The recordings of the Mountbatten Festival of Music are currently the highest selling compact discs from the Royal Marines. They are now produced entirely by the Royal Marines Band Service through its own recording label 'Chevron'.

Royal Air Force Concert Tour
by Colin Dean

Although of much more recent origin, this concert tour has now become an established fixture in the military band calendar, dating from 25th/26th September 1984 when the Massed Bands of the Royal Air Force performed at the Royal Albert Hall in London. The four UK based bands took part under the baton of the Principal Director of Music, Wing Commander Eric Banks. The programme comprised many of the RAF favourites such as the 'Battle of Britain Theme', '633 Squadron' and 'The Dambusters' (Eric Coates), a march without which no RAF concert would be complete. John Heddle Nash appeared as the guest baritone and 'Crown Imperial' (Walton), 'Rule Britannia' (Arne) and 'Pomp and Circumstance No. 1' (Elgar) formed the finale, as they have done at many of these concerts.

Warrant Officer John Lambert appeared as the vocalist at the 1985/6 concerts and included one of his favourite party pieces, 'Where is the Life?' from *Kiss Me Kate*. In 1987 Wing Commander Banks shared the conducting with Lieutenant Colonel James M. Bankhead, Commander and Conductor of the United States Air Force Band. One of the features of the concerts has been the use of a professional compere, with varying degrees of success, it might be added. Many thought the best presentation was in 1988 when Wing Commander Banks himself stood in at very short notice as the gentleman booked was indisposed.

Wing Commander Barrie Hingley took over as Principal Director of Music in 1989 and a number of changes were made to the concert, not least in that it was repeated two days later at the International Conference Centre in Harrogate, thus beginning its expansion into a major concert tour. The conducting on these occasions was shared by the Directors of Music of each of the bands. The Royal Air Force Squadronaires took part for the first time playing 'In the Mood' and were joined at the Royal Albert Hall by a virtuoso percussionist from Canada, Peter Appleyard.

The 1989 concerts also saw the introduction of a series of first performances of newly commissioned works including Laurie Johnson's suite 'To the Few'. This is in three movements, opening with 'Scramble' depicting a Spitfire in action, after which 'Juke Box' combined the RAF Squadronaires with the massed bands to represent the dance bands of the day, with a final salute in the last movement entitled 'Fly Past'. The 1990 concert continued the theme of introducing new music with Ron Goodwin's '15th September 1940' while the Beverley Sisters appeared as guests, singing songs from the war years, with the 'Squads' again featured, this time with the voice of Emer McParland.

Another work specially commissioned by RAF Music Services was included in 1991 with Edward Gregson's 'The Sword and the Crown', a dramatic piece based on music he had originally composed for 'The Plantagenets' trilogy in Stratford-on-Avon and conducted by the composer himself at the Royal Albert Hall. A sequel to this work, 'The Kings Go Forth' was played at the 1996 concerts. Yet another first performance came in 1992 with 'Days of Glory', a suite in four movements by Richard Harvey and conducted by Dr James Croft of Florida State University, who had jointly commissioned the work with the RAF.

The compere in 1990 and 1991 was the highly popular Roy Castle, who brought his trumpet to join with the Squadronaires in 'The Birth of the Blues' and with principal trumpet Sergeant Geoff Lawrence for a virtuoso duet in Hogey Carmichel's 'Stardust'. The 1993 concerts introduced the baritone voice of Junior Technician Matthew Little and the now Corporal Little has since been a regular feature. Also lending vocal talents at that time was Joanne Pullen, a lady with strong connections with RAF music, as her father was an RAF Bandmaster, her mother a member of the Central Band of the WRAF and her brother a current member of the Central Band.

The 1995 concert celebrated the 50th anniversary of the end of the Second World War and featured the Central Band's 5-piece ensemble, while 1996 marked the 60th anniversary of the Spitfire and included two items from the 10-piece ensemble, 'Central Brass'. The 1997 concert included the Band of the USAF in Europe and 1998 marked 80 years of the RAF. 1999 was the 50th anniversary of NATO with a programme chosen to represent the countries that form the alliance. This included a dramatic descriptive home-grown work entitled 'Warcrye of Elfegen', an anagram of the composer Geoffrey Lawrence, principal cornet of Central Band.

By the end of the century in 2000 the tour was covering the Bridgewater Hall at Manchester, the Royal Concert Hall in Glasgow, the Symphony Hall at Birmingham, the Poole Arts Centre as well as the London and Harrogate venues. The theme was the 60th anniversary of the Battle of Britain, with the bands under Wing Commander Rob Wiffin proving once again to be a great credit to their service.

CHAPTER 6

MILITARY BANDS ON THE AIR

Brian Reynolds

It might surprise younger readers of this book that there should be a chapter on military band broadcasting. After all, as we enter the 21st century, studio broadcasting of music of any sort has all but disappeared and it is indeed a rare treat to hear a military band 'on the air'. However, this was not always the case and for several decades military bands were well represented on radio. Programme titles such as 'Marching and Waltzing', 'Listen to the Band' and 'Bandstand' are synonymous with the genre. One can only speculate as to the reasons for the decline in broadcasts of the music that we love. Some would say that it represents 'the changing taste of the listener' – a favourite BBC excuse, which is a far cry from the Reithian principle of providing the best for everyone. The BBC's monopoly in broadcasting has long gone and competition from commercial stations, in recent decades, appears to have brought the BBC to the view that they have to provide similar fare.

Another factor, which is perhaps the main reason for the decline, is 'money'. Military bands are expensive and whereas a thirty minute broadcast by a standard size band would have cost £37/10/– in 1952, this figure would, in the 21st century come nowhere near the requirement of ONE player and a band of, say 28 musicians would now cost between two and three thousand pounds.

All regular army bands have for several years been required by the Ministry of Defence to charge performance fees in line with the guidelines given by the union to its members. This is to ensure that service musicians (who are already receiving a salary) do not displace professional musicians as a form of 'cheap labour'. All performance fees (including those for broadcasts) are paid into the 'Regimental Band Fund' and are distributed in accordance to regulations laid down in the Ministry of Defence document 'Instructions for Bands'. This allows for a percentage to be paid to the director of music/bandmaster and members of the band.

Brass bands, on the other hand, are designated 'amateurs' – although you would hardly think so upon hearing the high standard that many achieve – and are not usually paid at the same rates as military bands. This is presumably why brass bands are still heard 'on the air' fairly regularly. A former 'Listen to the Band' producer told me that in the 1980s he had to 'save up' in order to use a military band once every six weeks.

To review the history of Military Band broadcasting, we start at the very beginning – a very good place to start! It has often been claimed that the first military band broadcast was by the Band of the Royal Air Force on 1st July 1923. In fact (and I am grateful to military historian, Alastair Mitchell for this information) it was the Band of the Irish Guards who first took to the airwaves on 26th June 1923. A typical example of a broadcast from the period is given below.

5th February 1925

Band of the Royal Air Force – Flight Lieutenant J. Amers

Overture	**The Earl of Essex**	*Mercadante*
Selection	**Coppelia**	*Delibes*
Suite	**Bal Costume**	*Rubinstein*
	In the Cloisters	*Terrance*
Cornet solo	**A Summer Night**	*Goring Thomas*
	Reminiscences of Chopin	*arr F Winterbottom*
	Rural Scenes	*A E Matt*
Selection from	**Album for the Young**	*Schumann*

It has to be said that during the 1920s and 1930s broadcasts by service bands were by no means as frequent as they were later to become. Radio consisted of many territorial stations, all with limited range (rather like today's local radio), some having their own 'house' military bands. London (whose station identification was 2LO) had the 2LO Military Band, conductor Dan Godfrey Jnr, and as an example, a broadcast on 1st February 1925 included:

Overture	**Maximilian Robespierre**	*Litolff*
Selection	**La Bohème**	*Puccini*
Suite	**Mascarade (Merchant of Venice)**	*Sullivan*
Persian Dance	**Khovantschina**	*Moussorgsky*
Selection	**Reminiscences of Ireland**	*arr F Godfrey*

This may well have been the forerunner of the Wireless Military Band which first appeared in 1927 under its Musical Director, Bertram Walton O'Donnell – one of three musical brothers whose names are synonymous with military band history. (Incidentally, contrary to some beliefs, this band never broadcast under the title 'BBC Wireless Military Band' – although the BBC prefix was substituted for 'Wireless' in 1936.)

From the outset, the BBC broadcast live events such as tattoos, and many complete band concerts were broadcast in this way from locations around the country, often featuring guest artists.

By the late 1920s, the number of 'local stations' had diminished in favour of larger regional stations with their wider catchment areas, and in the early 1930s the 'National' service was established together with a 'Regional' network which was able to share broadcasts with a number of regional stations.

The size of the potential audience had a considerable bearing on which bands were selected for use. 'Top' bands such as the Royal Air Force, Royal Artillery and

11.0 THE BAND OF THE ROYAL TANK CORPS

(by permission of Brigadier W. M. Sutton, D.S.O., M.C., A.D.C. and Officers of the Royal Tank Corps)

Conducted by Mr. D. J Plater
from the Grand Parade Bandstand,
Eastbourne

The March of the King's Men *Plater*
Overture, Orpheus in the Underworld
Offenbach, arr. Hibbert
Liselotte and Lancelot.............*Adam*
Selection, The Geisha.............*Jones*
Serenade and Waltz (The Student
Prince).........................*Romberg*
Suite, From Meadow to Mayfair
Eric Coates
1 Rustic Dance. 2 A Song by the
Way
Selection, Firefly...................*Friml*
Fantasia, Festivalia..........*arr. Winter*

1st July 1938

Grenadier Guards were utilised regularly in the 'National' service, whereas the lesser 'line' bands were generally not deemed to be of sufficiently high standard to broadcast outside the local region in which they were based. For example, the 2nd Battalion The Northumberland Fusiliers broadcast in the Northern Region and The Argyll and Sutherland Highlanders were heard (as you would expect) from the Scottish Region. In the regions, much use was also made of 'civilian' military bands such as the Manchester Police, Merseyside Military Band, the Leicester Imperial Band and the Birmingham Military Band – amongst others. However, the BBC really did not have a high opinion of the 'civilian' bands and felt that most of the 'line' bands were substandard.

Throughout the 1930s, the Wireless Military Band (later BBC Military Band) dominated the radio schedules, usually doing three broadcasts a week and averaging 150 programmes per year. Its major contribution to broadcasting therefore merits more detailed comment. Its conductor, Walton O'Donnell, took great pride in the view that because it consisted of very experienced musicians it could and should concentrate on a repertoire that was different and indeed more ambitious than that offered by service bands.

Their programmes consisted of a mixture of 'classical' works and the more 'serious' items of light music, many of which were quite obscure. Even bearing in mind the fact that 1930s light music concerts were generally more classical in style than they were later to become, the BBC Military Band's programmes were distinctly 'highbrow', as the following examples from their repertoire will indicate:

	Scènes Dramatiques	*Massenet*
Overture	**King Lear**	*Balakirev*
Symphonic Suite	**Louise**	*Charpentier-Cadesius*
Overture	**La Baruffe Chiozzotte**	*Sinigaglia*
Symphonic Poem	**Korsholm**	*Jarnefelt*

The Wireless Military Band conducted by B Walton O'Donnell.

Whilst the BBC were proud of their Military Band and agreed that a band of such 'pedigree' should perform music of the highest order in their programmes they were, by the mid-thirties, distinctly worried that the almost complete exclusion of more 'accessible' items could be alienating listeners. They felt that some lighter items such as military marches and musical comedy selections should be included for contrast and accordingly sent a memorandum to O'Donnell stating their views. The extensive reply, which they received, interesting as it is, would be far too long to incorporate in this chapter. However, in summary, he made the following points:

1   My aims have been to help the listener extend the repertoire of things he likes and will not tire of listening to, by introducing him to a large field of music which he has less opportunity of hearing but which he will like the better the more he hears it – the test of good music.

2   To help in a musical policy which will reflect credit at all times to the Corporation, bearing in mind that only the best in every way should be good enough for broadcasting.

3   To create in the Wireless Military Band, a combination whose work and performance will be of lasting pride to the BBC.

He disagreed with the BBC management viewpoint regarding musical comedy and marches, feeling the former to be more appropriate to light orchestras and considering the latter to be the province of service bands. Indeed, he expressed concern that the very title of the band gave the false impression that it was a 'marching band'!

For some reason, throughout the years military bands have always been equated with brass bands as far as the BBC is concerned. Indeed, to this day, there are many people who, surprisingly, are unaware of the difference! A BBC memorandum dated 14th June 1934 reads: 'So long as we have our own military band we do not want many outside military bands, therefore the order is: Wireless Military Band, then a brass band then, very occasionally a military band'. This would undoubtedly explain why, at a time when the airwaves were full of music, service bands made a relatively small contribution, with the majority of the programmes being confined to the regions.

It had been agreed in 1933 that the BBC would audition all staff bands in turn and then endeavour to distribute the broadcasts equally between those bands found to be acceptable. Such auditions would be directly related to the outcome of Kneller Hall inspections and in fact it became the role of the Royal Military School of Music to advise the BBC (following such inspections) as to which bands were suitable for broadcasting.

The BBC, having auditioned them, would place the satisfactory bands into three categories, A, B and C in accordance with their perceived standard. An amusing internal memorandum in the BBC files gives instructions for the Royal Artillery (Salisbury Plain) Band to be 'removed from Category C because the Royal Artillery Mounted Band – designated Category A is one and the same band'!*

As mentioned earlier, outside broadcasts of bands were quite commonplace at this time, and on one occasion the Kneller Hall Band participated in a seaside concert party to which they contributed a number of 'potted' versions of classical works – symphonies and even a piano concerto, condensed into a few minutes. BBC management was outraged at what they described as a 'disgraceful' performance and took the band off the broadcasting list. In 1936 the BBC had second thoughts (no doubt inspired by their need of Kneller Hall recommendations) and decided that a concert party was hardly the most appropriate form of broadcast to make such a judgement and that the band should be allowed to do a 'normal' broadcast. Once again, there is an amusing observation in a BBC memo written by Maurice Johnstone which reads:

> The last broadcast by the Kneller Hall band in 1932 was not considered satisfactory. Even I would have misgivings about the Band of the Royal Military School of Music playing a piece called 'A Visit to the Dentist'!

As the '30s progressed, military bands were gradually used more frequently in National broadcasting. An interesting statistic in the files is that in 1938 there were 123 performances by military bands, of which 58 were civilian. If the BBC Military Band's performances were taken into account, the total figure would be 273.

The outbreak of war in 1939 made a dramatic impact on BBC broadcasting with the closure of the Regional network and all broadcasting being confined to the 'National' service for a very limited number of hours. For some months the BBC

* This is all the more amusing as they were, in fact, totally different bands!

relied mostly upon their own musical resources, but by 1940 things had greatly improved; the 'National' became the Home Service and a new 'Forces programme' of continuous light entertainment was broadcast and was aimed particularly at the services.

During the '20s and '30s, minimal air-time had been given to dance bands; this was because Sir John Reith, who had ruled the BBC with a 'rod of iron' during this period being a man of deep religious convictions, felt that such music was a corrupting influence. (I wonder what he would have thought of today's 'pop' music!). Suddenly such bands were broadcasting as regularly as light orchestras. Military band shows followed suit and an average of three or four bands were heard each week. For the first time, some music programmes were given names, whereas previously the billings had nearly always been the title of the band.

As previously mentioned, Kneller Hall's recommendations were the basis of BBC auditions but, because inspections were suspended during the war, the recommendations were no longer forthcoming. In 1941 Dr Dennis Wright decided that the BBC could now recommend bands for broadcasting on the basis of their own assessments. The BBC obviously relished this independence, commenting (in an internal document) that musical standards were 'more appropriate than the 'spit and polish' gradings of Kneller Hall!' Instructions were given to the appropriate official to thank Kneller Hall for their help in the past, but the memo added, in a footnote, 'we don't have to tell them that we are not going to use them again after the war!'

Walton O'Donnell had left the BBC Military Band in 1937 having been promoted to the senior position of conductor of the BBC Northern Ireland Orchestra. Sadly, he died two years later. His place as conductor of the Military Band was taken by his brother, Percy, who maintained its high standards. However, times were changing; the BBC's responsibility was to the morale of the nation in war time, especially to the forces, and on 1st July 1940 a strict instruction went out to the BBC Military Band 'to play more marches' and, like it or not, they had to comply.

The previous week, the BBC had taken a major step in boosting morale in industry, by introducing 'Music While You Work', a programme of continuous tuneful and cheerful music played twice daily by light orchestras, dance bands, brass and military bands. Because of the significant contribution this programme made in the history of military band broadcasting, I shall be dealing with it in some detail later on. For now, it suffices to say that the BBC Military Band was 'conscripted' to play regularly on the show and, in common with other contributors, had to comply with the programme's policy of playing familiar music – marches, selections, community

3.0 'MUSIC WHILE YOU WORK'
BBC Military Band
Conductor, P. S. G. O'Donnell
Festival march: Ostend-Luxembourg
Philippe Meny
Selection: Véronique............*Messager*
Four dances from Merrie England
German
The shanty man.......................*Vinter*

27th June 1940

song medleys and light entr'actes – a very different repertoire from that to which they were accustomed, although the example on the previous page from the first week of the series is perhaps not typical as the BBC had not yet set its guidelines for the series.

After about a year they complained that they were being used too frequently in the series, they found the broadcasts arduous and considered the music that they were required to play to be 'beneath them'! Actually, the music was perfectly good, albeit lighter and more easily assimilated. Regrettably their attitude was all too typical of the musical snobbery that existed towards light music during its Cinderella-like existence. The BBC's attitude to their complaints is detailed in their files – 'if they feel that way about the programme, we won't use them'. They were taken off the show, making just one more appearance in October 1942.

It was in 1942 that the management of the 'Forces' programme expressed concern that military bands in general were playing too much symphonic music and not enough 'cheerful and attractive' music. It was also felt that there were insufficient band broadcasts, and consultations took place with the War Office, the Admiralty and Air Ministry with a view to increasing them. The War Office in particular expressed the view that they would welcome additional broadcasts. As a result military band broadcasts increased to about nine or ten per week!

**9.0   Band of the
BEDFORDSHIRE AND
HERTFORDSHIRE REGIMENT**
Conducted by Mr. J. Thorpe
Regimental Marches of the Bedfordshire
    and Hertfordshire Regiment...........*trad.*
Overture : Plymouth Hoe..............*Ansell*
Walter's Prize Song (The Mastersingers)
                                                Wagner
(Cornet soloist, Bandsman W. Parris)
Marche solennelle (posthumous)
                                        Edward German
Waltz and Polacca : Eugene Onegin
                                        Tchaikovsky

8th April 1942

**2.0   Band of the
BORDER REGIMENT**
Conducted by Mr. J. L. Wallace
Regimental March : D'ye ken John Peel ?
                                                trad.
Intermezzo : Naïla........................*Delibes*
Songs of the Hebrides *arr. Kennedy-Fraser*
Slavonic Dance No. 1.................*Dvořák*
Tarantelle de Belphégor.................*Albert*
March : Le rêve passe.................*Helmer*

8th April 1942

War time conscription into the services had meant that thousands of professional musicians, many from symphony orchestras, were joining the bands and there was a notable improvement in standards of playing – particularly noticeable in the case of 'line' bands; a number of new bands were also formed – the RAF Command Bands, for example:

2.0   Time, Greenwich
Band ' B ' of the
,R.A.F. FLYING TRAINING
COMMAND

(by permission of the Air Officer
Commanding-in-Chief).   Conductor,
Mr. Gilbert Vinter

March : Dunster Castle..............*Johnson*
Valse Septembre..........................*Godin*
Escena India...............................,*Vinter*
When the home bells ring again
Haydn Wood
(Soloist, J. O. Wildman)
Rhapsodic Dance : The Bamboula
Coleridge-Taylor
R.A.F. March Past............*Walford Davies*

8th October 1943

Obviously, with so many bands suddenly achieving broadcasting standard, it was logical that they should be allowed to contribute to the BBC's programmes at this time. It was also by no means unusual for a Guards band to broadcast twice in one day, thus making the most use of a band whilst it was available.

The reader may well be amazed that with the country at war it was possible to release bands for non-military purposes such as broadcasts, particularly when one recalls that, during the Gulf War, all bands were put on medical duty alert. However, both the War Office and the BBC were of the opinion that maintaining the morale of the nation was of the utmost importance and the stirring strains of a military band served that purpose admirably.

Earlier, I mentioned the flood of professional musicians joining the services. The well known light orchestra leader, Van Dam, suggested to the Royal Air Force the idea of forming a 25-piece orchestra to provide a variety of music for RAF personnel. The Organising Director of Music, Wing Commander R P O'Donnell (brother of Percy and Bertram) thought that this was a marvellous idea and the Van Dam orchestra joined the RAF 'en bloc'. However, the whole thing fell through when Van Dam failed his medical examination and the musicians were left without the special posting for which they had volunteered but, nevertheless, had to remain in the RAF for the duration of the war. Poor Van Dam was left without an orchestra! He subsequently formed one from musicians ineligible for the services.

Following the decision to increase greatly the use of service bands 'on the air', it was perhaps inevitable that the BBC Military Band's function would diminish and early in 1943 a decision was made to disband it. Naturally, the Musicians' Union, who had always discouraged the use of service bands for non-military use, protested vehemently but their pleas were in vain. The BBC acknowledged that the loss of the BBC Military Band would be a source of disappointment to many members of the public but this was considered to be the inevitable result of changing conditions. Nevertheless, they had to recognise the plight of the band members; some could be re-employed within their orchestras, but about twenty (all over military age) would have to seek employment elsewhere. With the wartime shortage of musicians, it was felt that most would find work without difficulty.

The war years saw a turning point in broadcasting. For security reasons, the numerous outside broadcasts that were predominant before the war were drastically reduced but there was still an abundance of music from the studios, although the BBC went to great pains to avoid identifying the source of the broadcasts. Indeed, unbeknown to the listeners at the time, a large part of their organisation, including London based staff orchestras, was transferred to Bangor in North Wales.

The BBC was also ill at ease about being seen to employ Italians; this meant that artists working under Italian stage names had to change them. Primo Scala (of Accordion Band fame) had to revert to his own name Harry Bidgood – he was the son of march composer Thomas Bidgood. The BBC even stated in the *Radio Times* that he had 'taken over' the Primo Scala band before the war! Violinist Alfredo Campoli became Alfred Campbell and, most amusing of all, Mantovani (who was allowed to retain his own name) had qualifying 'billings' in the *Radio Times* stating that he was 'British despite his Italian surname'! What nonsense – he was Annunzio Paolo Mantovani from Venice!

It was in 1940 that 'Music While You Work' was introduced – following a suggestion from the War Department that a programme of morale-boosting music designed for factory workers (particularly munitions) would boost output. The BBC liased with factories around the country and a number of ground rules were set – bright, tuneful and predominantly familiar music was required – nothing lethargic; in fact, all modern slow waltzes were banned, as were any pieces that had distracting characteristics such as over elaborate orchestration; it was important that the melody should be clearly audible above factory noises.

As previously stated, the BBC Military Band contributed regularly during the first eighteen months of the programme but service bands were used with increasing frequency. The twice-daily programme was enhanced by a further late night edition in 1942. So, by the end of the war, there were usually three bands heard in the series each week. All of the Brigade of Guards bands (as they were then known) took part, as did the Household Cavalry, most Corps bands and a considerable number of 'line' bands who suddenly found themselves broadcasting regularly for the first time, having achieved the required standards as a result of the influx of civilian musicians.

The various bands of the Royal Marines, Royal Artillery and Royal Air Force were also regular contributors as were several civilian bands such as the Metropolitan Police and London Fire Forces (as they were then called). One of the many rules of the programme was that it had to be non-stop. The penalty for not playing *segue* (the musical term for this) was exclusion from the series and indeed when one Guards Director of Music refused to comply with this rule, considering it, unmusical', the band was dropped from the series until he retired.

As far as I can ascertain, the only staff bands that did not contribute to MWYW were the Cambrai Staff Band of the Royal Tank Regiment and the Women's Royal Army Corps. The explanation for the first could have been that they were frequently stationed abroad. The WRAC's exclusion was more puzzling. According to Captain Edward Crowcroft (one-time Director of Music of the WRAC) they failed the audition – a fact that will astound enthusiasts of this wonderful band in later decades. It certainly appeared in other programmes.

During the war years MWYW listeners were also treated to the sound of a number of military light orchestras and dance bands – The Royal Artillery Theatre Orchestra, Dance Band of the Manchester Regiment, Dance Band of the RASC, and Welsh

Guards all contributed to the series. Others such as the RAOC Blue Rockets, the Blue Mariners and the Skyrockets were destined to become famous.

Following cessation of hostilities in May 1945, the BBC dropped the late night edition of 'Music While You Work' but the programme, having established itself as a firm favourite with domestic listeners, continued successfully for more than two decades; however the military band contribution was reduced to two per week until 1954, after which there was a weekly slot.

Being a 'live' programme, there was no opportunity to correct any mistakes and I possess a recording of one of our most distinguished bands (which shall be nameless) getting lost in a piece called 'The Dance of the Three Old Maids'. It took a good fifteen seconds for the band to correct themselves and one can only imagine the Organising Director of Music rapidly ageing during the piece!

Another incident occurred, as a result of the practice of writing out music in abbreviated form, using what are known as 'first and second time bars'. To the uninitiated I should explain that this meant that, instead of writing out a repeated section in full, just the part at the end which is different the second time is written. On one occasion when a Guards band was playing their final march the Director of Music, noticing that they were running a bit late, signalled to the band to go straight to the 'second time bar'. Unfortunately, half the band had their music written out in full and therefore there *was* no second time bar! The cacophony that followed necessitated the Director quickly stopping the band and going straight into 'Calling All Workers' – the programme's famous signature tune!

Harry Mortimer, the distinguished cornetist and Brass Band conductor, headed the unit which dealt with brass and military bands but he didn't allow his affiliations towards the former to be prejudicial towards military bands. As far as MWYW was concerned, military bands were used much more frequently than brass and almost exclusively for much of the '60s.

Many will recall the popular series 'Marching and Waltzing'. Originally starting out as a record programme during the war, it came into its own in the 1950s when it featured a brass or military band to play the marches, interspersed with waltzes played by the Raeburn Orchestra directed by Wynford Reynolds. When Reynolds died in 1958, other orchestras such as those of Anton and Louis Voss took part. Both band and orchestra were in the studio at the same time, a concept which had to be abandoned when, for economic reasons, the BBC decided to use their own regional orchestras to play the waltzes.

This meant the pre-recording of part of the programme. I happen to know that the BBC Midland Light Orchestra absolutely loathed playing 'Marching and Waltzing' because it meant that they would be playing in the same tempo for the whole session (including rehearsal). This would be particularly monotonous for horns and second and third violins relegated to playing 'chug-chugs' on the second and third beat of each bar.

'Marching and Waltzing' was not broadcast all year round and there were sometimes gaps of many years between series. It was just given a season from time to time; it has not been heard since the mid-80s. During its last season, bands and orchestra sometimes swapped roles with the band playing a waltz, and the orchestra a march. I suspect that this offered more variety to the musicians than to the listeners!

However, a novel variation of this programme was introduced during the 1970s called 'Brass and Strings and Other Things' – a cumbersome title later shortened to 'Brass and Strings'. Whilst brass or military bands alternated with the orchestra (usually the BBC Radio Orchestra) as in 'Marching and Waltzing', they were able to play a wider variety of music, not being confined to marches and waltzes.

The war-time pattern of increased military band broadcasting continued for many years after the cessation of hostilities and bands were still achieving an average of five or six broadcasts per week in 1953, after which there was a decline as budgets for light music programmes were reduced.

'Listen to the Band', radio's oldest and longest running band programme, and now the only surviving band series, also started during the war and, as today, was primarily a vehicle for brass bands in the early years. Military bands received regular representation in later years, and a fifty-fifty policy was operated until the 1980s. The title of the programme of course derives from the words of Lionel Monkton's 'Soldiers in the Park'. Like 'Marching and Waltzing', 'Listen to the Band' was a very sporadic series but has had a semi-permanent weekly slot on Radio Two for many years.

1.40 'LISTEN TO THE BAND!'
Band of the Coldstream Guards, con-
ducted by Lieut. Douglas A. Pope,
Director of Music; Coldstream Guards
Overture: My Old Stable Jacket
                              Manuel Bilton
My Lady Greensleeves
                              arr. Richardson
Russian Sailors'. Dance (The Red
    Poppy)..............................*Glière*
Selection: La Traviata...............*Verdi*
March Medley: Sousa on Parade
                              arr. Palmer
Coldstream March: Milanollo...*Hamm*   *12th January 1946*

Perhaps I should point out at this stage that Radio Two, which started in 1967, replaced the old Light Programme which in turn had been the successor to the 'Forces' programme of the war years. Many people regard the 22-year existence of the Light Programme as the 'Golden Years of Radio'.

In the early 1970s, as an alternative to 'Listen to the Band' there was a similar but slightly lighter series called 'Strike up the Band' and the familiar Gershwin tune of this name was its signature tune. There were a number of shorter-lived band pro-grammes over the years – a breakfast time programme in 1949 entitled 'Follow the Band' was sub-titled 'a radio route march' and, as you would expect, consisted entirely of marches or marching songs.

Also in 1949 the BBC gave an early morning weekly slot to military bands in the series 'Bright and Early' which commenced at 6.30 am and was as good a reason as any for getting up early on a Saturday morning – other days featured brass bands, organists, dance bands and light orchestras. The music was continuous and very similar to 'Music While You Work' – indeed it was organised by the same department. Military bands were featured every week in this 'slot' until 1953.

In addition to featuring all the top Regimental Bands, this was probably the last series regularly to include 'line' bands – including the 12th Royal Lancers (Prince of

Wales), The King's Royal Rifle Corps (60th Rifles), 1st Battalion The Durham Light Infantry, 2nd Battalion Parachute Regiment, 3rd Carabiniers (Prince of Wales's Dragoon Guards), 1st Battalion The Highland Light Infantry plus a few civilian bands such as the Nottingham City Police, the National Military Band and the Ford Motor Works Military Band under Major G H Willcocks, (which had started out during the war as the Ford Motor Company Home Guard Band).

6.30 a.m.   **Big Ben**
BRIGHT AND EARLY
Band of the 12th Royal Lancers
(Prince of Wales)
Conductor, Mr. H. E. Roberts

The Red Cloak....................*Mansfield*
Waltz: The Grenadiers......*Waldteufel*
Tunes from Rio Rita...............*Tierney*
The Mosquitoes' Parade.........*Whitney*
Selection: Swing Time..*Jerome Kern*
John Peel..........*arr. Clive Richardson*
March: Namur...........*W. V. Richards*
(BBC recording)   *6th May 1950*

After the conclusion of this series, the contribution of 'line' bands diminished sharply; I suppose this was inevitable since many were now returning to their pre-war status, the professional civilian players who had boosted them during the war having been 'demobbed', but the BBC wrongly assumed in ensuing decades that the majority of such bands were below broadcasting standard. It was certainly true of many, but there were a number of quite outstanding bands such as the 13th/18th Royal Hussars which was probably as good as or better than some of the 'Corps' bands! After the early 1950s the quota of brass and military bands reduced markedly and by 1960 was only four per week (of which two were often brass bands).

It was in 1953 that the BBC commenced their long running series 'Friday Night is Music Night' and, together with the BBC Concert Orchestra and guest singers, bands were a regular feature until well into the 1980s. Although this series is still running at the time of writing, the inclusion of a military band is a very rare event indeed. Looking at it from the BBC's point of view, the engagement of a professional band to play about three pieces did not make a lot of economic sense.

The title 'Bandstand' had been given to a variety of programmes over the years but became a regular feature in 1946 with (initially) several editions per week. It continued intermittently on the Light Programme until well into the 1960s and was sometimes of longer duration than other band programmes. Even as late as the 1960s it was often broadcast 'live' from a seaside location such as Eastbourne bandstand; some of the shows also had guest artists.

In 1965 it became 'Saturday Bandstand' – possibly to distinguish it from a new programme called 'Bandstand' which was introduced to the Third Programme (or Radio 3 as it became in 1967). As one would expect, this was a vehicle for more serious works for brass and military bands and was probably the closest the BBC had come to the old Wireless Military Band repertoire. A composition of mine called 'Elizabethan Tapestry', composed for the Queen's Silver Jubilee in 1977 and my most serious composition, was rejected from this programme for being 'too light' and it was used in 'Listen to the Band' instead!

The early 'Morning Music' programmes, which ran for about twenty years, gave surprisingly little representation to military bands, apart from a few spells in the late 1940s, but in 1966 after the programme was renamed 'Breakfast Special', military bands were added to the formidable list of contributors.

The 1960s heralded major changes in broadcasting policy; 'pop' music was rapidly infiltrating and influencing programmes and many traditional styles of music were deemed out of date by the BBC who, for the first time, no longer had a monopoly in radio broadcasting and found themselves competing for audiences with commercial stations. In 1967 'Music While You Work' ended and the last military band to broadcast was the Royal Engineers (Chatham) conducted by the then Captain Peter Parkes.

The BBC liked to broadcast these programmes 'live' but it wasn't always convenient for the bands. When a well known Director of Music asked to pre-record his programme because he would be playing on the bandstand at Victoria Embankment Gardens, London, 90 minutes after the broadcast, the BBC were not very pleased; they persuaded him that if he wished a continued association with the Corporation, it would be in his interests to co-operate. He did! Indeed, I can well remember listening to the Band of the Royal Army Service Corps (as it then was) playing 'live' from 10.30 am until 11.00 am and then going to Finsbury Circus Garden at 12.00 where the same band had arrived ready for a two-hour concert!

In 1982, 'Music While You Work' was revived for a week in celebration of the BBC's 60th anniversary and its success led to a daily resumption of the programme in January 1983 which lasted over a year. During this period, military bands contributed a number of editions and I had the pleasure of attending one programme given by the Band of the Welsh Guards. The Director of Music, Major Derek Taylor, tuned the band before the show by requiring each musician to play a note. When he reached the oboe player the sound emitted was oboe-like but unfortunately it came from the player and not his instrument! Major Taylor, whose musical qualifications were not for nothing, promptly shouted, 'You're out of tune'!

Further brief revivals of this series in 1990 and 1991 provided opportunities for the Kneller Hall Band and the Irish Guards to take part. Frankly, neither of these programmes was really in the spirit of the original series. The Irish Guards' inclusion of the 'Pique Dame' overture, which would not have been considered suitable in the 1960s brought about comments that it was more like 'Listen to the Band' without announcements. A typical example of a 'Music While You Work' programme had been as follows, broadcast by the Coldstream Guards Band on 9th December 1964 under the direction of Captain Trevor L Sharpe MBE.

March	**Flash of Steel**	*Gustave Colin*
Selection	**Bouquet de Paris**	*Ronald Hamner*
	How Soon	*Mancini arr Sharpe*
	Mexican Serenade	*Jack Coles*
Selection	**Italian Holiday**	*arr Sharpe*
	Portuguese Party	*Gilbert Vinter*
Selection	**New Moon**	*Sigmund Romberg*
March	**Wein Bliebt Wien**	*Schrammel*

Eric Coates' march 'Calling All Workers' opened and closed each programme.

By the late 1970s the regular band programmes were 'Bandstand' on Radio 3 and 'Friday Night is Music Night'. 'Strike up the Band' had ended and 'Listen to the Band' returned after a long absence but included more military bands than previously. With longer programmes, it became the practice to interview the Director of Music – a nice touch! 'Brass and Strings', which was generally thought of as a replacement for 'Marching and Waltzing', ran for several years and was broadcast late on Sunday nights, but the latter returned for a spell in the '80s.

Brass and Strings – 19th July 1975
Royal Artillery Mounted Band
Director of Music: Captain Terry Kenny

Zacatacas	*Codina*
Happy Music	*James Last*
The Trains That Have Departed	*Yarhakis arr. Kenny*
The Masterpiece	*Mauret arr Parnes*
Merry Matelots	*Chris Siegal*
Red Sombrero	*Ronald Binge*
Clarinade	*Brian Reynolds*
Hang 'em High	*Frontiere*
Adelita	*Trad arr Kenny*
Magic Carousel	*Alex Smith*

Maybe it could be described as a 'death throe' because the few remaining band programmes featured military bands with ever decreasing frequency. By the early 1990s, bands had virtually disappeared from 'Friday Night' and the only remaining programme 'Listen to the Band' rarely featured military bands – there were just two in 1999! It is a sad fact that many of our top bands, including some of the Household Division bands have not been heard on the radio (other than on records) for over a decade and it now looks as if military band broadcasting (as far as the BBC is concerned) is regarded as a thing of the past.

Although not transmitted in Britain, mention must be made of 'Mainly Military' which has been broadcast on British Forces Broadcasting Service (BFBS) since 1986 and is still going strong. The programme is produced and presented by Major Richard Powell, formerly an RAOC officer and a past chairman of the United Kingdom (Founder) Branch of the International Military Music Society.

'Mainly Military' started with five series of thirteen one-hour programmes when Richard was stationed in Cyprus, followed by a further five series presented from Brunei, his next station. Now retired from the army, Richard continues to make the programme (on computer) from a studio in Cambridgeshire for at least 26 weeks of the year.

The emphasis has always been on true military music including corps of drums, pipes and drums, trumpets, bugles and soldiers' songs, with an emphasis on recordings of 'live' events such as the Edinburgh Tattoo, with less of what Richard will call the 'sittin' doon' music. The programmes in 2000 concentrated on march-pasts and their source material.

Finally, several IMMS members have written to the BBC asking why so few service bands are now featured in 'Listen to the Band'. The answer one correspondent received from the Radio 2 Controller's Special Assistant (what's so special about him?) says it all: 'the programme is dedicated to brass bands and not wind bands' (a term usually given to civilian bands that have the same instrumentation as the military band) and 'the programme's remit is to present the best of brass band music.' What short memories they have!

Acknowledgements: *Radio Times*
BBC Written Archives
British Bandsman
So I think I'll become a Musician (Louis Mordish)
   publ Stainer & Bell

CHAPTER 7

THE ROYAL TOURNAMENT

COLIN DEAN

Introduction

Tournaments, Tattoos and Beating Retreat all feature massed bands in a glorious splash of music and colour – but is there really a difference between them? The answer is very much 'yes' as regards their origins, although the strict military purpose has been rather overtaken by their value as public spectacles.

When we think of tournaments it probably conjures pictures of the great jousting events of centuries before, something from which the Royal Tournament was not that far removed.

Tattoo is believed to be derived from the Dutch expression '*Doe den tap toe*' which means 'Turn off the taps' or, if you prefer, 'Time gentlemen, please', and has its origin as a signal for soldiers to leave the taverns and return to their quarters for the night. In time, tattoo came to mean the period between the calls First Post and Last Post, which are thought to have been sounded to signal the first and last sentry posts visited by the Picquet Officer while inspecting the sentries posted for the night.

Retreat is said to date from a signal given by beat of drum to order troops to break off fighting as darkness fell. What is more certain is that it signalled the end of the working day and the lowering of the unit flag.

While both retreat and tattoo have always been the responsibility of the drums, pipes or bugles, and while they still have their place today in regulating a soldier's life, they have both been developed and embellished by the addition of military bands into a display of music and marching for the entertainment of guests or the public.

Generally speaking, Tattoo has now come to mean a display illuminated by searchlights or floodlights, usually in one of the garrison towns and often featuring massed bands from a number of units, as well as other displays such as musical rides, drill, dogs, motor cycles, battle scenes and historical pageants. Beating Retreat on the other hand, is normally confined to music and performed in the early evening by the massed bands, drums and pipes of a particular unit such as the Royal Marines or one of the divisions of infantry.

The distinction between the ceremonies has become further confused by matinée performances of tattoos and by retreat ceremonies held under floodlight, as well as by the sounding of the call Retreat at tattoos and Last Post at beating retreats, and in some cases with both calls played at the same ceremony.

The next three chapters give a brief picture of some of these great spectacles that thrilled the young and old alike throughout the 20th Century.

The Royal Tournament

The Grand Military Tournament and Assault-at-Arms started in 1880 as just that – a tournament of skill-at-arms between members of the forces encompassing equestrian events, fencing, tug-of-war etc. with the object of raising money for service charities.

With the need to attract the general public to increase the revenue, the Musical Ride of the 1st Life Guards was included in 1882 and other displays were added over the years so that the competitions have played less of a part. However, right up to its demise in 1999 the Royal Tournament continued to include horse jumping, fencing, tug of war etc. and, of course, the Royal Navy Field Gun Competition which was without doubt the toughest and most competitive team event of the 20th Century. In its latter years the Royal Tournament came to be largely associated with the appearance of massed bands although, as we shall see, this is something that only developed as a regular feature since the last war.

The Massed Bands of the Brigade of Guards first appeared at the Tournament on 18th May 1900 when they entertained the audience for half an hour prior to the arrival of the Prince of Wales for the official opening. As an aside, two performances that year were interrupted for news to be announced of the Relief of Mafeking and the crossing of the Vaal River by Lord Roberts' forces in South Africa.

In the early years of the century there were intermittent 'turns' in addition to the regular programme items, normally at the performances attended by the King and the Prince of Wales, and these generally included the Brigade of Guards until 1908. They often performed the popular 'British Army Quadrilles' by Louis Jullien, a descriptive fantasia depicting a soldier's day from reveille, through various national airs, trumpet calls and a battle scene, to the final victory and Handel's 'See the Conquering Hero'. In 1905, under the new name of The Royal Naval and Military Tournament, the Guards performed the 'Grand Military Tattoo' with music specially composed and arranged by the Senior Bandmaster, Lieutenant John Mackenzie Rogan, Coldstream Guards, to include Beethoven's 'Creation Hymn' and Monk's 'Abide with Me'.

There was to be a break of fifteen years until the Guards next appeared. On 1st June 1923 in the presence of the Duke of York, distant trumpets sounded 'Assembly' and the Band of the Grenadier Guards marched into the arena playing 'The British Grenadiers' to herald the beginning of a descriptive fantasia entitled 'Episodes in a Soldier's Life'. The Grenadiers were followed by the bands of the Coldstream, Scots, Irish and Welsh Guards in turn, each playing their own national airs. The sound of more than 250 musicians then echoed through the vast building of Olympia, finally quietening as the bands played 'Abide with Me' and trumpets sounded 'Last Post'

'Britannia's Muster' at the Royal Naval and Military Tournament of 1910. State Trumpeters are present and the Band of the Coldstream Guards can be seen in the foreground. The resident band that year was the 21st Lancers under Bandmaster R P O'Donnell.

Buglers of the Royal Marine Light Infantry under Bugle Major H.E. Lidiard taking part in a display of drill and handling of arms by the King's Squad at the 1920 Royal Tournament at Olympia.

(Photo: Royal Marines Museum)

representing the camp at night. The bands finally marched out of the arena playing Kenneth Alford's 'Cavalry of the Clouds'.

A musical ride was normally provided by one of the regiments of Household Cavalry and by the cavalry of the line regiment stationed at Hounslow, and one or both of these regiments would normally find the resident band.

A pageant was introduced in 1896 and these were later to include such themes as 'The Inauguration of the Australian Commonwealth' (1901), 'Rise of the Royal Artillery' (1904), 'Ye Tournament in Ye Olde Days' (1907) and 'Call to Arms 1588' (1912). Naval themes were also included such as 'Armada to Present Day' (1905) and 'Neptune's Soldiers' (1921), the latter telling the story of the Royal Marines from 1664 with music arranged by Major Charles Hall of the 2nd Life Guards who found the resident band that year. Scenes were set in the City of London depicting the recruiting of The Duke of York and Albany's Maritime Regiment of Foot, followed by a display of pike drill by men of the Chatham Division, Royal Marine Light Infantry. Detachments then entered depicting Royal Marines over different periods and the various army regiments which served as marines, the pageant ending with a display of arms drill by the King's Squad.

'Grand Pageant – Scotland' was presented in 1927 with episodes depicting the Battle of Killiecrankie, Highland Dancing ('The Expression of Unity, Vigour and Joy') and the unity of the Scottish regiments as part of the United Kingdom. The official programme tells us this latter episode was 'emblematic of the final disappearance of Scottish prejudice against England as a foreign nation' – some may disagree with that today! This scene featured Massed Pipes and Drums 100 strong, drawn from the Scots Guards, The Royal Scots, Royal Scots Fusiliers, King's Own Scottish Borderers, The Black Watch, Highland Light Infantry, Seaforth Highlanders, Gordon Highlanders, Queen's Own Cameron Highlanders and the Argyll and Sutherland Highlanders. Detachments wearing the uniforms of the Peninsular wars performed various evolutions, after which they were joined by soldiers representing the present day for the final tableau as the band played 'Scots Wha Hae Wi' Wallace Bled'.

Many of the pageants depicted historical scenes relating to particular regiments. In 1930 it was the turn of 2nd Bn Royal Fusiliers (City of London Regiment) and the west end of the arena was constructed to represent the Tower of London, patrolled by sentries and warders in the uniforms of 1685. The Regimental Call and Long Reveille sounded and echoed in the distance as the gates of the Tower were opened. Headed by their drums, 'Our Royal Regiment of Fusiliers' entered carrying fusils and escorting the Trayne of Artillery as was their original purpose. The drums of the regiment then entered playing 'Rule Britannia', leading historical detachments from various periods. Finally the band and drums led in detachments wearing Field Service Dress, Full Dress, and Foreign Colonial Service Dress of the day. The detachments formed line, advanced in review order and presented arms, before marching past with 'drums beating, colours flying and bayonets fixed', as when exercising their privilege to march through the City of London.

The Royal Tournament 1935 included a display by the Massed Drums and Fifes of the 167th Infantry Brigade, comprising the 1st, 2nd, 3rd and 4th City of London Regiments which formed the territorial battalions of the Royal Fusiliers. The display commemorated the 250th anniversary of the formation of the regiment at the Tower of London. The Regimental Call and Advance were sounded and the massed drums, under the command of Drum Major W Bulgin, marched into the arena playing 'Fighting with The Seventh Fusiliers', changing to slow time with 'Garb of Old Gaul' and breaking into the lively quickstep 'Hurrah' before marching out to the Regimental March, 'The British Grenadiers'.

In 1936 2nd Bn Royal Norfolk Regiment took part in 'Armada Days in Norfolk' which depicted the visit of the Queen's General in 1588 to inspect the trained bands. The pageant opened with Pikemen of the Yarmouth Detachment practising pike exercise to the 16th century fife march, 'The Willow Tree', after which the Band and Drums under Mr E C H Burgess and Drum Major W T Cubitt marched into the arena to 'Royal Standard' (Keith) and then played the following music to accompany the pageant itself:

Entry of the Yarmouth Detachment	**The Pikeman's March**	*Traditional*
Entry of the Mayor's Procession	**March from 'Le Cid'**	*Massenet*
Entry of the Queen's General's Party	**Spirit of Pageantry**	*Fletcher*
Air during the General's Inspection	**The Song of the Bow**	*Aylward*
Serenade by the Waits	**All in a Garden Green**	*16th Century Melody*
Exit of the Mayor's Party	**Long Live Elizabeth**	*German*
Exit of the Queen's General and Troops	**The Passing Pageant**	*Lumley-Williams*
Exit of the Band and Drums		
Slow March	**Merrie England**	*German*
Regimental March	**Rule Britannia**	*Arne*

In 1937 a display by the King's Squad from the Depot Royal Marines, Deal, was accompanied by a 60-strong band of the Royal Marines drawn equally from the Chatham, Portsmouth and Plymouth Divisions playing 'HM Jollies' (Alford), a slow troop 'Sea Soldiers', 'On the Quarter Deck' (Alford) and 'A Life on the Ocean Wave' (Russell).

Music took an increasing role in the Royal Tournament of 1938 with the Mounted Band of the Royal Scots Greys (2nd Dragoons) headed by the black drum horse 'Lairdsburn', leading in 32 men of the regiment for the musical ride in what must have been a particularly memorable spectacle. A Royal Air Force Band took part that year for the first time, accompanying 128 recruits for a display of physical exercise. Another display featured Massed Pipes and Drums and Highland Dancers from 1st Bn Scots Guards, 2nd Bn Scots Guards, 2nd Bn The Cameronians (Scottish Rifles), 1st Bn Highland Light Infantry, 2nd Bn Seaforth Highlanders and 1st Bn Queen's Own Cameron Highlanders.

In 1939 the King's Squad was accompanied by the Band of the Royal Marines (Chatham Division), augmented by musicians from Portsmouth and Plymouth, playing 'The Vedette' (Alford), 'Trumpet Voluntary' (Clarke), 'A Life on the Ocean Wave' (Russell) and 'The Bride Elect' (Sousa). An RAF Band again accompanied the physical training.

Following the Second World War, the Royal Tournament resumed in 1947 much as it had been in 1939 with an augmented Band of the Royal Marines (Chatham Group) accompanying the King's Squad and the Central Band of the Royal Air Force playing for the physical training. Massed pipes and drums from eight Scottish

Massed Bands of the Royal Naval School of Music at the Royal Tournament of 1948.
(Photo: Royal Marines Museum)

regiments marched into the arena, as they had done in 1938, playing 'King George V's Army' (MacLennan).

Massed Bands finally arrived at the Royal Tournament as a regular programme item in 1948 with the Sunset Ceremony performed by Massed Bands of the Royal Naval School of Music. The Staff Band of the RNSM was augmented by representative ranks temporarily drawn from the Fleet and from Royal Naval and Royal Marines establishments. The music played in the display was as follows:

Phase 1 – Fanfare by the trumpeters. Quick and slow troop by four bands which merge into two.

	Fanfare	*Frederick Curzon*
March On	**Nancy Lee**	*Adams*
Slow March	**By Land and Sea**	*Alford*

Phase 2 – Military ceremony of 'Beating the Retreat'.

'Beating the Retreat' by the drummers.

Quick March	**Imperial Echoes**	*Safroni*

Phase 3 – Naval Sunset Ceremony. Short musical programme by one composite band culminating in sunset call.

Grand March	**St George's Day** (dedicated to the Royal Marines)	*Thomas Wood*
	Fanfare	*Leon Young*
Traditional	**Rule Britannia**	*Arne*
Evening Hymn	**The Day Thou Gavest Lord is Ended**	*Scholefield*
Ceremonial Setting	**Sunset**	*A C Green*

The programme drew particular attention to the fact that the medal ribbons worn by the bandsmen had been won as part of the fighting crews of HM ships and that, in both world wars, musicians had operated calculating instruments of the gunnery control system in all the larger warships. Two hundred and twenty five NCOs and musicians were killed in action during the Second World War, a casualty rate of 11.5% of the total personnel of the Band Service. The Memorial Silver Trumpets purchased in their memory were used in the display, along with the Memorial Silver Drums which similarly honoured those who fell in the First World War.

The Royal Naval School of Music returned in its role of accompanying the King's Squad in 1949 with a band of about 100 strong. A display was also given that year by the Massed Drums and Pipes of the Brigade of Guards, comprising the Corps of Drums of 1st Bn Welsh Guards and the Guards Depot, and the Pipes and Drums of 1st Bn Scots Guards and 1st Bn Irish Guards. The massed drums marched on playing 'Gommecourt' (Winter) after which the pipes took over with 'Australian Ladies', the strathspey 'Arniston Castle', the reel 'Rejected Suitor' and the march 'Monte Caterelto', before the drums again took over to march out to 'San Lorenzo' (Silva).

The Massed Bands of the Royal Air Force at the Royal Tournament in the 1950s.

The Royal Tournament moved from Olympia to Earl's Court in 1950, the year that saw the first appearance of the Massed Bands of the Royal Air Force, who combined their display with continuation drill by the Royal Air Force Regiment. The Massed Bands were under the direction of Wing Commander A E (George) Sims, MBE, the Organising Director of Music RAF, and this was the first occasion that the new full dress uniforms were worn by the Regional Bands and the Central Band of the Women's Royal Air Force. The music programme was:

	Fanfare	*Sims*
March On	**Radio**	*Johnson*
Slow March	**Superna Petimus**	*Sims*
Quick March	**March of the Royal Air Force Association**	*Sims*
March on by the RAF Regiment	**Cavalry of the Clouds**	*Alford*
Ceremonial	**Eventide**	*Scull*
	Royal Air Force General Salute	*Sims*
March Off	**Royal Air Force March Past**	*Davies/Dyson*

1951 was the turn of the army with the Band and Trumpeters of the Royal Military School of Music, Kneller Hall, comprising 40 student bandmasters and 220 pupils, under the Director of Music, Major Meredith Roberts, MBE, Royal Artillery. Their programme was as follows:

Fanfares	**Crowning**	*Bullock*
	Jubilant	*Bliss*
Marches	**The School March**	*arr Roberts*
	The Road to the Isles	*Fraser*
	Men of Harlech	*Traditional*
	The Minstrel Boy	*Traditional*
	Trombones to the Fore	*Scull*
Finale Music	**The Yeoman of England**	*German*
	There'll Always be an England	*Parker*
	Here's a Health unto His Majesty	*Traditional*
	The Last Post	*arr Tulip*
	God Save the King	*arr Roberts*

The Kneller Hall Band proved a particular success, with its vast array of uniforms representing most regiments and corps of the army. They were invited to return again the following year and the marches this time were chosen to represent countries of the Commonwealth with 'Waltzing Matilda' (Australia), 'Trek Song' (South Africa), 'God Defend New Zealand' and 'We're on the Way' (Canada), but rather strangely the march chosen to represent 'The (British) Nation' was Bagley's 'National Emblem', an American march with the first section based on the Star Spangled Banner.

The coronation year of 1953 saw the first tri-service massed bands, which included the Royal Marines, the army represented by 4th/7th Royal Dragoon Guards and the Royal Berkshire Regiment (Princess Charlotte of Wales's), and Numbers 1 and 2

The Band and Trumpeters of the Royal Military School of Music, Kneller Hall, at the Royal Tournament in 1951 or 1952.

Regional Bands of the RAF. Detachments from the Brigade of Gurkhas, Pakistan, Ceylon and Southern Rhodesia formed an illuminated crown for the finale as the bands played 'Crown Imperial' (Walton) and 'Rose of England' (Novello).

Massed bands had now become synonymous with the Royal Tournament and their appearance settled to a general pattern of each service participating every third year, albeit with a few missed turns during the early 1960s.

Perhaps the most memorable display by the Massed Bands of HM Royal Marines took place in 1968 and marked the forthcoming retirement of Lieutenant-Colonel F Vivian Dunn later that year. Colonel Dunn, or Sir Vivian as he became on 1st January 1969, had been the Principal Director of Music of the Royal Marines since 1953 and was generally regarded as the architect of the modern Band Service.

The display featured various aspects of Royal Marines music, introduced by a fanfare, 'The Royal Tournament'. The Corps of Drums then marched into the arena playing 'Bugles and Drums', halted for their usual immaculate drum beating display and marched off to 'Bugle Bells'. While this display was in progress, a stage was constructed in front of the main arena doors for a full Royal Marines Symphony Orchestra. Colonel Dunn then conducted the Orchestra in a selection of such pieces as the Finale from the 'New World Symphony' (Dvořák), 'William Tell' overture (Rossini), and items by Elgar, Offenbach, Wagner and Tchaikowsky.

Next came the 'Oceanaires' Dance Orchestra under Bandmaster D A Drake, mounted on vehicles at the Warwick Road end of the arena. Meanwhile, the orchestra had exchanged strings for brass and woodwind instruments and donned helmets and accoutrements to conclude the display with the glorious sight and sound of the massed bands playing:

March	**A Tribute to Alford**	*arr Dunn*
March	**Cavalry of the Steppes**	*Knipper arr Woodfield*
Fanfare for Bugles, Trumpets and Band	**For a Royal Birthday**	*Dunn*
Combined setting for Bugles and Band	**Sunset**	*Green*
Traditional Air	**Rule Britannia**	*Arne arr Sargent/Arnold*
	National Anthem	
Regimental March	**A Life on the Ocean Wave**	*Russell arr Alford*
March of the Royal Marines Commandos	**Sarie Marias**	*Toonsetting arr Dunn*

The orchestra and large dance band appeared again in 1984 and 1987 respectively, both under Lieutenant David Cole, but this time just in accompanying roles as the Royal Navy Display Team danced the Hornpipe.

One of the principal milestones in the history of the Royal Tournament was the appointment of a Producer in 1974. Major Michael Parker (now Sir Michael) held this

The Massed Bands of the Royal Marines and the Marine Band of the Royal Netherlands Navy end the 1981 Royal Tournament with 'The Battle of Trafalgar'. (Photo: Colin Dean)

appointment for 26 years right through to the final Royal Tournament in 1999 and introduced themes and spectacular finales to the show, the first in 1974 being a musical representation of 'The Battle of Trafalgar' by the Massed Bands of HM Royal Marines. This naval equivalent of '1812' was specially written by a former Royal Marines musician, Albert Elms, and was presented with large models of HMS *Victory* and the French ship, *Redoubtable* firing at each other across the massed bands.

The Battle of Trafalgar was musically re-fought in 1981 and 1993, on the latter occasion combined with celebrations of the 50th Anniversary of the Battle of the Atlantic. Other navy years generally incorporated mast manning into the finale but in 1990 the theme was 'The Sea Soldier', telling the history of the Royal Marines, perhaps with a glance back to 1921 and 'Neptune's Soldiers'.

While the Royal Marines and RAF comprised largely the same bands each year, there was much greater scope for the army to provide contrasting massed bands. A particular favourite was always the Massed Bands and Bugles of the Light Infantry Brigade or, latterly, the Light Division, who appeared on five occasions and whose green uniforms and fast-moving drill never failed to impress.

The Massed Bands of the Royal Armoured Corps took part in four Royal Tournaments, providing perhaps the most impressive spectacle of all with their colourful full dress uniforms. In 1975 they marched on playing Rodney Bashford's specially written 'Royal Tournament March' (subtitled 'Cavalry Walk') and were joined by the Pipes and Drums of the Royal Scots Dragoon Guards (Carabiniers and Greys) in

The Mounted Band of The Blues and Royals and the Massed Bands of the Royal Armoured Corps at the Royal Tournament 1991, headed by Major Roger Tomlinson. The drum horses are (left to right) Winston, Queen's Royal Irish Hussars; Belisarius, The Life Guards; Janus, The Blues and Royals and Dettingen, Queen's Own Hussars. (Photo: Colin Dean)

'Morning Has Broken'. To conclude, the massed bands featured 'Post Horn Galop' played on rifles which were all fired at the end of the piece.

The 1991 Royal Tournament was especially memorable, because the massed bands comprised all regiments of the Royal Armoured Corps, each wearing its traditional full dress uniform. Along with the Mounted Band of The Blues and Royals, their display featured the music of Mozart to mark the 200th anniversary of the composer's death. Some licence was taken by including the 'Steptoe and Son' theme in the style of Mozart while oboe and trombone duetists rode in on a rag and bone cart to play the beautiful 'La Ci Darem La Mano' from *Don Giovanni*. Added poignancy came midway through the Tournament when drastic defence cuts were announced which meant that most of the regiments on parade were to be amalgamated. Together with the expected demise of regimental bands, it was clear that history was before us and that such a spectacle would never be seen again.

The first of Major Parker's finales in army years was in 1975 with 'The Retreat from Moscow'. The Massed Bands of the Royal Armoured Corps were dressed as Russian and French soldiers and re-fought the Battle of Borodino with specially arranged music culminating in the final part of the '1812 Overture'. The bands were conducted by Captain Brian Keeling, Royal Tank Regiment, who rode in for the finale on horseback dressed as Napoleon.

In 1978 a composite band from the Foot Guards was joined by bands from the other divisions of infantry (less the Scottish Division) for Beethoven's 'Wellington's Victory'. The finale in 1982 was to have marked the centenary of the charge at Kassassin in 1882 but the Egyptians objected and a 'Carlton-Browne' at the Foreign Office intervened to have it stopped. 'The Retreat from Moscow' was substituted since the Foreign Office presumably raised no objection to offending the French!

The Massed Bands of Cavalry and Corps at the Royal Tournament of 1982. (Photo: Colin Dean)

1985 marked the tercentenary of twelve regiments whose history was taken as the theme, along with that of the Band of the Grenadier Guards which was also celebrating its 300th anniversary, with much of the music specially written by Lieutenant-Colonel Derek Kimberley MBE, Grenadier Guards. 'The Drum' was the theme in 1988 with a spectacular opening sequence bringing together all aspects of drumming from Red Indian and Chinese drummers to the modern drum horse and the massed corps of drums of 10 battalions. The finale celebrated the 400th anniversary of the Defeat of the Spanish Armada in 1588 with music specially written by Major Roger Tomlinson, The Blues and Royals, and with 'Drake's Drum' linking it to the central theme.

The theme in 1991 was 'The Horse' with the finale culminating in 'Light Cavalry', while 'War and Peace' in 1994 took us from the four horsemen of the Apocalypse to the prospects of peace brought about by NATO. The last army theme of 'Firepower' in 1997 concluded with '1812' played by the Massed Bands of the Household Division.

Aside from the finales, the concept of a musical theme to the massed bands item had started in 1988 when the display by the Massed Bands of the Infantry was based on the music of Sir Arthur Sullivan, while in 1994 the music of Elgar was chosen, with the Massed Bands of the Household Division conducted by Lieutenant-Colonel Roger Tomlinson, Principal Director of Music (Army), in the guise of Elgar himself.

From 1989 the Massed Bands of the Royal Air Force combined their display with the continuity drill of the Queen's Colour Squadron RAF, thus returning to the tradition started by their original appearance in 1950. In 1989 the music for their display was 'Songs of the Early Airmen', based on songs adapted by the RAF in the years between the wars and specially arranged for the bands to play and sing by the Principal Director of Music, Wing Commander Barrie Hingley MBE. The RAF Squadronaires also appeared at the 1989 Royal Tournament and in most RAF years since.

In 1992 the massed bands played Gershwin's 'Rhapsody in Blue' as the finale to the first half, with the piano solo played by Flight Lieutenant Stuart Stirling on a platform which was slowly lowered from the roof. Disaster struck on the night of the Queen's visit when a thunderstorm caused a power cut in the Earl's Court area just as this was about to start, leaving Flight Lieutenant Stirling marooned just below the roof. Wing Commander Hingley took the swift decision to signal the bands to march off and the platform was winched down during the interval, no doubt to the relief of the intrepid pianist.

The themes for the RAF years were generally based around such topics as 'Heroes of the Air', 'The History of Flight' and the two world wars, with much use made of lasers and special effects and with music often taken from the classical repertoire, including Sir William Walton's 'Spitfire Prelude', extracts from Gustav Holst's 'Planets' suite, Wagner's 'Götterdämmerung' and Saint Saens' 'Organ Symphony'.

In 1996 the Royal Air Force bands were joined by the massed bands of the Commonwealth Air Forces comprising bands from Australia, Canada and India to continue the long tradition of including bands from overseas, dating back to displays by the Pipe Band of the Pakistan Police and Massed Pipers and Drummers of the Arab Legion in 1955. Since then, bands from throughout the world have come to Earl's Court bringing their own individual styles, including the Fort Henry Guard from Canada, Malaya Police, King's African Rifles, Queen's Own Nigeria Regiment, Fiji Military Forces, Jamaica Regiment, Royal Brunei Malay Regiment, Royal Barbados Police, Kenya Army Band and the South Australia Police, not forgetting the Papua New Guinea Constabulary with their dancing cymbal player. The Massed Bands of the Australian Defence Force celebrated their country's forthcoming bicentennial in 1987.

In 1971 the Fanfara of the 3rd Bersagleri Regiment from Italy brought a completely new style to the Royal Tournament by playing while running and, not to be outdone, the Charanga (mounted band) of the Portugese Republican Guard played at the trot and canter when they visited in 1973 and 1986. Other visitors from Europe have included the Marine Band of the Royal Netherlands Navy and the French Foreign Legion, the latter in 1995 along with the US Army Band Europe and the Central Band of the Russian Federation. 1989 saw the Massed Bands of ten NATO countries taking part.

Other musicians from afar, although very much part of the British Army, were the Band, Bugles, Pipes and Drums of the Brigade of Gurkhas who appeared at the Royal Tournament on a number of occasions, their first individual display being in 1960 under the direction of Major J P C (Bill) Bailey MBE when their programme comprised:

Band and Bugles	**Paris Belfort**	*Farigoul*
Pipes and Drums	**Dovecote Park**	*Bradford*
Band and Bugles	**Raglan**	*Stevens*
	Little Bugler	*Duthoit*
Pipes and Drums	**Skye Boat Song**	*Trad*
	Bonawe Highlanders	*Bowman*
Massed Bands	**Scotland the Brave**	*Trad*
	The Road to the Isles	*Fraser*
	The Steamboat*	*Tchaikowsky*

The Royal Tournament itself was the theme for its final year in 1999, in celebration of its 119 years of history. The performance opened by tracing the Tournament's history with a representation of a competition popular in the early days, 'Cleaving the Turk's Head', followed by a parade of all the performers in the order that their unit first took part, headed by the Household Cavalry (1882) and the Royal Horse Artillery (1896) and accompanied by music appropriate to the periods.

The Queen and the Duke of Edinburgh attended on 26th July 1999, while the final performance on 2nd August 1999 was attended by the Princess Royal. As the Finale approached on these special days, the haunting theme from '1492 – Conquest of Paradise' (Vangelis) was played quietly in the background as The King's Troop, Royal Horse Artillery appeared through a white mist to ride slowly into the arena as if representing the ghosts of the RHA Batteries that had taken part since 1896. The Troop marched past, leaving the arena at the Warwick Road end and were followed

---

* This march appears in the *Nutcracker* ballet. It is, of course, possible that Tchaikowsky may have borrowed it from a piper.

by the Household Cavalry with the Mounted Band of The Blues and Royals, the Musical Ride and a further composite troop.

The massed bands of the three services and the pipes and drums then took up '1492' and slow marched into the arena for the finale, directed by Lieutenant-Colonel R A Waterer OBE, Principal Director of Music, Royal Marines. At the end of the finale the massed bands and the performers remained in the arena, with those in the rear half retiring a few paces to create an 'avenue' along the length of the arena. The royal guests then drove very slowly around the arena and through the avenue created between the bands, each section of the performers giving three cheers in turn as the car passed. A memorable end to 119 years of history.

By way of an appendix to this chapter there follows a summary of the massed bands which appeared at the Royal Tournament in the post-war years.

Year	Bands	Director
1948	Massed Bands of the Royal Naval School of Music	
1950	Massed Bands of the Royal Air Force	Wing Commander A E Sims, MBE
1951	Band of the Royal Military School of Music, Kneller Hall	Major M Roberts, MBE
1952	Band of the Royal Military School of Music, Kneller Hall	Major M Roberts, MBE
1953	Tri-Service Massed Bands	
1954	Massed Bands of HM Royal Marines	Captain W Lang, MBE
1955	Massed Bands of the Royal Air Force	Wing Commander A E Sims, OBE
1956	Massed Bands and Bugles of the Light Infantry Brigade	WO1(BM) C D Jarrett
1957	Massed Bands of HM Royal Marines	Lieutenant-Colonel F V Dunn, CVO
	Massed Drums, Pipes and Bugles of the North Irish Brigade	
1958	Massed Bands of the Royal Air Force	Wing Commander A E Sims, OBE
	Massed Pipes and Drums of the Scottish Regiments	
1959	Massed Bands of the Army	Captain W Williams, MBE
1960	Massed Bands of HM Royal Marines	Lieutenant-Colonel F V Dunn, CVO OBE
1961	Massed Bands of the Royal Air Force	Wing Commander J L Wallace, OBE
1962	Massed Bands of HM Royal Marines	Lieutenant-Colonel F V Dunn, CVO OBE
	Massed Pipes and Drums of Scottish and Irish Regiments	
1963	Massed Bands of the Royal Armoured Corps	Captain T L Sharpe, MBE
1964	Massed Bands of HM Royal Marines	Lieutenant-Colonel F V Dunn, CVO OBE
	Massed Bands, Pipes and Drums of the North Irish Brigade	
1965	Massed Bands of the Royal Air Force	Wing Commander J L Wallace, OBE

1966	Massed Bands of the Royal Artillery	Captain R Quinn, MBE
	Massed Bands and Bugles of the Light Infantry Brigade	WO1(BM) R A Ridings
1967	Massed Bands of the Royal Air Force	Wing Commander J L Wallace, OBE
1968	Massed Bands of HM Royal Marines	Lieutenant-Colonel F V Dunn, CVO OBE
1969	Massed Bands of the Royal Armoured Corps	Captain C V Wright
1970	Massed Bands of the Royal Air Force	Wing Commander R E C Davies
	Massed Bands and Bugles of the Light Division	WO1(BM) J C Mutlow
1971	Massed Bands of HM Royal Marines	Major P J Neville, MVO
	Massed Pipes and Drums of the Scottish Division	
1972	Massed Bands and Drums of the Infantry	Captain T A Kenny
1973	Massed Bands of the Royal Air Force	Wing Commander R E C Davies, OBE
	Bands, Bugles, Pipes and Drums of the Royal Irish Rangers	
1974	Massed Bands of HM Royal Marines	Lieutenant-Colonel P J Neville, MVO
1975	Massed Bands of the Royal Armoured Corps	Captain B T Keeling
1976	Massed Bands of the Royal Air Force	Wing Commander R E C Davies, OBE
1977	Massed Bands of HM Royal Marines	Lieutenant-Colonel P J Neville OBE MVO
1978	Massed Bands of the Infantry	Captain D R Kimberley, MBE
1979	Massed Bands of the Royal Air Force	Wing Commander J W Martindale
1980	Tri-Service Massed Bands	Lieutenant-Colonel J R Mason, MVO
1981	Massed Bands of HM Royal Marines	Lieutenant-Colonel J R Mason, MVO
1982	Massed Bands of the Army	Major D Snowden
1983	Massed Bands of the Royal Air Force	Wing Commander E Banks, MBE
	Massed Pipes and Drums of Scottish Regiments	
1984	Massed Bands of HM Royal Marines	Lieutenant-Colonel G A C Hoskins, MVO
1985	Massed Bands of the 'Tercentenary' Regiments	Lieutenant-Colonel D R Kimberley, MBE
	Massed Bands and Bugles of the Light Division	Captain G H Leask
1986	Massed Bands of the Royal Air Force	Wing Commander E Banks, MBE
1987	Massed Bands of HM Royal Marines	Lieutenant-Colonel G A C Hoskins, MVO
1988	Massed Bands and Drums of the Infantry	Major R G Tomlinson
1989	Massed Bands of the Royal Air Force	Wing Commander H B Hingley, MBE
1990	Massed Bands of HM Royal Marines	Lieutenant-Colonel J M Ware

1991	Massed Bands of the Royal Armoured Corps	Major R G Tomlinson
	Massed Pipes and Drums	
1992	Massed Bands of the Royal Air Force	Wing Commander H B Hingley, MBE
1993	Massed Bands of HM Royal Marines	Lieutenant-Colonel J M Ware, OBE
1994	Massed Bands of the Household Division	Lieutenant-Colonel R G Tomlinson
	Massed Bands and Bugles of the Light Division and the Brigade of Gurkhas	Captain R J Owen
1995	Massed Bands of the Royal Air Force	Wing Commander R E Wilkinson
1996	Massed Bands of HM Royal Marines	Lieutenant-Colonel R A Waterer
1997	Massed Bands of the Household Division	Lieutenant-Colonel D E Price
1998	Massed Bands of the Royal Air Force	Wing Commander R K Wiffin
1999	Tri-Service Massed Bands	Lieutenant-Colonel R A Waterer, OBE

CHAPTER 8

TATTOOS AND PAGEANTS

COLIN DEAN

Aldershot Tattoo

The origins of the tattoo go back to a visit to Aldershot by Queen Victoria in 1894 when her third son, HRH the Duke of Connaught, was the General Officer Commanding. The Duke arranged for a drill display to be presented in the afternoon followed by bands playing at night with torch-bearing soldiers interspersed between their ranks. In 1900 the tattoo became part of the Aldershot Military Fete held in the grounds of the GOC's residence at Government House, with bands up to 1,500 strong.

The impressive sight of the Massed Bands of Aldershot Command at a rehearsal for the Tattoo in June 1914, conducted by Mr Henry Sims, Royal Artillery Mounted Band. (Photo: Royal Military School of Music)

After the Great War, the idea of a searchlight tattoo was revived in 1919 and the following year saw the addition of a musical ride of the 3rd (King's Own) Hussars clad in uniforms from their history, as well as the first use of aeroplanes in an illuminated display.

In its early years the tattoo was mainly attended by what might be termed the gentry, but as it was becoming an increasingly popular public spectacle the venue moved to Cove Common in 1922. With great unemployment in the wake of the war, gangs of Aldershot unemployed men cleared and levelled Rushmoor Arena in time for the 1923 Tattoo, with circles of benches around the arena and a grandstand which was erected by Humphreys Ltd of Knightsbridge.

The attendance at the first post-war tattoo in 1919 was 25,000 and by 1938 this had increased to 531,850 with 61,159 vehicles being accommodated in the car parks surrounding Rushmoor Arena. About 5,000 troops were involved in the production with a further 3,600 staff being employed in support. All the troops were provided with supper on their return to barracks after the tattoo, something that entailed a march of up to five miles.

The tattoo was held on a vast scale and featured the bands, drums, pipes and bugles of the battalions within Aldershot Command, most of which have long since disappeared into the history books by disbandment or amalgamation. To give an idea of the sheer size of the musical forces, the following took part in the 1926 Tattoo:

Massed Bands

1st Cavalry Brigade:
1st Royal Dragoons — Bandmaster S S Smith
10th Royal Hussars (Prince of Wales's Own) — Bandmaster M Roberts
17th/21st Lancers — Bandmaster F J Allsebrook, MM
Royal Artillery Mounted Band — Bandmaster T J Hillier

1st Guards Brigade:
1st Bn The Middlesex Regiment
(Duke of Cambridge's Own) — Bandmaster J W Clark

2nd Infantry Brigade:
2nd Bn Royal Fusiliers
(City of London Regiment) — Bandmaster R Tulip
1st Bn The King's Regiment (Liverpool) — Bandmaster G Passelow, MM
1st Bn The Lincolnshire Regiment — Bandmaster C S Trowt
1st Bn Seaforth Highlanders — Bandmaster G V E Grayson

3rd Infantry Brigade:
2nd Bn The East Lancashire Regiment — Bandmaster W M Fryer
1st Bn Royal Sussex Regiment — Bandmaster S A Guilmant
1st Bn The York and Lancaster Regiment — Bandmaster G Hart
2nd Bn The Gordon Highlanders — Bandmaster W Bartlett

5th Infantry Brigade:
1st Bn The Cameronians (Scottish Rifles) — Bandmaster H E Dowell
1st Bn The Gloucestershire Regiment — Bandmaster S Yorke, DCM
2nd Bn The Dorsetshire Regiment — Bandmaster G E Hudson
2nd Bn The Rifle Brigade (Prince Consort's Own) — Bandmaster S J Young

6th Infantry Brigade:

1st Bn The Devonshire Regiment	Bandmaster H Carotti
1st Bn The Northamptonshire Regiment	Bandmaster W Cresswell
2nd Bn The Queen's Own Royal West Kent Regiment	Bandmaster A D W Hunt
2nd Bn The King's Royal Rifle Corps	Bandmaster W J Dunn, MC
Royal Army Service Corps	Bandmaster C J Crosbie
Royal Army Medical Corps	Bandmaster E U Lane

Massed Drum and Fife Bands

2nd Bn Grenadier Guards	Sergeant Drummer E Allwood
2nd Bn Coldstream Guards	Sergeant Drummer W Gooden
1st Bn Irish Guards	Sergeant Drummer G D Smith
2nd Bn The Royal Fusiliers (City of London Regiment)	Sergeant Drummer C Hobbs
1st Bn The King's Regiment (Liverpool)	Sergeant Drummer C H Andrews
1st Bn The Lincolnshire Regiment	Corporal B A Kime
1st Bn The Devonshire Regiment	Sergeant Drummer A S Sonds
1st Bn The Gloucestershire Regiment	Sergeant Drummer R H Mason
2nd Bn The East Lancashire Regiment	Sergeant Drummer H Nicks
1st Bn The Royal Sussex Regiment	Sergeant Drummer W E Marrison
2nd Bn The Dorsetshire Regiment	Sergeant Drummer E Inkpen
1st Bn The Northamptonshire Regiment	Sergeant Drummer F Hunt
2nd Bn The Queen's Own Royal West Kent Regiment	Sergeant Drummer T H Cousins
1st Bn The Middlesex Regiment (Duke of Cambridge's Own)	Sergeant Drummer G W Goodwin
1st Bn The York and Lancaster Regiment	Sergeant Drummer L A Headly

Massed Pipe Bands

1st Bn Scots Guards	Sergeant Piper J D McDonald
2nd Bn Scots Guards	Sergeant Piper A McIntosh
1st Bn Irish Guards	Sergeant Piper T Atkins
1st Bn Seaforth Highlanders	Sergeant Piper D McLennan
2nd Bn Gordon Highlanders	Sergeant Piper C Turnbull
1st Bn Argyll and Sutherland Highlanders	Sergeant Piper R T Ancell

Buglers

2nd Bn The King's Royal Rifle Corps	Sergeant Bugler R B Brookes

Massed Trumpeters

1st Royal Dragoons	
10th Royal Hussars (Prince of Wales's Own)	Sergeant Trumpeter A Frape
17th/21st Lancers	

The names of some of the bandmasters may be familiar. Mr Roberts of the 10th Royal Hussars was to become Lieutenant-Colonel Meredith Roberts, Director of Music at Kneller Hall, while Mr Samuel Smith and Mr Horace Dowell were to become Directors of Music of The Life Guards and Scots Guards respectively. Mr Richard Tulip became Professor of Piano at Kneller Hall and is particularly remembered for having arranged one of the best loved settings of Evening Hymn and Last Post.

It is interesting to note that four of the bandmasters had won gallantry awards including the Senior Bandmaster, Mr William James Dunn, MC, the only Bandmaster ever to be awarded the Military Cross*. Captain 'Paddy' Dunn was later to be appointed Director of Music of the Royal Horse Guards (The Blues) and his son, Lieutenant-Colonel Sir Vivian Dunn became the first Principal Director of Music of the Royal Marines. The Massed Pipe Bands were led by Sergeant Drummer W Ritchie, VC, of 1st Bn Seaforth Highlanders.

The scene was set for the 1926 Tattoo with selections played by the massed bands, concluding with 'Oriental Scenes' conducted by Mr Dunn. This made use of five West African drums which had been taken from the Palace of King Prempeh at the fall of Kumassi during the Ashanti War of 1874, the largest of which was originally festooned by a ring of human ears! The music was performed with a background of scenery specially erected by the Royal Engineers and added atmosphere was provided by the presence of camels.

The programme notes for the 1938 tattoo help conjure the spectacle presented to the audiences by the huge massed bands picked out by searchlights:

The Massed Bands of the Aldershot and Eastern Commands

Preceded by a fanfare sounded by the Tattoo Trumpeters, the immense body of musicians who compose the Massed Bands of the Aldershot and Eastern Commands make their entrance through the main castle gate. With nearly a thousand men on parade in their pre-war uniforms, the bands of twenty Infantry battalions, four Bugle bands, and eight Drum and Fife bands fill the arena with a magnificent and imposing array of military musicians.

While the bands enter, eight at a time, to the quick march 'Lancastria' by Chandler, the arena is illuminated only by spotlights until the whole vast concourse is assembled. Only when the bands reach their position at the halt do they take up the march and while the volume of music increases the general lighting of the whole arena is slowly imposed.

To the strains of the march from Mozart's 'Figaro', the Massed Bands advance to the forefront of the arena where they halt to play the principal orchestral selection, the 'Slavonic Rhapsody' by Friedemann. Immediately afterwards they break into the quick march 'The Standard of St. George', and give one of those inspiring displays of marching and counter-marching that dazzle the eye as they change from quick to slow time with the great square of scarlet and gold diminishing, revolving and extending again. The combined Band and Bugle march, 'Tudor Rose' by Adams, is played during the counter-marching before the bands form up again at the rear of the arena to provide the musical setting for the next item. Every note of music heard in the Tattoo is memorised by the bandsmen.

---

*Although Paddy Dunn was the only man to be awarded the MC as a Bandmaster, it is worth mentioning that this award also went to Lieutenant William Victor Richards of the Dorsetshire Regiment, a former Bandmaster of the 1st Battalion and perhaps best known as the composer of the march 'Namur'.

The tattoo often opened with a display by the band and bugles of one or more of the Light Infantry or Rifle regiments, marching in their unique style at 140 paces to the minute in what were described in the programmes as 'Bugle Marches and Band Accompaniment'. As an example, in 1929 the bands and bugles display comprised:

2nd Bn The Duke of Cornwall's Light Infantry
1st Bn The King's Own Yorkshire Light Infantry
2nd Bn The King's Shropshire Light Infantry
1st Bn The Royal Ulster Rifles

The Little Bugler	*Duthoit*
Sambre et Meuse	*Planquette*
Marching thro' Georgia	*arr Miller*

The Massed Drums and Fifes of the Aldershot Command would generally Beat Tattoo. In 1932 the drums of 14 battalions entered from the woods playing 'Land of My Fathers' and 'Sweet Polly Oliver' and halted facing the grandstand to beat Tattoo with 'Sarony'. They then advanced, wheeled and counter-marched playing 'Marche Militaire' (Schubert) before marching out of the arena.

The Mounted Band of the Royal Scots Greys (2nd Dragoons) at Aldershot in 1937. The Bandmaster is Mr A W Crofts and the black drum horse is 'Lairdsburn'. The band took part in the tattoo that year although this photograph may have been taken at the Aldershot Horse Show – members of the musical ride with lances can be seen behind the band. (Photo: Royal Military School of Music)

Massed mounted bands were another regular feature of the tattoo in the days when every cavalry regiment had a mounted band, bringing their unique sight and sound with the colourful full dress uniforms, the jingle of harness and, of course, the drum horses in front. The mounted bands display in 1928 featured:

1st King's Dragoon Guards
11th Hussars (Prince Albert's Own)
17th/21st Lancers
Royal Artillery Mounted Band

139

Royal Artillery March	*Traditional*
Cavalry Brigade March	*Anon*
Trumpet Fanfare	*Anon*
Parade March	*Mollendorf*
Slow March – Dover Castle	*Carter*

Massed pipes and drums were also a regular feature, often accompanying a display depicting scenes from the history of the one of the Scottish regiments. The Coronation Tattoo of 1937, for example, saw what was described as the biggest massed band of pipes yet seen at Aldershot, playing as 2nd Bn Seaforth Highlanders presented a stirring spectacle symbolic of the raising of the regiment in 1778. On parade were the massed pipe bands of:

2nd Bn Scots Guards
1st Bn The Royal Scots (The Royal Regiment)
2nd Bn The Royal Scots Fusiliers
2nd Bn The Cameronians (Scottish Rifles)
1st Bn Highland Light Infantry (City of Glasgow Regiment)
2nd Bn Seaforth Highlanders (Ross-shire Buffs, The Duke of Albany's)
1st Bn Queen's Own Cameron Highlanders

March	**Mackenzie Highlanders**
March	**25th K.O.S.B.'s Farewell to Meerut**
Strathspey	**Miss Ada Crawford**
Reel	**Mistress MacLeod of Raasay**
March	**Caber Feidh**
March	**Murray's Welcome**
Slow March	**Loch Duich**

The Pipes and Drums of 1st Bn Royal Irish Fusiliers in front of the impressive scenery erected for the Aldershot Tattoo 1937.
(Photo: Royal Military School of Music)

The pageants depicted in the tattoo through the 1920s and 30s covered many centuries of history – the Crusades, the Romans in Britain, Battle of Hastings, Battle of Agincourt, the Field of the Cloth of Gold, Queen Elizabeth's Visit to Tilbury, Legend of Drake's Drum, Siege of Namur, Battle of Dettingen, the Passage of the Douro, Retreat to Corunna, the Duchess of Richmond's Ball, the Battle of Inkerman, Gordon and the Sudan, right up to the Great War.

The Tattoo in June 1939 was to be the last before the outbreak of war and a version of the 'Changing of the Guard' symbolically portrayed the move to the khaki-clad mechanised force which was replacing the colour and spectacle that had so much been part of the British Army. The 'Old Guard' entered from behind a facade of Elizabethan houses, headed by a battery of Royal Horse Artillery, a troop of the Royal Horse Guards and a guard of 1st Bn The Black Watch in full dress uniform. From the opposite end of the arena the 'New Guard' entered led by a detachment of the 12th Royal Lancers in six armoured cars followed by six tractor-drawn guns of the 24th Field Regiment, Royal Artillery and a guard of 1st Bn The Black Watch in service dress.

The Old and New Guards slow-marched forward in turn to present arms, while a light tank moved into position in the centre of the arena in front of the massed cavalry bands (dismounted) and the Royal Artillery Mounted Band. The Commanding Officer of the Old Guard handed over the national flag to his opposite number who placed it on the tank as the massed bands played 'O God, Our Help in Ages Past'. A drive past of mechanised units followed and the Old Guard, led by the RA Mounted Band, marched past to the music of the Cavalry Bands, after which The Black Watch were played past to 'Hielan' Laddie' by the massed pipe bands.

With the growing expectation of war, the massed bands marched off at the end of the tattoo playing 'Who's Afraid of the Big Bad Wolf?', something that was to be recalled a year later when a number of the bandsmen who took part were to meet again in prisoner-of-war camps in Occupied France.

The event was revived to an extent in 1961 with the Aldershot Army Display which took place on Queen's Parade. The success of the display eventually led to its pre-war home of Rushmoor Arena being completely refurbished and the event returned there in 1972 and continued until 1984. The massed bands by now largely comprised the various staff bands stationed in and around the Aldershot area, rather than the bands from the many infantry brigades of earlier years.

In 1979 a SSAFA Aldershot Tattoo was held over two days with massed bands of the Royal Marines and the army under Major Tony Richards, The Life Guards, concluding with a spectacular musical representation of the Charge of the Light Brigade.

Tidworth Tattoo

The Tidworth Tattoo was first presented by Southern Command in 1923 and took a similar format to the Tattoo at Aldershot. While a brief history of the Aldershot Tattoo has been given, by way of contrast, the Tidworth Tattoo will be illustrated with details of just one performance: that held to mark the Silver Jubilee of King George V in 1935.

The Massed Bands and Drums at the Tidworth Tattoo 1934. (Photo: Royal Military School of Music)

1   9.30 pm   Cavalry Trumpeters of the 2nd Cavalry Brigade

The tattoo opened with massed mounted trumpeters and kettle-drummers of 4th/7th Dragoon Guards, 3rd King's Own Hussars, 9th Queen's Royal Lancers and 12th Royal Lancers sounding fanfares and then leaving the arena playing two trumpet marches. The fanfares were composed by Trumpet Major E V Moon, 4th/7th Dragoon Guards.

2   9.33 pm   Beating Tattoo with Massed Drums, Fifes and Bugles of
                Southern Command

2nd Bn The King's Regiment	2nd Bn The Hampshire Regiment
1st Bn The Suffolk Regiment	1st Bn The Prince of Wales's Volunteers
1st Bn The Green Howards	2nd Bn The Loyal Regiment
1st Bn The Royal Welch Fusiliers	1st Bn The York and Lancaster Regiment
1st Bn The Royal Sussex Regiment	1st Bn The Rifle Brigade

under Drum Major E Connolly, 2nd Bn The Loyal Regiment

The drummers, drawn up at the castle entrance, beat 'Drummers' Call' and buglers sounded 'First Post'. The drums and fifes then played the Risings, 'I Passed By Your Window', in slow and quick time, changing to 'The Rose of Tralee' before counter-marching to 'Gommecourt' (Winter). Finally they wheeled at the centre of the arena and retired to the trees at the back playing 'For Flag and Empire' (Turpin).

3   9.40 pm   Motor Cyclists – Despatch Riders Royal Signals, Salisbury Plain Area

4   9.50 pm   Activity Ride by 9th Queen's Royal Lancers

5   9.56 pm   First Entry of the Massed Bands of the Southern Command

4th/7th Dragoon Guards	1st Bn The Royal Sussex Regiment
3rd King's Own Hussars	2nd Bn The Hampshire Regiment
9th Queen's Royal Lancers	1st Bn The Prince of Wales's Volunteers
12th Royal Lancers	2nd Bn The Loyal Regiment
Royal Artillery (Salisbury Plain)	1st Bn The York and Lancaster Regiment
2nd Bn The King's Regiment	1st Bn The Argyll and Sutherland Highlanders
1st Bn The Suffolk Regiment	1st Bn The Rifle Brigade
1st Bn The Green Howards	Royal Tank Corps
1st Bn The Royal Welch Fusiliers	

under the direction of Bandmaster T Francis,
Royal Artillery (Salisbury Plain) Band.

The bands advanced from the back of the arena playing the old imperial Russian slow march, 'Preobrajensky' (Donajowski), breaking into quick time with the stirring march 'Action Front' (Blankenburg) and the popular 'Sing As We Go' before halting in front of the stands to play the overture 'Zampa' (Herold). The bands marched out of the arena to the famous French band and bugle march '56 Brigade'.

6   10.11 pm   Physical Training Display by 1st Bn The Royal Sussex Regiment Performed to the music of the Massed Bands of 8th Infantry Brigade.

7   10.19 pm   Musical Ride by the 4th/7th Dragoon Guards

The ride consisted of 48 men in review order with 8 trumpeters and was accompanied by the Massed Bands of 2nd Cavalry Brigade.

8   10.30 pm   Infantry Drill by 1st Bn The Argyll and Sutherland Highlanders (Princess Louise's)

The battalion was represented by 4 companies, the pipes and drums and military band. The pony 'Cruachan' gifted to the battalion by the Colonel-in-Chief, The Princess Louise, Duchess of Argyll, marched at the head of the pipes and drums. The King's and Regimental Colours were carried on the parade which was under the command of a field officer who, together with the Adjutant, was mounted. The battalion wore the full dress uniform which had been worn on all ceremonial occasions prior to the great war and marched on to parade to the march of the 1st Battalion, 'The Campbells are Coming'.

The companies formed into line and the battalion gave a general salute with the pipes and drums playing 'Lochleven Castle', after which drill movements were carried out in quick time to the tunes 'Captain Towse VC' and 'The Pathan March', the latter being an old Indian tune adapted for playing on the pipes. In conclusion, the companies each marched past to their own march:

A Company:	**The Cameron Men**
B Company:	**Glendaurel Highlanders**
C Company:	**Bonnie Dundee**
D Company:	**Scotland the Brave**

The battalion marched out of the arena to 'Hielan' Laddie', the march of the 2nd Battalion.

9   10.43 pm   Display of Fireworks

Massed Mounted Bands at the Tidworth Tattoo, probably 1933, made up of 4th/7th Dragoon Guards, Royal Scots Greys (2nd Dragoons), 11th Hussars (Prince Albert's Own) and 16th/5th Lancers.

10   10.46 pm   Second Entry of the Massed Bands

The bands entered in four separate groups from different points of the arena, each group playing famous old regimental marches representative of England, Ireland, Scotland and Wales:

Bands of the 2nd Cavalry Brigade playing 'The British Grenadiers', 'Rule Britannia' and 'John Peel'.

Bands of the 8th Infantry Brigade playing 'Garry Owen', 'St Patrick's Day' and 'Come Back to Erin'

Bands of the 9th Infantry Brigade playing 'Men of Harlech', 'God Bless the Prince of Wales' and 'Ap Shenkin'

Bands of the 7th Infantry Brigade playing 'Hielan' Laddie', 'Cock o' the North' and 'Hundred Pipers'

When the four groups had assembled together in the centre, the lights were dimmed and, as if in the distance, came the strains of the highland patrol, 'Wee Macgregor' (Amers). The music gradually increased in volume and, when it was at its height, the whole of the massed bands moved forward and counter-marched to the back of the arena with the music of the patrol dying away again into the distance. Under the trees at the back of the arena the bands played the second movement of the London Suite ('Westminster') by Eric Coates.

11   11.01 pm   Quebec – 13th September 1759

A representation of the battle and the death of General Wolfe.

12   11.16 pm   Drive by 'L' (Nery) Battery, Royal Horse Artillery

The following music was played for the drive:

Bonnie Dundee	**Flowers that Bloom in the Spring**
A Hunting We Will Go	**Cockles and Mussels**
Dorothy	**The Campbells are Coming**
I'm Going to Marry Yum Yum	**Royal Artillery Slow March**

13   11.26 pm   Grand Finale

At the conclusion of the RHA Drive the battery formed two groups of three guns at opposite ends of the arena. The massed mounted and dismounted bands, already formed up at the back of the arena, stepped off to the band and bugle march 'Tidworth' (Stopford) and 'Silver Jubilee March' (Plater). The bands then played 'Land of Hope and Glory' (Elgar) after which 'Last Post' was sounded and the audience was invited to join in singing the evening hymn, 'The Day Thou Gavest', and 'God Save the King'. Finally, the troops dispersed with the bands playing a medley of tattoo tunes.

As with Aldershot, the Tidworth Tattoo was also revived during the 1960s and 70s.

Wembley Torchlight Tattoo

The Wembley Torchlight Tattoos took place at the newly opened Wembley Stadium as part of the Empire Exhibition in 1924 and 1925. The 1924 event included massed bands of the:

Irish Guards
Royal Marines, Chatham Division, Royal Marines, Portsmouth Division
Royal Marines Depot, Deal, Royal Naval School of Music
Central Band of the Royal Air Force

In addition there were the corps of drums of twelve battalions and the pipes and drums of seven battalions. The Tattoo opened with 'Retreat' sounded by massed buglers and beaten by massed drums and fifes, after which the massed bands played selections taken from:

The Parade of the Tin Soldiers	*Jessel*
Gems of Sullivan	*arr Godfrey*
Selection of Regimental Marches	
Henry VIII Dances	*German*
Reminiscences of Ireland	*arr Godfrey*

The conducting was shared at alternate performances by Lieutenant C H Hassell, Irish Guards, Lieutenant B W O'Donnell, RM, and Flight Lieutenant J Amers, RAF.

Next came a representation by the Brigade of Guards of Guard Mounting in Colour Court at St James's Palace one hundred years earlier in 1824, supported by the Band of the Scots Guards playing instruments from the 18th century including the serpent, ophicleide and jingling johnnie. The massed bands and torchbearers followed the beating of tattoo by playing 'The Duke of York', 'Sambre et Meuse', 'El Abanico', 'The Great Little Army', 'National Emblem' and 'The Liberators'.

The tattoo reached its conclusion with a military fantasia depicting Balaclava, commencing with the Russian army on the march including Cossacks, trick riding and Russian dancing. The scene then changed to the British camp at night with camp songs such as 'Here's a Health unto His Majesty', 'The Minstrel Boy', 'Early One Morning' as well as 'Last Post' and 'Lights Out'. The morning gun signalled the dawn of the next day, 'Reveille' and 'Stables' were sounded and the camp in motion was depicted with part of the Allegro from 'Der Freischutz' overture. 'The Alarm', 'Assembly', and 'To Horse' were then sounded to signal the advance of the British Army:

Cavalry	(11th Hussars)	**Light Cavalry Overture**
Artillery	('O' Battery RHA)	**Keel Row, Bonnie Dundee**
Massed Drums	(Grenadier Guards and	
	Coldstream Guards)	**The British Grenadiers**
Welsh Brigade	(23rd Foot (Royal Welch Fusiliers))	**Men of Harlech**
Highland Brigade	(93rd Foot (Sutherland Highlanders))	**Hielan' Laddie**
Irish Brigade	(88th Foot (The Connaught Rangers))	**St Patrick's Day**

A French regiment of the line advanced to 'Marseillaise' and the battle commenced. Scenes then represented Florence Nightingale's camp and a victory march with the massed bands playing 'Old Comrades' and the pipes, 'The 79th's Farewell to Gibraltar'. Finally, the army at rest led into 'Abide With Me' as the evening hymn and finally 'Last Post'.

The 1925 Tattoo featured the Massed Bands of the Brigade of Guards under the Senior Director of Music, Lieutenant Frederick Wood, Scots Guards, along with the Central Band of the Royal Air Force and massed drums and pipes. A choir of 230 also took part, opening the tattoo by singing with the bands such songs as 'Jolly Good Luck to the Girl who Loves a Soldier', 'Ship Ahoy', 'Tommy Atkins', 'Soldiers of the King' and 'I'll Make a Man of You'. 'Soldiers of the King' brought the Tattoo to a close with 'a Finale of Dedication, Remembrance and Hope'.

Northern Command Tattoo

This tattoo was held in Knavesmire, York, during the 1920s. In 1926 it opened at 9 pm with a short selection played by the Band of the Royal Corps of Signals under the Bandmaster, Mr Randolph Ricketts, well known as a march composer under the name of Leo Stanley. The massed drum and fife bands then marched into the arena playing 'Roehampton' (Turpin) and 'Toy Drum Major' (Nicholls), followed by five guards which were mounted outside representations of the Minster and the four gates of York. As these guards were mounted the drums beat retreat.

Next came the massed bands of eight regiments numbering 400 bandsmen under Mr W Cheeseman, 8th King's Royal Irish Hussars, playing 'Sons of the Brave'

(Bidgood), 'Mayblossom' (Weir) and 'National Emblem' (Bagley). The finale featured 'The Glory of Yorkshire' in a pageant of Yorkshire regiments from the crusades to the great war, all set against the scenic representation of the Minster.

By 1935 the tattoo had moved to Woolaton Park, Nottingham, described as a beautiful and natural setting with a lake and wooded background. The firing of a maroon and sounding of a fanfare heralded the opening. As the guard turned out from the castle gate, Retreat was sounded and the massed corps of drums of nine battalions advanced playing Sousa's 'El Capitan'. Drummers' Call was beaten, Buglers of 2nd Bn The King's Shropshire Light Infantry sounded the fanfare 'Lilywhite' and the massed drums gave a short display including 'Sweet Lavender' (Burdett), 'Belphegor' (Brepsant) and 'Sing As We Go' (Parr-Davies).

Marching on to 'Entry of the Gladiators' (Fucik), the massed bands and drums numbering 622 under Mr R C Hanney, 16th/5th Lancers, gave the audience *the spectacular splendour of brilliant uniforms and glittering instruments with the feast of music, both in stirring marches and the selection'*. The 'Introduction to Act 3 of Lohengrin' (Wagner) was followed by 'Grenadier du Caucase' (Meister), 'The Colours' (Stanley), 'Blaze Away' (Holzmann) and 'Officer of the Day' (Hall). The whole arena was thrown into darkness for the finale as the evening hymn, 'The Day Thou Gavest', was sung. 'Reveille' was then sounded and the whole scene was bathed in golden light, before a roll of drums signalled the National Anthem.

Woolwich Searchlight Tattoo

Woolwich Tattoos were held from 1929 to 1938 and revived in 1952 with an 'At Home' held in conjunction with the Royal Artillery Association Rally, with many parts of the barracks opened to the public. Events took place throughout the day, including the musical drive, a band display, guard mounting by the Boys Battery and highland dancing. The final event was the Tattoo by the Massed Bands of the Royal Artillery (Woolwich, Aldershot, Portsmouth and Plymouth) on the impressive setting of the Front Parade from 10 to 10.30 pm.

The Tattoo itself resumed in September 1953 at Woolwich Stadium and was rather naturally dominated by the Royal Artillery with the massed bands, The King's Troop and displays of firepower. Guest bands also appeared including the 751st United States Air Force Band and the Royal Military Band from the Netherlands. An interesting display was included in 1958 by the Royal Air Force Escaping Society which included a number of members from the resistance movements who came from the continent to re-enact a landing and escape with the aid of a Lysander aircraft.

The Gunners have continued to hold 'At Homes' or massed bands displays at Woolwich on a regular basis, usually on the Front Parade.

Edinburgh Military Tattoo

The first Edinburgh Tattoo was held in 1950 although its foundations really date back to 1947 when Scottish Command staged floodlit displays of piping and highland dancing on the esplanade of the castle at 10 o'clock on some evenings as the army's contribution to the Edinburgh Festival. On other evenings pipe bands would beat retreat at various locations in the city. In 1948 and 1949 the displays were extended to include physical training, drill and guard changing, with the venue split between the esplanade and the Ross Bandstand in Princes Street Gardens.

In 1950 the Tattoo was established on the castle esplanade on each evening (except Sundays) from 21st August to 9th September, starting at 10 pm and lasting for seventy minutes. This first Tattoo opened with a historical pageant depicting the Installation of the Governor of Edinburgh Castle and the displays included:

The Massed Pipes and Drums

1st Bn The Royal Scots (The Royal Regiment)
1st Bn Highland Light Infantry (City of Glasgow Regiment)
1st Bn The Gordon Highlanders
7th/9th Bns The Royal Scots (TA) – 'The Dandy Ninth'
2nd Scottish General Hospital RAMC (TA)

Retreat March	**The Green Hills of Tyrol**
Slow Marches	**My Home, Lord Lovat's Lament, Skye Boat Song**
Quick Marches	**Blue Bonnets over the Border, Bonnie Dundee, Barren Rocks of Aden, The Black Bear, The 79th's Farewell to Gibraltar, Corn Riggs are Bonnie**

The Massed Bands

Royal Scots Greys (2nd Dragoons)
9th Queen's Royal Lancers
1st Bn The Royal Scots (The Royal Regiment)
1st Bn Highland Light Infantry (City of Glasgow Regiment)

The bands were under Bandmaster C A Holt, Royal Scots Greys, and the music programme was selected from the following:

Slow Marches	**Road to the Isles, Garb of Old Gaul, Lament for Maclean of Ardgour**
Quick Marches	**The Great Little Army, On the Quarter Deck, Colonel Bogey**
Static	**Handel's 'Largo'**

The Mounted Band of the Life Guards

The band was led by Major Albert Lemoine in a display entitled 'She Shall Have Musick':

The Life Guards Regimental Slow March	*Traditional*
March – Coburg	*Traditional*
Quick March – Imperial Echoes	*Safroni*
A Fanfare for a Ceremonial Occasion	*Ketelbey*
Auld Lang Syne	*Traditional*

Edinburgh Military Tattoo 1989. The Massed Pipes and Drums. (Photo: Colin Dean)

Perhaps the real magical moment of the Edinburgh Tattoo comes when the fanfare has sounded, the gates of the castle have opened and the searchlights pick out the massed pipes and drums marching out across the drawbridge on to the esplanade. There can be little doubt that this is what most visitors associate first and foremost with the tattoo.

The Massed Pipes and Drums of the Scottish Regiments have always formed the backbone of the tattoo but from 1951, when the Argyll and Sutherland Highlanders of Canada took part, they have frequently been augmented by bands from the Commonwealth. The Massed Pipes and Drums of the Commonwealth took part in the 1955 Tattoo with the 1st and 2nd Battalions The Black Watch (Royal Highland Regiment) of Canada, The 8th Punjab Regiment of the Pakistan Army, representative pipers from the Royal Inniskilling Fusiliers, Royal Irish Fusiliers (Princess Victoria's), the Brigade of Gurkhas, Australia, New Zealand and South Africa, with the 1st Bn Gordon Highlanders representing Scotland. At the 50th anniversary Tattoo in 2000 there were seven pipes bands from the Commonwealth along with all but one of the Scottish regiments.

The Brigade of Gurkhas have also been seen regularly since their 60-strong pipes and drums appeared in 1953, while the Royal Air Force and the Boys' Brigade have been included a number of times. The Edinburgh City Police Pipe Band took part in 1957 but were not to reappear until 1995 in their new guise as the Lothian and Borders Police.

Massed military bands have also been a regular feature in the tattoo, with the bands of what is now the Scottish Division making regular appearances, usually in support of one of the principal staff bands from the three services, and adding

Edinburgh Military Tattoo 1999. Drummers from the Massed Pipes and Drums. (Photo: David Robertson)

The 17th Century Band of the Scots Guards as part of the Edinburgh Military Tattoo 1992 which celebrated the 350th anniversary of the formation of the regiment. (Photo: Colin Dean)

greatly to the visual spectacle with their distinctive uniforms and tartans. The Band of the Scots Guards has taken part no less than seventeen times from their first appearance in 1952 up to 2000, including six times in the 1950s, five of which were under the baton of the legendary Lieutenant-Colonel Sam Rhodes.

Royal Marines bands first appeared in 1951 and have taken part in 12 tattoos, in the early days supported by a number of army bands and on three occasions under Lieutenant-Colonel F Vivian Dunn, Principal Director of Music. Shortly after the 1965 Tattoo Colonel Dunn took the Band of the Royal Marines School of Music and the Pipes and Drums of the Royal Scots Greys (2nd Dragoons) and 2nd Bn Scots Guards on a three-month tour of North America, with much of the 'spare' time during the tattoo period spent on rehearsals. From 1975 the Royal Marines have provided their massed bands, thus avoiding the problems of combining their drill with that of the army, although in 2000 the Band of the Royal Marines Scotland joined with the Scots Guards and the Lowland and Highland Bands.

The Band of the Royal Air Force Regiment took part in 1952 to accompany a drill display but their first appearance as part of the massed bands was not until 1960 as part of a tri-service band. The Regiment Band returned in 1964 under Flying Officer Eric Banks who proved to be another tattoo stalwart, as he was back with the band in 1968 and 1971 as Flight Lieutenant Banks. The Central Band of the Royal Air Force took part for the first time in 1985 – under Wing Commander Banks. The 1994 Tattoo was the only occasion that the Massed Bands of the Royal Air Force have appeared, with an ambitious display to a selection of Scottish music specially arranged by the Principal Director of Music, Wing Commander Barrie Hingley MBE.

The Massed Bands of the Royal Air Force conducted by Wing Commander Barrie Hingley at the Edinburgh Military Tattoo 1994. (Photo: Colin Dean)

Mounted bands were a fairly regular feature in the 1950s with The Life Guards appearing in 1950 and 1957, and the Royal Horse Guards (The Blues) in 1951 and 1954. They were not to appear again until 1993 when the Mounted Band of The Blues and Royals took part in what was perhaps the most memorable tattoo of them all. Appearing with them were the bands of the Royal Scots Dragoon Guards (Carabiniers and Greys) and all regiments of the Scottish Division who were taking their public farewell as they were all to disband shortly afterwards. Rather surprisingly the military bands did not play on their own but were used to accompany the massed pipes and drums of all the Scottish regiments, also together for the first time in the tattoo.

Overseas bands have been a regular feature of the tattoo since 1952 when the Royal Military Band from the Netherlands and the mounted band, La Fanfare de la Garde Républicaine à Cheval, from France appeared. One of the most popular visitors has been HM Kongen's Garde from Norway who first took part in the tattoo in 1961 and returned for the sixth time in 2001.

One of the more recent innovations has been for the finale to include a specially written arrangement combining the bands, pipes, Kevock Choir and on occasions, Scottish fiddlers. WO Michael McDermott, Royal Marines, specially composed 'A Tribute to HM The Queen' for the 1997 Tattoo, Major David Marshall, Coldstream Guards, arranged 'O Waly Waly' and 'Hector the Hero' for 1998, while Major Malcolm Torrent, The Life Guards, arranged 'I'm a Doun o' the Lack of Johnnie' for the 50th Tattoo in 1999.

The drum horse 'Ramillies' and Trumpeters of the Royal Scots Dragoon Guards (Carabiniers and Greys) in the 1994 Edinburgh Military Tattoo. (Photo: Colin Dean)

The 2000 Tattoo featured the voice of Mairi MacInnes in 'Land of Light' which had been arranged by Lieutenant-Colonel (Retd) David Price OBE who, as Captain Price, had first become involved in the tattoo in 1980 as Director of Music, Scottish Division, when he conducted the pre-tattoo singalong. He was the Senior Director of Music for the tattoo on three occasions and following his retirement was appointed as the Tattoo Musical Adviser.

SSAFA Searchlight Tattoo at the White City

The SSAFA Tattoos were held annually at the White City Stadium in West London from 1952 to 1959 and featured massed bands on a grand scale, on each occasion under the baton of Wing Commander A E 'George' Sims, Organising Director of Music RAF.* The Central Band of the Royal Air Force always took a prime role in the massed bands which largely comprised bands from up to eleven cavalry regiments, all wearing their pre-1914 full dress uniforms. In 1953, for example, the music for the massed bands item was:

Entry of the Bands	**The Standard of St George**	*Alford*
Slow March	**Superna Petimus**	*Sims*
Quick March	**Imperial Echoes**	*Safroni*
Static	**Prelude to Act 3 Lohengrin**	*Wagner*
	Long Live Elizabeth	*German*
The Bands march out to	**Action Front**	*Blankenburg*

All the usual tattoo items were included, such as the Musical Drive by The King's Troop, Royal Horse Artillery, drill from the RAF, motor cycles and Musical Rides by the Household Cavalry and by the Metropolitan Mounted Police, the latter wearing the uniforms of famous cavalry regiments.

Massed pipes and drums were a regular feature and the Massed Bands of the Royal Marines would often perform Beating Retreat. The Massed Bands and Bugles of the Light Infantry Brigade took part in 1957 and the Massed Bands and Drums of the Parachute Regiment in 1956, 1958 and 1959. An unusual but very effective item in 1957 featured eighty cavalry trumpeters drawn from ten cavalry regiments sounding harmonised settings of the trumpet calls: 'Reveille', 'Stables', 'Boot and Saddle', 'General Parade' and 'Officers' Mess'.

Particularly popular was the jazz and distinctive marching style of the 751st United States Air Force Band which appeared at the tattoo on a number of occasions, latterly as the Third Air Force Band, performing such hits as 'Tiger Rag', 'St Louis Blues' and, of course, 'The Saints Go Marching In'.

Interestingly, efforts were made by the organisers to transfer the occasion to Aldershot to resurrect the Aldershot Tattoo but these were refused by the ministries.

Colchester Searchlight Tattoo

Much of the success of the Colchester Tattoo was due to the close partnership which existed between the garrison, Colchester Community Fund and various local drama groups. The tattoo was illuminated by the Second World War searchlights of 873 Movement Light Squadron, Royal Engineers which gave the tattoo a wonderfully old fashioned style, reminiscent of the pre-war tattoos and arguably creating much more of an atmosphere than some of the more elaborate lighting systems used elsewhere.

---

*It is believed that Wing Commander Sims directed the massed bands on each occasion but the programme for 1952 has not yet been traced.

The first tattoo was produced in 1960 in the historic setting of the Lower Castle Park, adjacent to Colchester Castle, although its origins go back to the early 1950s when a Military Display and Gymkhana was presented in the stadium on Abbey Field. In the early days the bands were mostly drawn from the infantry battalions which formed part of Colchester Garrison, such as in 1962 when the tattoo opened with massed bands comprising:

Band of 1st Bn Royal Fusiliers (City of London Regiment)
Band of 1st East Anglian Regiment (Royal Norfolk and Suffolk)
Band and Drums of 3rd East Anglian Regiment (16th/44th Foot)
Band of 2nd Green Jackets (KRRC)

Old Panama	*Alford*
Scipio	*Handel*
National Emblem	*Bagley*
Gladiators Farewell	*Blankenburg*

Separate displays were given by the 2nd Green Jackets and by the bands of the East Anglian Regiment with all bands coming together for the finale with:

The Great Little Army	*Alford*
Old Comrades	*Teike*
Trumpet Voluntary	*Clarke*
Abide with Me & Last Post	
God Bless the Prince of Wales	*Roberts*
National Anthem	
The Vanished Army	*Alford*

The 1963 Tattoo included a display by the Band, Drums and Pipes of the Royal Inniskilling Fusiliers, while the massed bands of five battalions performed '1812' as the finale. The Queen's Division of Infantry was formed on 1st July 1968 and their massed bands and drums appeared together for the first time at the tattoo that year, made up from nine of the division's twelve battalions:

1st, 2nd and 4th Bns The Queen's Regiment
1st and 2nd Bns Royal Regiment of Fusiliers
1st, 2nd, 3rd and 4th Bns Royal Anglian Regiment

The 2nd Anglians were worked doubly hard as, with 1st Bn Prince of Wales's Own Regiment of Yorkshire and 1st Bn Green Howards (Alexandra, Princess of Wales's Own Yorkshire Regiment), they also appeared in the opening item as the Massed Bands and Drums of 19 Infantry Brigade who were stationed at Colchester. Also taking part were the Band and Bugles of 2nd King Edward VII's Own Gurkha Rifles whose Director of Music, Major E J H ('Dinty') Moore directed the massed bands in the finale which included 'Goodbye Dolly Gray' and 'Tipperary'.

The Bands and Drums of the Queen's Division were to play a major role in the tattoo. One of the marches they played in 1969 was Kenneth Alford's 'The Vanished Army' in a clever presentation devised by the senior bandmaster, WO1 Derek Kimberley, Royal Regiment of Fusiliers. As the bands marched across the arena,

Colchester Searchlight Tattoo 1982 – The Massed Bands and Drums of the Queen's Division. (Photo: Colin Dean)

sections fell out into the shadows at intervals to reduce the size of the band gradually, with all sections coming together in a flood of light as the march reached its climax. The Queen's Division were joined for the finale by the bands of 19 Infantry Brigade for 'Salute the Prince of Wales' which was specially arranged and conducted by Bandmaster Kimberley to mark the investiture that year. The 1969 Tattoo also included a pageant showing the links between the soldiers and citizens of Colchester since Roman times, one of many such items in which local drama groups took part. In fact, their participation was to become a feature of the tattoo.

The Band of the Grenadier Guards appeared in 1972 under their Director of Music, Captain Peter Parkes who, as Major Parkes, returned in 1974 and 1975 in the appointment of Resident Tattoo Director of Music.

The Silver Jubilee was celebrated in 1977 with a Pageant of Royal Jubilees comprising tableaux representing the six monarchs who reigned for 25 years or more, to the accompaniment of suitable music from the massed bands. The Tattoo was held annually up to 1978 when it became biennial, an improvement on the original plan which had decreed that it should only be held every three years.

In 1982 the theme for the finale was 'Colchester AD 60 And All That', a most effective presentation in which the various figures and statues from Colchester's historic past which adorn the Victorian town hall, 'came to life' in the arena. The music was specially composed by John Lewis and directed by Major Tony Richards, The Life Guards, in his fourth consecutive appearance as Tattoo Director of Music. A particularly poignant moment came during the finale as Buglers of 1st Bn Royal Green Jackets sounded Last Post from the distant slopes of Upper Castle Park. The battalion's band had also been due to take part in the tattoo but had been blown apart by terrorists in Regent's Park just two weeks before.

155

Colchester Searchlight Tattoo 1984 – a section of the massed bands including the Staff Band of the Women's Royal Army Corps, led by Drum Major Frances Tull. (Photo: Colin Dean)

In 1984 the Tattoo moved from the Castle Park to Abbey Field which had the advantage of being more spacious and convenient for the participants, although it somehow wasn't quite the same as the more historic former setting. 'Royal Colchester' was the centrepiece that year with a procession of the various monarchs who had visited Colchester since the legendary figure of 'Old King Cole' and Cunobelin (AD 10–41). As a change from '1812' and 'Waterloo', the finale depicted the 'Battle of Abu Klea' in 1885 when the Essex Regiment fought the Dervishes. The battle was re-enacted in front of an impressive scenic background which included

Colchester Searchlight Tattoo 1986 – Massed Cavalry Bands under Captain David Marshall, Royal Tank Regiment.
(Photo: Colin Dean)

live camels, to music composed by the tattoo's Director of Music, Major Gordon Turner MBE, Royal Corps of Signals.

'Carmina Burana' proved an effective accompaniment to 'Seven, Seventy Summers Since' in 1986 which depicted an attack on Colchester Castle by King John in 1216, while the 1988 Tattoo commemorated the 400th anniversary of the 'Defeat of the Spanish Armada' to music composed and arranged by Major Roger Tomlinson, The Blues and Royals, which was different from that which he wrote for the Royal Tournament.

The massed bands re-fought the Battle of Arnhem in 1990 but depicting an Allied defeat proved a bad omen as this was sadly to be the last Colchester Tattoo.

Cardiff Searchlight Tattoo

This tattoo was held in the grounds of Cardiff Castle with the historic Norman Keep providing an impressive background but with the regular inhabitants of Castle Green, the peacocks, refusing fully to surrender their territory. Peacocks would often stray into the arena during performances and occasionally 'march' at the head of the massed bands, stealing much of the Senior Drum Major's glory! Indeed, part of the entertainment came from watching members of the arena party trying to chase them out of the arena before the motorbikes could roar in.

The first Cardiff Tattoo was held in September 1963 on a fairly modest scale but it was nearly washed out before it started, as the first two performances had to be cancelled due to heavy rain which had left the arena waterlogged. However, a small profit was made and from 1964 the tattoo was produced by Major Aubrey Jackman and held in alternate years, although the biennial sequence was disturbed with a special tattoo in 1969 to mark the Investiture of the Prince of Wales.

The 1964 Tattoo opened with three fanfares. Trumpeters of the 3rd Carabiniers (Prince of Wales's Dragoon Guards) under Bandmaster Michael Pryce sounded 'Arrival' (Jacob) from the base of the steps to the keep, Mounted Trumpeters of the Royal Horse Guards (The Blues) sounded 'Welcome' (Thirtle) from the arena and fanfare trumpeters sounded 'Ceremonial' (Ketelbey) from the South Gate, conducted by Bandmaster Terry Kenny, The Welch Regiment.

Next came the ceremony of retreat with the Corps of Drums of 1st Bn The Welch Regiment, 1st Bn The Sherwood Foresters and 2nd Bn The Parachute Regiment, headed by their respective mascots, with the bands of 15th/19th The King's Royal Hussars and 1st Bn The Welch Regiment. Tent pegging, fire fighting, gymnastics and unarmed combat led up to the interval, after which came a support weapons race, a display portraying Dick Turpin, motor cycles and a display by The Welch Regiment. Finally came the massed bands of the regiments already mentioned, along with the Welsh Guards and 1st Bn The Lancashire Fusiliers, all under Captain Arthur Kenney, Welsh Guards.

Entry of the Bands	**Trombones to the Fore**	*Scull*
Quick March	**Wheels**	*Petty arr Kenney*
Slow March	**Cardiff Castle**	*Kenney*
Band and Bugles March	**Mechanised Infantry**	*McBain*
The Bands halted to play	**The Grand March from Tannhauser**	*Wagner arr Ravenor*

157

Trumpeters of the Royal Horse Guards (The Blues) sounded First Post to begin the Muster Parade and all troops entered to 'The Little Bugler' (Duthoit). The evening hymn, 'Cwm Rhondda', was sung ('Land of Hope and Glory' at the afternoon performance) and trumpeters sounded 'Last Post'. 'Lights Out' was sounded from the top of the keep and as the trumpeters played 'Reveille', the arena was again illuminated. After 'Land of My Fathers' and the National Anthem the parade marched off to 'Under the Banner of Victory' (von Blon) and 'We'll Keep a Welcome' (arr Kenney).

The regiments of Wales naturally played a major part, in particular the Band of the Welsh Guards who took part in every tattoo. The musical arrangements were always in the hands of the Director of Music, Welsh Guards, with Major Derek Taylor taking this role for the six tattoos from 1975 to 1985. At the start of the finale on his final appearance at the tattoo he found himself joined on the rostrum by a scantily clad 'kissogram' girl, delivering a note conveying the good wishes of his band. The photograph made the front page of the local paper with the appropriate headline *'A Bareskin Surprise for the Major'*!

1st Bn Welsh Guards performed the Changing the Guard in 1973 and 1983 in front of a huge scenic facade of Buckingham Palace which was positioned in the arena on the back of lorries. In 1968 and 1981 they Trooped the Colour, albeit on a much reduced scale. The Battle of Rorke's Drift was re-enacted in 1968 by 1st Bn South Wales Borderers and in the centenary year of 1979 by their successors, 1st Bn Royal Regiment of Wales.

Cardiff Tattoo 1981 – Drummers of 1st Bn Royal Regiment of Wales (24th/41st Foot). (Photo: Colin Dean)

Most of the displays seen in tattoos appeared at Cardiff at one time or another, including the Field Gun Competition by two crews from Fleet Air Arm in 1969. One of the more unusual overseas visitors was the United States Air Force Pipe Band, who appeared in 1968.

Cardiff Tattoo 1985. Cavalry Trumpeters of the 5th Royal Inniskilling Dragoon Guards and Fanfare Trumpeters of the Welsh Guards prior to sounding the opening fanfares.
(Photo: Colin Dean)

Large scale displays by massed bands and drums always formed the mainstay of the Tattoo and included musical representations of the Battles of Waterloo and Trafalgar, and the Retreat from Moscow in 1812, with the appropriate scenery and period clad troops. Amongst the more unusual items were massed xylophones in 1969 with Kenneth Alford's 'Mac and Mac', and 'Dixieland Festival' (arr Green) in 1975 when the bands joined with a six-piece Dixie band formed from musicians of the Royal Artillery Mounted Band and the Welsh Guards, which was positioned on the back of a truck.

A very impressive Finale Muster Parade would always close the tattoo and normally included 'Cwm Rhondda' as the evening hymn. Fourteen Cardiff Tattoos were held in all, the last being in 1987.

The Band of the Brigade of Gurkhas and Bugles of 2nd King Edward VII's Own Gurkha Rifles at the Cardiff Tattoo 1985.
(Photo: Colin Dean)

159

Military Musical Pageant at Wembley Stadium

The spectacle of massed bands in a half-time marching display formed a regular part of the major sporting events held at Wembley Stadium but in 1969, perhaps with a glance back to the tattoos of 1924/5, the bands were to form a central, rather than supporting role. The pageants took place every two years up to 1985 and were probably the largest and finest massed bands displays of them all.

The first pageant in 1969 opened with a number of fanfares and routine calls, after which massed bands drawn mainly from the Infantry and Kneller Hall marched on playing a selection of marching songs associated with soldiers, most of which were arranged by the then Captain Trevor Sharpe, Coldstream Guards, who conducted the item.

Next came the Massed Bands and Bugles of the Light Division, which proved to be a special favourite of the audiences at all of the Wembley Pageants, marching at 140 paces to the minute with the distinctive and stylish drill of the Bugle Majors. A massed corps of drums of seven battalions then marched on, to be joined by the Pipes and Drums of 1st Bn Scots Guards and 1st Bn Irish Guards and the first half of the pageant concluded with a display by the Mounted Band of the Life Guards led by Major 'Jacko' Jackson and the new drum horse, 'Hector'.

The Massed Bands, Drums and Pipes of the Guards Division opened the second half and, after some community singing, all the bands came together for the finale with Tchaikowsy's '1812' Overture, conducted by Lieutenant-Colonel 'Jiggs' Jaeger, Irish Guards and embellished with the voice of the Guns of The King's Troop, Royal Horse Artillery.

The 1969 Pageant was produced by Captain Michael Parker but Major Aubrey Jackman took over for the 1971 spectacle, which featured even more bands. This was to set the pattern for future pageants with opening fanfares, individual displays by the Household Division, the Light Division and massed pipes and drums, and all bands coming together to conclude each half.

The finale to the first half of the 1971 Pageant was Eckersburg's musical fantasy 'The Battle of Waterloo' with massed bands of over 1400 musicians representing the opposing armies, conducted by Major Jimmy Howe, Scots Guards. Members of the Household Cavalry bands represented Wellington, Napoleon and their mounted staff officers, the Band and Drums of 3rd Bn The Parachute Regiment were dressed in period uniforms as the British square to provide the rattle of musketry and the Guns of The King's Troop made their presence felt as only they can.

To complement the mounted bands in the second half of the pageant, the Cambrai Staff Band of the Royal Tank Regiment was mounted on ferret scout cars of the Royal Yeomanry with bandsmen sitting on either side of the vehicles and the Director of Music, Captain Roy Hunt and the bass drummer riding in a Landrover. '1812' was the centrepiece again in 1973 and the Rhine Staff Band rode on the armoured vehicles.

The massed bands in 1975 were under the baton of Lieutenant-Colonel Trevor Sharpe, Coldstream Guards, with 'Tunes of Glory' forming the finale to the first half with a cavalcade of wartime songs and music from 1900-45. Vintage horse-drawn and motor vehicles were driven around the speedway track to add to the atmosphere as the three wars of that period were depicted. Finally, the bands played

Laurie Johnson's 'Battle Pageant' with the Guns of The King's Troop 'conducted' by Captain Terry Kenny, then Director of Music of the Royal Artillery Mounted Band. Bandstand Grand in the second half featured instrumental sections of the massed bands with the trombones in 'Peanut Vendor', xylophones in 'William Tell' and 'Post Horn Galop', all ending with Handel's 'Music for the Royal Fireworks' which was accompanied by a spectacular pyrotechnic display.

1977 was Silver Jubilee year and the first performance of the pageant was attended by Her Majesty the Queen and preceded by a review of the Reserve and Cadet Forces. Since 1971 the Household Division had provided the first display after the fanfares and in 1977 they were joined by massed bands from the Royal Marines and the Royal Air Force, the latter wearing their new busby head-dress for the first time. After a short marching display the bands combined with over a hundred fanfare trumpeters to play Gordon Jacob's 'Ceremonial Music' and Albert Ketelbey's 'Knights of the Queen'. The huge massed bands that brought each half of the Silver Jubilee Pageant to its conclusion played such suitably patriotic music as 'Homage to the Queen' (Arnold arr Dunn), 'Vivat Regina' (Johnson), 'Salute the Sovereign' (arr Sharpe) and, of course, 'Pomp and Circumstance No. 1' (Elgar).

Intricate marching displays present problems at the best of times but in 1979 a display considerably more ambitious than hitherto was presented with massed bands numbering over a thousand musicians marching as one to such music as 'Marching around the Shows' (arr Sharpe), 'Under Freedom's Banner' (Nowowieski) and 'Steadfast and True' (Teike). Also included as novelty items were 'The Sign of the Swinging Cymbal' and 'Merry Matelots' (Kenny), the latter being a duet (many times over!) between piccolo and euphonium. 1979 marked the centenary of the massacre of the 24th Foot at Isandhlwana and their gallant defence of Rorke's Drift the following day. This action was commemorated with part of Edward German's 'Welsh Rhapsody' and John Barry's dramatic music from the film 'Zulu' as the battle was re-enacted by today's successors, 'B' Company, 1st Bn Royal Regiment of Wales.

Part of the massive massed bands at the Wembley Military Musical Pageant 1981.
(Photo: Colin Dean)

The Household Division display in 1981 took the form of a representation of the Lord Mayor's Show with a procession around the arena and included specially commissioned music from Captain Roger Swift, The Light Infantry, to mark the forthcoming marriage of the Prince of Wales and Lady Diana Spencer, who were present at the first performance. This 'Royal Celebration' featured the Guns of The King's Troop and the Honourable Artillery Company, as well as a full peal of church bells. Bands, pipes and drums from Canada took part and Tchaikowsky's 'Capriccio Italien' and '1812' concluded the two halves of the 1981 Pageant, both under the baton of Lieutenant-Colonel George Evans, The Blues and Royals. '1812' was given a particularly spectacular presentation with 'Russian' cavalry charging around the perimeter and a massive firework representation of Moscow burning.

The Massed Bands of the Household Division at the Wembley Military Musical Pageant 1983, conducted from his charger by Major Tony Richards, The Life Guards. (Photo: Colin Dean)

The battle music in 1983 was Beethoven's 'Wellington's Victory at Vittoria', specially arranged for the occasion by Lieutenant-Colonel Rodney Bashford and performed to suitable thunderous accompaniment with the massed corps of drums dressed to represent the opposing armies. A particularly memorable moment in the 1983 Pageant came in the finale when the massed pipes and drums joined the bands playing 'Crags of Tumbledown Mountain', led by pipers of 2nd Bn Scots Guards under Pipe Major Jimmy Riddell who had composed the march on the mountain in the Falklands a few days after the battle the previous year.

The fanfare for the 1985 Pageant was followed by massed corps of drums from twelve battalions, in a display conceived largely through the inspiration, determination and sheer enthusiasm of Major Richard Powell, RAOC. This was believed to be the largest such gathering since the 1930s and, for many in the audience, all that followed was an anticlimax. The display was unique in post war years and deserves to have its music listed here in full:

Quick March	**The Thunderer**	*Sousa*
Slow March	**See the Conquering Hero Comes**	*Handel arr Hall*
Quick March	**The Adjutant**	*Birkett*
Slow March	**Annie's Song**	*Denver*
Historic	**The General**	*Traditional*
	The Rogue's March	*Traditional*
March Off	**Ca Ira**	*Traditional*
	Aces High	*Goodwin arr Hall*

Part of the Massed Corps of Drums at the 1985 Wembley Military Musical Pageant. (Photo: Vic Hillsdon)

The 1985 Pageant marked the 300th anniversary of twelve regiments as well as the birth of Handel, and the first half came to a spectacular conclusion with a representation of the celebrations of the peace of Aix-La-Chapelle for which Handel wrote the Royal Fireworks Music. Bands from outside the Commonwealth took part for the first time with the Royal Military Band of the Netherlands and the 33rd United States Army Band, Europe. The finale took the theme of 'War and Peace' but somehow did not match the magnificence of the first half. Both performances took place in constant rain, albeit stopping for the duration of the interval on the Saturday! Sadly, the 1985 Pageant was to be the last.

Luton Musical Pageant

The Luton Pageant was held annually from 1971 for ten years and then continued on roughly a biennial basis until 1993. The normal venue was Luton Town Football Ground although the 1979 Pageant was held indoors at the Shaw and Kilburn Autorama. The pageant followed a similar pattern to the Wembley Pageants and,

Lt Col George Evans, OBE, with the massed bands at the 1982 Luton Musical Pageant, shortly before his retirement from the army. (Photo: Colin Dean)

although on a smaller scale, there was little lacking in the way of quality. The finale of the 1991 Pageant was Eckersburg's fantasy, 'The Battle of Waterloo', with the battle re-enacted by members of the Napoloenic Association in what must have been one of the finest presentations of this music.

The Musical Director each year until 1982 was Lieutenant-Colonel George Evans, Director of Music, The Blues and Royals, and later of the Royal Military School of Music, Kneller Hall. Following his retirement, Colonel Evans returned to Luton as the commentator for the 1985 Pageant and as producer in 1989.

South Norfolk Tattoo

This tattoo has been held at the Attleborough Training Centre, normally every two years, since 1975. The first tattoo included the bands of the Corps of Royal Engineers (Chatham), The Light Infantry, the Band, Pipes and Drums of the Royal Irish Rangers and the Kneller Hall Trumpeters, all under the baton of Lieutenant-Colonel Trevor Sharpe MBE.

The musical centrepiece in 1989 was a pageant entitled 'Salute to Sousa', with the massed bands of eleven regiments playing the composer's marches as a host of local community groups depicted Sousa's family and the carnivals, circuses etc, which are associated with his music. The bands were under Lieutenant-Colonel Peter Hannam BEM, Welsh Guards, who was the musical director for five consecutive tattoos from 1983.

To mark the tenth tattoo in 1991, the finale was a composite of previous finales, with extracts from the 'Royal Fireworks Music' (twice), '1812' (twice), 'Songs from the Second World War', 'Wellington's Victory', 'Last Night of the Proms', 'Crown Imperial' and a 'Classical Cavalcade'. The event was renamed the Breckland Tattoo in 1993, with tri-service massed bands under Major David Marshall, Coldstream Guards, who had taken part in the first tattoo in 1975 as one of the Kneller Hall Trumpeters.

Massed Bands at the South Norfolk Tattoo at Attleborough in 1991. (Photo: Colin Dean)

The London District Tattoo was held on Horse Guards Parade on a number of occasions from 1948. In 1950 it took place on four Saturdays in July commencing at 8 pm, and included the Massed Bands, Drums and Pipes of the Brigade of Guards, the Musical Drive by The King's Troop and the Musical Ride of the Household Cavalry, although the equestrian displays could only be carried out at the trot in view of the hard surface of the parade ground.

The Bath Searchlight Tattoo began on a small scale in 1954, and was held for several years in the pleasant tree-surrounded area in Royal Victoria Park as part of the Bath Festival.

The Berwick Military Tattoo started as an annual event in 1995 at the barracks at Berwick-on-Tweed and, despite being in England, the Tattoo has a distinctly Scottish flavour, usually featuring a band from the Scottish Division and King's Division, as well as pipes and drums and local TA and police bands.

Finally, the **Royal Military Tattoo** was held on Horse Guards Parade in July 2000 and depicted the Defence of the Realm from the time of Alfred the Great to the present day. The Massed Bands were found from the three services including mounted bands, corps of drums, pipes and drums and the Light Division.

165

Dover Tattoo 1986 at Fort Burgoyne with Bands from the Welsh Guards, The Queen's Regiment and the Royal Irish Rangers. (Photo: Colin Dean)

Countless other tattoos were held throughout the country during the 20th century at places including Belfast, Brighton, Chester, Derby, Dover, Eastney, Inverness, Plymouth, HMS *Vernon* at Portsmouth, Shoeburyness, Shrewsbury, Sunderland … the list is endless.

CHAPTER 9

BEATING RETREAT ON HORSE GUARDS PARADE

COLIN DEAN

Massed Bands of HM Royal Marines

The first occasions that the Royal Marines performed Beating Retreat on Horse Guards Parade were on 23rd and 24th June 1950. The bands on parade were those of Chatham Group, Portsmouth Group, Plymouth Group and the Royal Naval School of Music, all under the direction of Major F Vivian Dunn, Director of Music, Portsmouth Group.* They were formed as individual units within the massed bands and thus at one point of the parade they were easily split into separate component bands.

The programme of music in 1950 was as follows:

Fanfare by the Memorial Silver Trumpets of the Royal Naval School of Music

Quick March	**HM Jollies**	*Alford*
Troop	**By Land and Sea**	*Alford*
Bugle March	**Mechanised Infantry**	*McBain*

Fanfare by the Memorial Silver Bugles of the Royal Marines
Beating Retreat by the Corps of Drums

(a)	At the Halt	
(b)	**British Grenadiers**	*Traditional*
Quick March	**Imperial Echoes**	*Safroni*
Troop	**The Tudor Maiden**	*Traditional arr Dunn*
Quick March	**Old Panama**	*Alford*
Quick March	**The Standard of St George**	*Alford*
Finale	**Trumpet Voluntary**	*Jeremiah Clarke*
	The Day Thou Gavest	*Scholfield*

*Later Lieutenant-Colonel Sir Vivian Dunn, KCVO, OBE. This was prior to his appointment as Principal Director of Music in 1953.

167

Combined setting for band and bugles

Sunset	*Green*
Fanfare for Military Band and Trumpets	*Bliss*
Rule Britannia	*Arne arr Wood*
God Save the King	

On leaving Horse Guards Parade on completion of the Ceremony

Regimental March   **A Life on the Ocean Wave**   *Russell*

The Royal Marines have returned to Horse Guards Parade in 1958 and at roughly three-yearly intervals since, and the parade became a celebration of the birthday of HRH The Duke of Edinburgh, Captain General Royal Marines.

The basic form of the ceremony has remained much the same through the years with 'Drummers Call' beaten and 'Band Call'/'Fall In' sounded prior to the massed bands marching on, normally to 'Sarie Marais'. Each performance except 1982 has included at least one march composed by Kenneth Alford (the pen name of Major F J Ricketts, a former Director of Music of the Plymouth Division, Royal Marines), with titles such as 'The Vedette', 'HM Jollies', 'On the Quarter Deck', 'Voice of the Guns' and the slow march 'By Land and Sea'.

Similarly, there have been few parades which did not include a march by Sir Vivian Dunn, 'The Captain General' being played regularly for very good reasons, as well as such marches as 'Soldiers of the Sea', 'The Admiral's Regiment' and 'Under

The Massed Bands of the Royal Marines, with 72 Buglers at their head, march off after Beating Retreat in 1984. (Photo: Colin Dean)

168

the White Ensign'. In 1999 a pastiche of his many marches was specially arranged by Warrant Officer 'Mac' McDermott.

In fact, a considerable number of the marches played over the years have been composed by Royal Marines, which ably demonstrates the wealth of composing talent at all levels of the Band Service, since their ranks ranged from Musician and Bugler to Lieutenant-Colonel:

> **Silver Bugles** (Paul Neville)
> **Zeebrugge** (Peter Sumner)
> **Per Mare Per Terram** (Sidney Rose)
> **Wembley Way** (Albert Elms)
> **On Parade** (Albert Elms)
> **San Carlos** (John Ware)
> **Up Periscope** (Paul Baker)
> **Semper Supremus** (David Harris)
> **Navy Blue** (Trevor Brown)
> **Soldier 'n Sailor Too** (Alan Piner & Michael McDermott)
> **Belle Isle** (Michael McDermott)
> **Royal Salute** (Richard Waterer)
> **Gibraltar** (Richard Waterer)
> **Golden Reserve** (Chris Gould)

The focal point of the ceremony is the Beating Retreat by the Corps of Drums and, again, many of the drum beatings and bugle fanfares have been composed by serving members of the Bugler Branch including:

Bugle Fanfares: **Crowned Laurel** (Angrove)   **Salute to Swordfish** (Lawton)
Drum Beatings: **Highland Slow** (Piner)   **The Duchy of Cornwall** (Cullen)

It has to be said that the bands have slowly been encroaching into this part of the ceremony since 1978 when the theme 'Sailing' (Sutherland) was added, with the drums beating a bolero rhythm. Subsequent years have included equally effective music at this point with 'Aranjuez' (Rodrigo), 'Escort to the Colours' (Adams), 'Bolero' (Ravel), 'Olympic Theme' (Williams), 'Jurassic Park' (Williams) and '1492' (Vangelis).

The Corps of Drums rejoin the bands for a further marching display, which has normally involved them splitting into four bands before joining together and halting in front of the dais with the fanfare team at the head. The finale has included 'Homage to the Queen' (Malcolm Arnold), 'Ceremonial Music' (Gordon Jacob), 'March of the Pacemakers' (Gordon Langford), 'Royal Review' (Arnold Steck) as well as music by Sir Edward Elgar, Sir William Walton and Sir Arthur Bliss. The Evening Hymn, 'Sunset' and 'Rule Britannia' form the traditional end to the finale before the massed bands take their leave to 'A Life on the Ocean Wave'.

A tremendous amount of planning goes into the display and the 1999 Beating Retreat was accomplished, by skilful musical arranging and careful attention to drill, with only two commands – both to step off from static positions – and no bass drum signals were necessary at all. A very impressive feat.

The finale to Beating Retreat in 1984 by the Massed Bands of the Royal Marines. The fanfare team is under Captain Keith Sharpe. (Photo: Colin Dean)

Household Division

On 2nd June 1966 the Household Brigade performed Beating Retreat on Horse Guards Parade, utilising the stands erected for the Queen's Birthday Parade, to raise money for army charities. Taking part in what was to become an annual event were Trumpeters of the Household Cavalry, the Bands of the Grenadier and Scots Guards, Massed Corps of Drums, and Pipes and Drums. The musical programme was

Fanfare by Trumpeters of the Household Cavalry

Drummers Call and Entry of the Massed Corps of Drums

	Hazelmere	*Birkett*

Retreat March of the Corps of Drums

The Carnival is Over	

Entry of the Pipes and Drums

	Blue Bonnets	*Traditional*
	Glendaruel Highlanders	*Fettes*

Entry of the Massed Bands

	Pentland Hills	*Howe*

Marching Display by the Combined Bands

Slow Troop	**May Blossom**	*Weir*
Quick Troop	**La Père la Victoire**	*Ganne*

Display by the Pipes and Drums

March	**The 79th's Farewell to Gibraltar**	*MacDonald*
Stathspey	**Because He Was a Bonnie Lad**	*Paton*
Reel	**The Piper of Drummond**	*Traditional*
Marches	**Bonnie Dundee, Dear Old Donegal**	*Traditional*

Finale	**Retreat**	
	Grand March from Aida	*Verdi*
	Evening Hymn	*arr Sims*
	National Anthem	
Dispersal		
Slow March	**My Home**	*Traditional*
Quick Marches	**Scotland the Brave**	*Traditional*
	By the Left!	*Bashford*

In the following year, 1967, Beating Retreat was extended to two nights, this time with the Mounted Band of the Life Guards, Trumpeters of the Royal Horse Guards (The Blues), the Bands of the Coldstream, Irish and Welsh Guards and Massed Corps of Drums. The massed mounted bands took part each year* from 1968, together with the Massed Bands of the Guards Division (less the Scots Guards in 1968) and the available Corps of Drums and Pipes and Drums.

In 1977 the final performance took place at 9.30 pm under floodlights. This proved a success and was extended to two nights from 1978 with just the one early evening performance. Up until 1980 the parade would end with the massed bands marching down The Mall with the mounted bands riding behind. At the Victoria Memorial the massed bands wheeled to the left and returned to Wellington Barracks, while the mounted bands wheeled right and played all the way back to Hyde Park Barracks, either together or with the two bands alternating. The sight and sound of the massed bands in the dimly lit Mall after the floodlit performances created a particularly special atmosphere for the spectators and, of course, meant that the marches had to be memorised by the musicians. This proved to be little problem, although the less played march 'The Bullfighters' (Kottaun) gave them something of a test in 1980. The mounted bands, it should be said, refrained from disturbing the Knightsbridge hotel dwellers after these late performances.

By way of compensation for the loss of the march back, from 1981 the massed bands have marched from Wellington Barracks to Horse Guards prior to the parade. The early evening performance was dropped from 1993.

The pattern of the event changed considerably from year to year but it has frequently opened with a display by the Massed Mounted Bands of the Household Cavalry who have included a goodly sprinkling of German cavalry marches over the years, 1980 being a good example and including:

Trumpet March	**Bayrischer Defiler Marsch**	*Scherzer*
Set Piece	**Des Grossen Kurfursten Reitermarsch**	*Graf von Moltke*
Trumpet March	**Kesseldorf (1788)**	*Anon arr Keeling*

* There was no Beating Retreat in 1970.

The traditional military style of the cavalry began to change occasionally from 1988 when the mounted bands formed a large 'wheel' to the appropriate music of the 'Carousel Waltz' (Rodgers). The trumpeters were required to trot on some occasions (but not while playing!) to such music from the bands as 'Horse Brasses' (Tomlinson), 'Parade of the Tin Soldiers' (Jessel), 'Autumn' (Vivaldi) and 'Sabre Dance' (Khatchaturian). Soloists were even introduced, albeit dismounted, in 'Post Horn Galop' (Koenig) in 1996 and with xylophones in 'William Tell' (Rossini) the following year.

The Massed Corps of Drums form the central and essential part of Beating Retreat and the traditional retreat marches 'Land of My Fathers' and 'Sweet Polly Oliver' have been regular features, as well as 'The Ash Grove', and 'Flow Gently Sweet Afton'. Drum Major Stephen Ward, Coldstream Guards, was the Senior Drum Major from 1989 to 1991 and three of his own marches were included, 'Captain Nicholls', 'Colonel Heywood MBE' and the wonderfully titled slow march 'The Whistling Guardsman'.

The Pipes and Drums of the Scots and Irish Guards took part most years, with the addition in 1996/7 of the Scots Guards Association under Pipe Major, Captain Linden Ingram, and very smart they looked too. In 1985 a row of 20 Scots Guards Pipers, followed by 10 from the Irish Guards and 10 Drummers, marched at the head of the massed bands at one point playing a medley, 'Away the Pipes' which had been arranged by Cy Payne.

Being an annual event, this proved to be a test of the imagination of successive Senior Directors of Music to find something different each year, and styles varied considerably from the traditional military to a liberal helping of show music during

Major Peter Hannam, Welsh Guards, conducts the Massed Bands of the Household Division at Beating Retreat in 1990. (Photo: Colin Dean)

Lieutenant-Colonel David Price's tenure. There were some particularly inspired choices for the slow march with the soft playing of the bands highlighting the 'percussion' of several hundred guardsmen's boots. These included the overture to the 'Royal Fireworks Music' (Handel) in 1980, 'Fingal's Cave' (Mendelssohn) in 1989 and Bach's 'Air of Celebration' in 1992.

The Falklands War brought a number of changes to the 1982 printed programme, to make way for suitably patriotic music that captured the mood of the time. As the Pipes and Drums of 2nd Bn Scots Guards were heavily involved in the conflict, their part in the programme was replaced by six pipers from the Guards Depot who joined with the Band of the Scots Guards in a combined display.

Some may say that amplification does not have a place on Horse Guards Parade, although it has to be said that it has been used very effectively over the years, no more so than with tubular bells in 1977 in Albert Ketelbey's much loved 'Bells Across the Meadow'. In 1981 an amplified trumpet soloist was featured in Andrew Lloyd Webber's 'Don't Cry For Me, Argentina', a title that would certainly have been on the list of banned music the following year when the Falklands War was at its height. An outside soloist appeared in 1993 with Sergeant Edgar of The King's Regiment, then part of London District, playing the pan pipes in 'Highland Cathedral' while the 2000 parade included three violinists in 'Irish Jiggery', arranged by WO1 Jon Brigden, Bandmaster of The Blues and Royals

The finale could be anything from the wonderfully grand overture to Wagner's 'Rienzi' in 1979 and 1984, to 'Hootenanny' (Walters) in 1973. The Guns of The King's Troop, Royal Horse Artillery joined the bands in the '1812 Overture' in 1994 and again in 2000, on the latter occasion rather wisely after the mounted bands had departed.

The finale of Beating Retreat in 1992 with the Massed Bands of the Household Division conducted by the Senior Director of Music, Lt Col Peter Hannam, Welsh Guards. (Photo: Colin Dean)

Although occasionally sounded by the whole Corps of Drums, Retreat has more often been sounded on a single bugle from the roof of the Citadel. Other than 1990-92 when Lieutenant-Colonel Peter Hannam was Senior Director of Music, a setting of Evening Hymn and Last Post was normally included in addition, sometimes with Cavalry Last Post being used. In 1999 Beating Retreat reverted to its more correct time of the early evening.

Massed Pipes and Drums

The ceremony of Beating Retreat took place on Horse Guards Parade on 30th August and 6th September 1950 with the Massed Pipes and Drums of the Brigade of Guards, the London Irish Rifles and the London Scottish. A similar parade was held on 21st September with the 1st Bn Royal Ulster Rifles also taking part.

The Massed Pipes and Drums of the Royal Scots Greys (2nd Dragoons), Scots Guards, Lowland Brigade and Highland Brigade combined for Beating Retreat with a 'Big Blaw' on 10th July 1967. The Argyll and Sutherland Highlanders were not on parade as it was during this time that they were to distinguish themselves in Aden, but Drum Major Malloch represented the battalion as Senior Drum Major.

Her Majesty the Queen was received with a Royal Salute, 'St Andrew's Cross', and after the drum beatings that followed came the retreat march 'Torosay Castle', the slow marches 'The Red and Blue Hackle' and 'My Home' and the quick marches 'King George V's Army', 'Haughs of Cromdale' and 'Murray's Welcome'. The pipers then formed a large double circle to play 'The Brig o' Perth' and 'Thomson's Dirk', re-forming to 'Scotland's Gallant Soldiers' and 'Within a Mile o' Edinburgh Toon' before marching past to 'Highland Laddie'.

A similar parade was held on 7th June 1971, less than a month before the Royal Scots Greys were to amalgamate, and with the Lowland and Highland Brigades now joined as the Scottish Division. These parades were held for just the one performance but in 1990 the Scottish Division was joined by the Gurkhas and representatives from a number of its allied and affiliated regiments from the Commonwealth, for the customary three evenings. This time the military bands were also on parade under the Director of Music, Captain Geoffrey Kingston, King's Own Royal Border Regiment, who was said to have taken great pride in being the only man on parade dressed as an Englishman!

'The Saltire' (Kingston) opened the parade and the drums moved to the front for the focal part of the evening. Retreat was sounded by buglers positioned in front of the Guards Memorial and the Massed Pipes and Drums then advanced playing retreat marches representing three actions involving Scottish soldiers, 'The Highland Brigade at Magersfontein', 'The Bloody Fields of Flanders' and 'The Heroes of St Valery'.

The massed bands then stepped off for their part of the display with Major Jimmy Howe's 'Pride of Princes Street' and a number of Scottish songs, ending with the march 'Scottish Emblem' (Ellis). The Pipes and Drums again took centre stage playing 'Prince Charles' Welcome to Lochaber' and, after their set, re-formed to 'Jean Allan', composed by Major John Allan, the Director of Army Bagpipe Music, and 'The Top of Ben Lomond'.

Drum Majors and a Bugle Major during the finale of Beating Retreat by the Scottish Division in 1990.
(Photo: Colin Dean)

The pipes, drums and bands then combined, playing 'The Glendaruel High-landers', 'Atholl Highlanders' and 'Happy We've Been a' the Gither' and formed up for the finale in a giant thistle formation to play a new setting by Captain Kingston of the haunting theme 'Distant Hills'.

Light Division

Sounding Retreat by the Massed Bands and Bugles of the Light Division was first held on Horse Guards Parade in 1974 with 200 bandsmen and over 100 buglers on parade. The original use of the bugle for transmitting orders was ably demonstrated prior to the parade with buglers at Horse Guards sounding the 30 and 15 minute warning calls which were then picked up by more buglers in St James's Park and passed onto others at Wellington Barracks from where one section of the massed bands was to march.

A good number of bugle marches were played including many by composers who served with Light Division regiments such as 'Jellalabad' (James), 'Mechanised Infantry' (McBain), 'Tudor Rose' (Adams), 'Hark Forrard' (Plater) and the slow march 'Raglan' (Stevens), as well as medleys of the regimental marches of the former regiments. The Buglers were featured on their own in Koenig's 'Post Horn and Echo' after which they rejoined the bands at the double.

In 1979 the Light Division were joined towards the end of the display by the Band of the Brigade of Gurkhas and the Bugles of 1st and 2nd Battalions, 2nd King Edward VII's Own Gurkha Rifles (The Sirmoor Rifles). The Gurkhas gave their own short display playing 'Men of the Hills' (Bentley), 'Nilo Chari' (Moore),

'Clochemerle' (Roper) and 'Marching thro' Georgia' (arr Miller), before joining with the Light Division for the finale. The first performance that year was held in constant heavy rain and by the time the bands marched back down The Mall after the parade they looked as though they had just marched out of the lake! Perhaps when you are that wet you don't care any more, so when the bands played a selection of songs entitled 'Round the Counties', the buglers spontaneously burst *fortissimo* into song when they reached 'My Old Man Said Follow the Van'!

Massed Bands and Bugles of the Light Division Sounding Retreat in 1987. (Photo: Colin Dean)

Sounding Retreat was repeated in 1987 and in 1993, the latter occasion coming after the death knell had struck for regimental bands. At the conclusion of the parade, a snook was well and truly cocked as the bands marched off into the history books in slow time playing Berlioz' 'March to the Scaffold', with some Buglers seen marching with bowed heads.

Prince of Wales's Division

The Massed Bands and Drums of the nine regiments of the Prince of Wales's Division came to Horse Guards Parade in 1977, the first performance being held on Jubilee Day itself. The Corps of Drums marched on first to the traditional airs 'The Young May Moon', 'Come Lasses and Lads' and 'The Farmer's Boy', after which came the massed bands playing Major Alf Young's splendid march 'Royal Birthday'.

Much of the music had connections with the regiments on parade – 'Royal Welch Fusiliers' (Sousa), 'Triple Crown' (Brien), 'Rorke's Drift' (Ridings) and, of course, 'God Bless the Prince of Wales' which was played in a new setting by Gordon Langford to commence the finale. The parade ended in very effective style with the bandsmen singing the evening hymn, 'Now the Day is Over', in a setting with Last Post, conducted by the Director of Music, Captain Gordon Turner.

The Drums and Fifes lead out the Bandmasters to join the bands for Beating Retreat by the Prince of Wales's Division in 1983. (Photo: Colin Dean)

The next appearance of the Division came in 1983 under Captain Cliff Ross. Prior to the commencement, the bandmasters and fanfare trumpeters marched on from Admiralty Passage led by drums and fifes wearing uniforms of the regiments dating from the 17th and 18th Centuries. The display effectively turned the traditional format about-face by starting with a set piece, 'Dance of the Tumblers' (Rimsky-Korsakov) and with the corps of drums display coming immediately before the playing of the evening hymn. The central part of the display comprised music associated with the regiments that formed the Prince of Wales's Division, divided into their former brigade areas:

Wessex Music	**Barwick Green, Sempre Glevum, Farmer's Boy and Portsmouth**
Mercian Music	**Under the Double Eagle, The Miller of the Dee, Derby Ram, Staffordshire Knot, A Bridge Too Far**
Welsh Music	**Marching with Max Boyce, Men of Wales, Myfanway and Y'Ddraig Goch (The Red Dragon)**

After the finale the bands stepped off playing a medley of the regimental marches and marched past the saluting officer to 'God Bless the Prince of Wales'. Although a little unconventional, the 1983 Retreat worked well and was very successful.

Royal Artillery

Although the Royal Regiment does not Beat Retreat as such, its displays on Horse Guards Parade took a similar format. At the first of these in 1980 the three regular and two TA bands mustered 180 strong and marched on to a medley, 'Parade of the Nations', arranged by Sergeant Alan Roche of the RA Woolwich Band. There were separate displays by the Junior Leaders' Regiment RA and by Pipes and Drums from various Gunner units. The King's Troop, Royal Horse Artillery performed a shortened Musical Drive before adding their voice to the bands and herald trumpeters in the '1812 Overture', conducted by Major Stanley Patch.

Major Frank Renton was Director of Music for the 1986 parade when the Gunner bands were joined by the Staff Band of the Women's Royal Army Corps. An unusual feature of this parade was that a fanfare was sounded by six mounted trumpeters from The King's Troop.

Trumpeters of The King's Troop, Royal Horse Artillery with the Massed Bands of the Royal Artillery in 1986.
(Photo: Colin Dean)

By 1998 the Gunners had just the one regular band which was joined by the Bands of the Honourable Artillery Company, the South Nottinghamshire Hussars Yeomanry, the Lancashire Artillery Volunteers and the Band of the Sri Lanka Artillery. The parade was titled 'Firepower and Music', and included a number of compositions and arrangements by the Senior Director of Music, Major Geoffrey Kingston. A separate display was given by La Musique Principale de l' Armée de Terre which was said to be the first appearance by a French army band on Horse Guards Parade. Their programme comprised 'Sambre et Meuse', 'Infanterie de Marine', 'Marche du Souvenir', '56 Brigade', 'Marche Apothéose' and 'Grenadier du Caucase', with the band finally joining with the massed bands for the traditional '1812' finale.

178

Irish Regiments

One of the most memorable of Beating Retreats was performed on 8th June 1981 by the 5th Royal Inniskilling Dragoon Guards, Queen's Royal Irish Hussars, Irish Guards, Royal Irish Rangers, Ulster Defence Regiment and TA units, all under Major 'Mick' Lane, Irish Guards; 140 men of 1st Bn Irish Guards kept the west side of the parade ground, and Standard and Colour Parties were on parade, along with armoured vehicles.

There was a feast of Irish music from the moment the bands and bugles marched on playing 'Tipperary', 'If You're Irish', 'Begorrah', 'Paddy McGinty's Goat' and 'MacNamara's Band'. The bugles came to the fore to be featured in 'The Old 87th', 'Back to Donegal', 'Rangers' Waltz' and 'Jackets Green' and the massed pipes and drums marched on from the Horse Guards Arch playing 'South Down Militia' and joined with the bands in 'Green Glens of Antrim' and 'Star of County Down'.

The massed bands continued with 'The Kerry March' (Lane), 'Cormac of Tara' (Lane) and 'St Patrick's March' (Bidgood) and the pipes and drums took over again to play a set. 'Slattery's Mounted Fut' (French) and 'Holy Ground' led into the finale which included 'The Londonderry Air', 'Belmont' and 'Sunset'.

Queen's Division

The Queen's Division, then comprising The Queen's Regiment, Royal Regiment of Fusiliers and Royal Anglian Regiment, beat retreat in 1981 and 1985, joined by the Pipes and Drums of two battalions of the Ulster Defence Regiment which were affiliated to the Queen's Division.

The 1981 parade was preceded by a selection played by a Northumbrian piper from the Royal Regiment of Fusiliers which, by necessity, utilised the public address system. The Corps of Drums took a major role, playing two marches by William Turpin, 'For Flag and Empire' and 'Dinah's Delight', three retreat marches by Drum Major Joseph Winter, 'Mandora', 'Tournay' and 'Badajos', as well as the retreat risings 'Sarony'. The drums and flutes combined very effectively with the bands in Sir Malcolm Arnold's 'HRH The Duke of Cambridge' and Captain Peter Hannam's arrangement 'Hogan's Patrol'.

The forthcoming wedding of the Prince of Wales was marked by coupling the tunes 'Diana' and 'Charlie is My Darling' while the parade was brought to a conclusion with a finale including 'Il Silenzio' with cornet duetists on balconies on either side of the parade ground, and Purcell's 'Hymn of Dedication' which was to be played at the royal wedding.

The 1985 parade marked the tercentenary of some of the former regiments and the Corps of Drums again made a fine sight and sound, particularly when combined with the Massed Bands in Terry Davis' 'Wolfe's Patrol'. The display included a section comprising music associated with each of the regiments:

Royal Anglian Regiment   **The Lincolnshire Poacher, The Essex and La Mandolinata**

179

Royal Regiment of Fusiliers	**Blaydon Races, Let's All Go Down the Strand, Warwickshire Lads and She's a Lassie from Lancashire**
The Queen's Regiment	**Maybe it's Because I'm a Londoner, A Southerly Wind and a Cloudy Sky, Old Kent Road, Men of Kent and Sussex by the Sea**

Massed Bands and Drums of the Queen's Division Beating Retreat in 1985. (Photo: Colin Dean)

Royal Air Force

The only Beating Retreat on Horse Guards Parade by the Royal Air Force was held in 1992 to mark the 50th anniversary of the formation of the RAF Regiment. Heavy downpours preceded the first performance and those spectators who arrived early were entertained by fatigue parties with large brooms trying to sweep away the puddles on what was fast resembling 'Horse Guards Lake'! However, the rain stopped just in time and all was well.

The parade took the form of a pageant of the RAF with Horse Guards Parade lined with aeroplanes, tanks and other armoured vehicles as the massed bands led on the Queen's Colour Squadron and Representative Flights in uniforms spanning the last fifty years

The massed bands were featured in a short marching display playing Kenneth Alford's 'Eagle Squadron', a new slow march, 'Lord Trenchard', composed by Wing Commander Barrie Hingley, and 'The Pathfinders' by Malcolm Lockyer. The Queen's Colour Squadron then gave its usual immaculate display of drill and was followed by Pipes and Drums from the RAF and the Royal Air Force of Oman. The bands played a 'Fanfare of Commemoration' and Sir William Walton's 'Battle of Britain' theme during which there was a flypast by three Tornado jets. Two Queen's Colours and the National Standards of the RAF Regiment Associations were marched on parade for the finale and the playing of 'Abide with Me' as the evening hymn.

Tri-Service Massed Bands

The first tri-service beating retreat took place in 1989 with the army represented by the Royal Artillery Band, the Quebec Band of the Queen's Regiment and the Staff Band of the Royal Army Ordnance Corps. The individual services marched on separately and then combined with the fanfare trumpeters in a very effective Fanfare and Processional, 'Queen Alexandra', composed by Wing Commander Barrie Hingley who was Musical Director. Each service then gave a short individual display, followed by the Pipes and Drums of 1st Bn King's Own Scottish Borderers and the Drums and Pipes of 1st Bn Gordon Highlanders, and then the Queen's Colour Squadron RAF.

Tri-Service massed bands headed by Drum Majors of the Royal Marines and Royal Air Force, and Bugle Majors from the Light Division, marching to Horse Guards Parade for Beating Retreat in 1995.

(Photo: Colin Dean)

The display took a similar form in 1995 under the baton of Lieutenant-Colonel Richard Waterer, Royal Marines. This time the individual displays started with the Royal Marines playing 'HM Jollies' (Alford), Ceremonial Drum Beating and 'Famous Songs of the British Isles' (arr Dunn). The RAF then took over with 'Pathfinders' March' (Lockyer), 'The Trap' (Goodwin) and 'Glorious Victory' (Kendall).

Massed Bands of the Royal Marines, Light Division, Brigade of Gurkhas and Royal Air Force about to march onto Horse Guards Parade for the Tri-Service Beating Retreat in 1995. (Photo: Colin Dean)

The army was represented on this occasion by the Bands of the Light Division and the Brigade of Gurkhas, along with the Pipes and Drums of 3rd Bn Royal Gurkha Rifles. Buglers doubled on from the Archway and led the bands in 'Quick Silver' (McElligott), 'Sambre et Meuse' (Rauski) and the 'Red Poppy – Russian Sailors Dance' (Gliere arr Keeley), the latter being played in their own inimitable style of *alla accellerandi*, starting in slow time and gradually increasing to well over the prescribed 140 paces to the minute.

The finale on both occasions was Tchaikowsky's '1812 Overture', with added effects from The King's Troop, Royal Horse Artillery.

CHAPTER 10

THE INTERNATIONAL MILITARY MUSIC SOCIETY

Colin Dean

T he International Military Music Society began in its present form on 1st January 1977 although its roots go back to 1962 and the Military Band Historical Research Society, which was based in Leeds.

For annual membership fee of £1/2/6d members of the MBHRS received three editions of an informative *Military Band Journal* which varied in size anything up to 440 pages. In addition there was a library from which members were able to borrow books and recordings for an additional charge. Despite a seemingly impressive list of committee members, it eventually transpired that this society was in fact run by just one individual with some help from his son. Financial problems ensued which saw the MBHRS meet a sad demise, but the founder had done much service in bringing together men who shared an interest in military music.

A number of former members decided that they should try to keep together and, although the membership list had been lost, they managed to trace many of the addresses. Finding somewhere to hold meetings proved impractical, but a periodic newsletter was produced which was edited by Harry Plunkett with much help from George Brinckley. This was reproduced with a stencil typed by Mr Brinckley's neighbour and a Gestetner duplicating machine made available by a helpful and sympathetic scoutmaster in Hounslow in return for a small donation. However, the Scouts themselves had only obtained the machine after it was considered past its useful life and Mr Brinckley could only use it one day a week after the Scouts' meeting had finished at 9.30 pm. There were endless problems with the stencils tearing and breaking but Mr Brinckley persisted, often long into the night, and was generally covered with black ink by the end of the evening!

The next important development came about from a chance meeting on 1st June 1967 when George Brinckley was at Horse Guards Parade to watch Beating Retreat and found himself sitting near Jack Steeple, a member of the Military Historical Society committee. As they chatted during the hour before the ceremony, George enquired about the possibility of some of the former MBHRS members holding meetings in the MHS room at the Duke of York's Headquarters in Chelsea. After further negotiation with the secretary and other MHS committee members, it was agreed that the best course of action would be for them to become members of the MHS and form themselves into a Band Section. This put them on a more formal footing and enabled them to have a section for band notes in the professionally produced bulletin and to hold regular meetings at the Duke of York's Headquarters.

This arrangement continued satisfactorily for nine years although there was a feeling that the Band Section was making slow progress, as it was not its own master and appeared to be the poor relation of the parent society. In addition, many members were unhappy at paying the bulk of their subscriptions for literature on such things as the manufacture of badges and buttons, which were of less interest to them.

The idea of forming an independent society began to emerge, but it was felt to be vital to find someone of sufficient stature who would lend his name to the new society, to help it become established. Lieutenant-Colonel Sir Vivian Dunn KCVO, OBE, FRAM, former Principal Director of Music, Royal Marines, was approached and invited to attend a meeting to be held on 25th September 1976 at George Brinckley's house in Harlington, Middlesex, to discuss the possibilities of forming a separate society. Those present that day were:

Sir Vivian Dunn	G J Brinckley	H L S Plunkett
R H P von Motz	A R Drane	B L Arnold
A Froom	J T Simmonds	S L Kretschmer
G L Drew	R T Griffiths	E W J Bevan
G H Clark	W H Barnett	B W Alim

Sir Vivian was very keen to become involved and agreed to be elected President of the new society, subject to conditions that it would be properly run. The fifteen founder members laid down the basis of the new society and elected the first committee. George Brinckley agreed to become chairman, at Sir Vivian's virtual insistence, with Harry Plunkett combining the roles of secretary, treasurer and editor of the Society's newsletter/journal, *Band Call*. The society was to be known as the International Military Music Society and the inauguration date was fixed as 1st January 1977.

Once officially established, the IMMS was able to hold quarterly meetings at the National Army Museum in Chelsea. One of the first of these meetings featured an illustrated talk by John Browning, assisted by Stan Templeman, about music at the Shrewsbury Flower Show and, unknowingly at the time, this was to sow the seeds for what was to become an event central in the Society's calendar, of which more later.

The appointment of Squadron Leader Edward Bevan as editor of the journal in December 1978 coincided with the change of name to its present title of *Band International*. Having successfully overseen the formation of the Society, George Brinckley stood down as chairman after his three-year tenure. He was later to become the Society's only Honorary Life Member in recognition of the considerable role he played in establishing it.

He was succeeded by John Trendell, a historian who specialised in the Royal Marines Band Service, being the author of *A Life on the Ocean Wave* and *Colonel Bogey to the Fore*, the latter being a biography of the composer Kenneth J Alford. John successfully took on the task of developing the society from a small group of enthusiasts and expanded membership around the world. Overseas branches began to emerge with particularly strong support in Canada and the Netherlands.

One of the Society's early successes was the production of a series of five long playing records taken from vintage 78 rpm recordings by bands including the Grenadier Guards, Coldstream Guards and the Wireless Military Band.

John Trendell was succeeded as chairman in 1986 by Harry Harding, a former Grenadier Guardsman who had the distinction of having taken part in the last King's Birthday Parade (Trooping the Colour) before, and the first after, the Second World War. Between these ceremonial events he had been amongst the first wave of Guardsmen to secure the liberation of Brussels in 1944 and was later to return to make his home in Belgium. Despite the distance involved, he rarely missed an IMMS meeting in England. Harry was also President of the Antwerp Branch of the Royal British Legion and was appointed MBE on 31st December 1991 in recognition of his work for ex-servicemen.

Since its inception the Society had been governed by a committee in London but as the overseas element continued to expand Harry Harding oversaw the establishment of an International Committee comprising representatives of each of the branches, and this has governed the Society since 1st January 1988. At the same time the United Kingdom members were formed into a branch of their own, which gave considerably more scope for organising UK-based activities. Although, at that stage, officially the youngest branch, Sir Vivian Dunn wished it to be known as the United Kingdom (Founder) Branch to emphasise that the Society had started in this country.

A branch Newsletter was first published in January 1988, edited by Philip Mather who combines his editorial skills with playing euphonium in the Band of the Lancashire Artillery Volunteers. The Newsletter started life being produced on a proverbial battered typewriter but modern technology was soon to take over when the Branch funds were of sufficient size to purchase a computer.

Quarterly meetings continued to be held at the National Army Museum, save for a short spell at the Imperial War Museum while the NAM was refurbished, until Lieutenant Colonel George Evans OBE, a Vice President of the Society, arranged for Kneller Hall to be available for meetings, the first being held there in March 1989.

Major Richard Powell took over the reins as Chairman in November 1992 and, despite being a piper, injected his own irrepressible enthusiasm into building on the foundations laid by his predecessor. Richard has produced and presented regular series of military music for British Forces Broadcasting Service (BFBS) since 1986, usually under the title 'Mainly Military', and had much involvement with tattoos and other such events.

Mention has already been made that the subject of one the Society's first meetings was the Shrewsbury Flower Show, where three of the finest military bands are engaged to play on the bandstand on the two days of the Show. The bands provide continuous music from 10.30 am to 7.30 pm, originally with a further performance on the bandstand by the massed bands but now ending with a massed bands display in the Show's arena, concluding with the '1812 Overture' accompanied by a magnificent firework display. John Browning's talk prompted a small group of members from London to attend the Show on a regular basis and a rapport was soon established with some local members. Word of this feast of military music rapidly spread and the number of IMMS members attending increased each year. Most travelled considerable distances and thus arrived at Shrewsbury on the previous day, so the idea emerged of arranging to meet socially on the eve of the Show, and the buffet evening at the 'Buck's

Head' has been a regular fixture since 1993. In 1998 the UK members were joined by 50 members from the Netherlands branch and, to help our guests feel welcome, the Band of The Blues and Royals under Captain Bob Owen played the fine march 'IMMS Holland' by Henk Van Lijnschooten on both days of the Show.

The UK Branch visited the Netherlands to attend the Breda Tattoo in 1999 and 2000, further strengthening the friendship which exists between the two branches, while the Dutch were back here again in 2000 for Beating Retreat, the Colonel's Review of Trooping the Colour and a visit to the Royal Marines School of Music at Portsmouth.

The Society now has branches in Australia, Brazil, Canada, Denmark, France, Germany, Italy, the Netherlands, Norway, Portugal, South Africa, USA and, of course, the United Kingdom (Founder) Branch. In addition there are representatives in Belgium, Hungary, Japan and Switzerland.

The aims of the Society are to bring together those who enjoy military music throughout the world, to provide a source of expertise for those seeking information and to encourage research into the historical aspects of military music. Three editions of the journal *Band International*, edited by Major Gordon Turner MBE since 1988, are issued to all members each year.

The United Kingdom (Founder) Branch is now led by Lieutenant Colonel (Retd) George Evans, OBE, formerly The Blues and Royals, as Branch President and John Ambler as Chairman. It continues to arrange quarterly meetings for members at Kneller Hall and the list of speakers who have addressed the Society reads like a 'Who's Who' of military music over the last 25 years. In addition, numerous visits have been made to bands including the Royal Marines at Deal, Portsmouth

and Lympstone, the Royal Air Force at Uxbridge, Northolt and Cranwell, and more than half of the current army bands. Some have even invited us back a second time!

2002 represents the Silver Jubilee of the Society and happily coincides with the Golden Jubilee of Her Majesty the Queen. The United Kingdom (Founder) Branch is marking the IMMS anniversary with this book and a compact disc called 'The Founders'. This is a unique recording for which the Principal Director of Music of each of the services has selected a programme of his choice. The centrepiece of the celebrations will be based around the Shrewsbury Flower Show on 14th to 17th August 2002 with events which will bring members from many overseas branches to join together in a truly international gathering.

Lt Col Sir Vivian Dunn, KCVO, OBE, FRAM, the first President of the International Military Music Society.

SUBSCRIBERS

Percy Acres
John Ambler, UK Chairman
D J Ashcroft
Michael J Austin
Nicholas J Austin
Bernard M Baker
Malcolm J Baker
Eric Balmer
Geert Bergsma
Mr Steven Black
David & Fiona Bowman
Raymond Bridger
George J Brinckley
J Brodie – RCT & RCMP Bands
Gordon Brown Esq
Reg Burnett
Major Donald Carson MBE
John Carver
Victor Childs
F A Chown (late RAF)
Bill Clare
David Edward Clark
Major K E C Cross
John Currie
John Curtis
Ron Darling, Royals Band
J L Davies
Ex Royal Marine J Eggleton
John Elms
Peter Elsdon
David Emanuel
Wilf Farrell
Tony Fleming
Major L M Garwood MBE
C Gracey, ex REME Band
Jim Hamilton, Scotland
Michael Hardiman
Harry Harding MBE

N Hayes
Roy Hayes
Pat Higgins
The Highland Band
Brian Hill
William Hill
Mr Victor Hillsdon
Thomas Hinchsliffe
Terry Hissey
F Holloway, ex Grenadier
Peter Hopker
Jim Hutcheson, Canada
Michael Hyde
Mr Rodney Illsley
Peter Jackson, RAF 49/51
D E Johnson
Barry Knight, Band QO RWK
Lanois, Jean-Marc
Alan Le Vicount
BFL
Major D D A Linaker
Alan Littell
David E Loftus
Dr D G Mackay
G E Mansfield BEM (MIL)
Philip Mather
D R McAndrew
H Meadowcroft BEM, Ex RE
BM P R Meakin, PATE'S CCF
D L Messer
Dr Roy Millington
Mr Alastair Mitchell
Keith H Moss
Robert von Motz
Mr Barry Northey
C W Oliver, Capt QRR (Retd)
Mr A D Osbourn
Raymond L Oxley

J G Padget
Fred Palfrey
Peter Penwarden
N Peters, ex RAF
Robert Pinder
George S Pringle
Norman Read
Robin Ridewood
Miss Joan E Robinson
Anthony E Salmon
Philip L Scowcroft
H G (Bert) Sealey
Philip Shannon MBE
L V ('Curly') Shaw
S G Sheppard
Ron Shooter
A P Simkins
Henry George Smith
Stuart Stredwick
Frank E Sumner
Robert Suttie
Paul Taylor
John N Thwaite
David Tribe
Fred Tudor, Oswestry
Frank Tyler
Don Vaughan, ex RE
William Francis Wadge
J G Walker
Lt Col (R) R Walton
Dr J W Watkins
P G Watkins
Kenneth Webb
Mrs Susan A White
David Willmore
Lt Col L M Wilson MBE
W S Wolfe

INDEXES

DIRECTORS OF MUSIC/ BANDMASTERS AND PERFORMERS

MUSIC